Art

Drama

Architecture

Music

Art, Drama, Architecture and Music

An Anthology of Miron Grindea's
ADAM Editorials

Volume II

Selected and edited by
RACHEL LASSERSON

VALLENTINE MITCHELL
LONDON • PORTLAND, OR

First published in 2006 in Great Britain by
VALLENTINE MITCHELL
Suite 314, Premier House, 112–114 Station Road,
Edgware, Middlesex HA8 7BJ

and in the United States of America by
VALLENTINE MITCHELL
c/o ISBS, 920 NE 58th Avenue, Suite 300
Portland, Oregon, 97213-3786

Website: http://www.vmbooks.com

British Library Cataloging in Publication Data:

Grindea, Miron
    Art, drama, architecture and music : an anthology of Miron
    Grindea's ADAM editorials
    vol. 2
    1. English literature – History and criticism 2. French
    literature – History and criticism 3. Music – History and
    criticism 4. European literature – History and criticism
    5. Great Britain – Intellectual life – 19th century 6. Great
    Britain – Intellectual life – 20th century 7. France –
    Intellectual life – 19th century 8. France – Intellectual
    life – 20th century
    I. Title II. Lasserson, Rachel III. ADAM international review
    820.9

ISBN 0-85303-666-7 (cloth)
ISBN 0-85303-667-5 (paper)

Library of Congress Cataloging-in-Publication Data:

A catalog record for this has been applied for

Printed in Great Britain by
MPG Books Ltd, Bodmin, Cornwall

CONTENTS

LIST OF ILLUSTRATIONS

PLATES
(between pages 108 and 109)

1. Portrait by Dorel Pascal, MG's nephew, 1957
2. Picture of MG by a young Persian artist he discovered on the New York subway, 1963
3. MG's Romanian passport and Press Association card
4. MG's identification papers and travel pass of pre-war Romania
5. MG's journalist papers
6. MG with Princess Margaret
7. MG with Natalie Clifford Barney, in her garden
8. MG with Yehudi Menuhin and M. Celak, during the Enescu Festival
9. Portrait of MG by Daghani
10. MG with Olga Rudge, Pound's partner
11. MG visiting the dying Pound

These volumes are dedicated to the memory of
Miron Grindea, and to his great-grandchildren
Joshua, Raphael and Rebekah.
May they be inspired by his unique legacy.

ADAM

International Review

Edited by Miron Grindea

VICTOR HUGO and ENGLAND

English Versions of Victor Hugo's Plays
by Victor Bowley

La nouvelle bataille d'Hernani
par Jean-Jacques Bernard

A chronological English bibliography on Victor Hugo

2/6

VICTOR HUGO AND ENGLAND

Nos. 229–230, Vol. XX, 1952–

ALAS, VICTOR HUGO

Je m'ignore; je suis pour moi-même voilé.
Dieu seul sait qui je suis et comment je me nomme.

The hundred-and-fiftieth anniversary of Victor Hugo's birth, which inspired celebrations at the Bibliothèque Nationale and elsewhere, could not have been better marked in this country, we think, than by the publication of a valuable thesis by Dr Victor Bowley on 'Victor Hugo in the light of English criticism and opinion during the nineteenth century'. Having discovered its manuscript in the London University Library, we consider it a duty to bring this work to the notice of any publishing body, either here or abroad, who might be interested in comparative literature. At all events, a great part of the current issue is based on this scholarly piece of research, which was completed in 1944 and which, when published, will form a lively companion to Mr Kenneth Ward Hooker's earlier PhD thesis on 'The fortunes of Victor Hugo in England' (Columbia University Press, 1938). These two works, together with Professor Heywood Thomas's book, *L'Angleterre dans l'œuvre de Victor Hugo* (E. Droz, Paris, 1935), help one not only to trace the headway made by the chief of the French Romantic school in this country but also to understand the different forms which the Romantic impulse took on both sides of the Channel.

It was ominous for Victor Hugo's reputation that his name was first introduced in England by Stendhal. As Professor Moraud, in his *Le Romantisme français en Angleterre de 1814 à 1848*, aptly observes: 'On ne peut s'empêcher de regretter que notre romantisme n'ait trouvé d'autre interprète français en Angleterre que Stendhal. Dans l'ensemble, il a plutôt desservi qu'aidé nos poètes romantiques.'

As early as 1823, the future builder of the *Chartreuse* relished presenting Hugo as one of the most promising bores of the century. It is true that the *Edinburgh Review* presented Hugo as 'superior to his contemporaries in creative imagination – being in fact the only one of them who seems to see his way with some clearness, or to possess the power of inventing, brooding over, and working out with patience one leading view …'; yet it soon became evident that, whereas the liberal and the radical press were ready to give Hugo a fair and even a cordial hearing, the Tory publications had declared an anathema on all his works right from the beginning.

The Hunchback, translated by William Hazlitt the younger, was a success, but it started the long and often irritating line of comparisons with English literary idols which was to dog Hugo's footsteps on English soil and arouse the wrath of British 'purists'. His comparison with Scott and Tennyson provoked a great deal of angry controversy and discord; but when his plays were compared to Shakespeare's, and when Sidney Colvin tried to convince his readers that the French poet was 'undeniably of the brotherhood of Isaiah, of Aeschylus, of Dante', this was going too far. Furthermore, from 1834 his reputation suffered a sharp decline owing to the stigma of immorality which was attached to his plays. The obliging critics then turned round and combed *Notre-Dame* for evidence of the author's 'depravity'. Quasimodo's marriage scene and Frollo's meditations were pronounced unfit for the youthful eye or for the girlish ear. An unsparing condemnation of most of his writings was all that Hugo got from the English press until G. H. Lewes's epoch-making article, 'The French Drama, Racine and Victor Hugo', in the *Westminster Review*, September, 1840, marked the turn of the tide.

It is worth remembering that in the eighteen-thirties a real 'campaign' of verse translations had popularised Hugo's lighter poetry and found him hob-nobbing with Felicia Hemans and Miss Rossetti in some of the reviewers' columns. Lewes, who was to turn against Hugo later, came out with an explanation for the English dislike of French poetry – 'The French,' he said, 'have not a poetical language, as distinct from that of everyday, and thus the same words which have convulsed us today in some exquisite witticism, we shall read tomorrow in the stately lines of Racine – how can a smile be avoided?' He also exposed the fallacy in the Englishman's picture of 'English nature' – which was 'a sort of Wordsworth world, very pleasant scenery, with very clean, very simple, very honest non-sensual peasants, who knew no vice and had great coxcombry in clean linen' – and French Art, which appears to be nothing else but 'a very crowded saloon, with ormolu, knick-knacks, rococi, etc., filled with very insipid, heartless people, who won each other's money, seduced each other's wives, and cut each other's throats with perfect grace and nonchalance'. It was this sort of prejudice which caused the *Westminster Review* to describe Scott as 'healthy, whole and sound', while *Notre-Dame* revealed 'a sickly glare and oppressive atmosphere'.

Being thus accustomed to mitigate his aesthetic judgements with moral and political considerations, the nineteenth-century Englishman could hardly be blamed for believing most of the fairy-tales about

'French fickleness and immorality'. Strangely enough, however, this limitation of vision and an inability to read French poetry in the original enabled the public to formulate what was substantially a correct estimate of Hugo's bulk of stilted mannerisms and verbosity. Also, the average Englishman's charge against Hugo's many inflated digressions, fallacies and unrealities was, after all, made almost at the same time in a similar vein by many a Frenchman.

To sum up: although it cannot be claimed that the work of Victor Hugo exercised any *sacrées* in the *New Monthly*, Stendhal displays his cynical animosity towards the young poet and literary leader by proclaiming that, although Hugo's excellence in the manipulation of French verse could not be denied, this quality was not sufficient to save his compositions from being 'supremely tiresome'. Yet the English critics of that time thought him to be a literary figure of sufficient importance to justify them in devoting lengthy articles and studies to the examination and evolution of his vast output. Any alphabetical review of the eminent literary men of the nineteenth century who wrote about Hugo and his works takes us first to Matthew Arnold, a vigorous opponent of the Frenchman and author of a scathing article published in *The Nineteenth Century* (1879) on *Hernani*: 'We poor old people,' he wrote, 'should pluck up courage to stand out yet, for the few years of life which remain to us, against that passing illusion of the confident younger generation who are newly come out on the war-path, that Mr. Victor Hugo is a poet of the race and lineage of Shakespeare.' (But then, Arnold found French poetry deficient in 'high seriousness' and fatally damaged by the 'incurable artificiality' of the rhyming Alexandrine; as for Hugo himself, he was 'the average sensual man, shouting and impassioned'.)

Alfred Austin disliked Hugo intensely, yet, when the centenary of the poet's birth was celebrated all over the world in 1902, the Poet Laureate made up with the following over-enthusiastic sonnet:

> POUR LE CENTENAIRE DE V.H.
> *Honneur et gloire à toi, France, à toi qui prodigues*
> *Aux grands porteurs de lyre et la gloire et l'honneur!*
> *Ils sont plus à tes yeux, que roi, pape, empereur:*
> *Tu les ceins de lauriers en dépit des intrigues.*
> *Pour toi les cœurs loyaux sont pleins de noble ardeur;*
> *Et tu séduis si bien l'âme la plus profonde.*
> *Qu'on te pardonne tout, France, et qu'au loin le monde*
> *Dans les siècles sans fin proclame ta grandeur.*
> *Si tu voulais un peu connaître, aimer, toi-même,*
> *Ceux chez qui, douce France, on te connaît, on t'aime,*

Et voir que l'Angleterre, ô soeur, ne te haït pas,
Si tu lui témoignais l'amitié qui l'anime.
Alors plus de discorde! et l'idéal sublime
Dont fut épris Hugo, régnerait ici-bas.
(Translation from English by Emile Blémont)

Robert Buchanan, whose poetry dealt largely with the humble life of the poor, found a bond of sympathy with the author of *Les Pauvres Gens* and *Les Misérables*. Edward Dowden, author of the well-known *History of French Literature* (1897), showed at the beginning some appreciation of Hugo's lyric poetry, while denouncing him as a thinker and quoting many pages of his last works 'piled up with synonyms and common-places in endless variations'. W. E. Henley, himself the author of sonnets and other poems written in the old French forms, showed, however, little sympathy for the works of Hugo and made no effort to conceal his dislike of the author ('How hard it is for decent people to have anything to do with him').

George Moore was, as is well-known, a Balzac addict. He had declared in his *Confessions of a Young Man* (1888) that 'Reading Hugo was like being in church with a strident-voiced preacher shouting from out of a terribly sonorous pulpit'. As to the man himself: 'He shouts and raves over poor humanity, while he is gathering coppers for himself; he goes in for all-round patronage of the Almighty in a last stanza; but of the two immortalities he evidently considers his own the most durable.' The stream of frenzied appreciation grows shallow and muddy in the sandbanks of abuse. Algernon Charles Swinburne, who, himself a fine French scholar and author of poems in French, was far and away the most enthusiastic disciple of Hugo in England:

O, le plus haut poète du cœur.
Tu es notre chef et seigneur.
Tu es seigneur et roi ...
Loué au-dessus des hommes sois-tu!

Unfortunately, this adulation of the French poet sometimes overstepped the bounds of reason, leaving the reader bewildered and dazed with a profusion of uncritical expressions. One cannot therefore be surprised when a Francis Trollope jumped to the other extreme and found much of Hugo's work indecent and unbearable. In fact, the British bulldog was always ready to snap at the Frenchman's heels. He was thus exposed as being 'cased in a proof-panoply of self-esteem, self-sufficient, pompous, proud, vain, self-complacent, a braggart and an egoist'. F. W. H. Myers describes him as having 'arranged all voices of heaven and earth in a cantata of his own glory'.

Hugo had to wait long for his English success; it was not until after 1870, when the 'halo of exile' had been exchanged for a more solid crown, that he found wide public support and had a sonnet written to him by Lord Tennyson:

> Victor in Poesy, Victor in Romance,
> Cloud-weaver of phantasmal hopes and fears,
> French of the French, and Lord of human tears ...

although the then Poet Laureate privately regarded him 'without enthusiasm', preferring de Musset; but even this crown was suspiciously elaborate. It toppled easily, and by the centenary, in 1902, Gosse was writing that the English genius shrank from Hugo's 'grandiose forms of speech' and 'theatrical superficiality', while the Academy spoke of 'the deliberate grotesque sensationalism of Barnum and Bailey'.

Victor Hugo suffered by being often translated too late and usually badly. If *Les Misérables* had appeared shortly after 1848, it might have been the battle-cry of a movement. As it was, its appearance in 1862 drew attacks from the *Edinburgh, Athenaeum, Cornhill, Westminster* and many others. Meredith was a notable exception when he called it 'the master-work of fiction of this century – as yet'.

This long list, by no means complete, of entries and comments gives, we hope, some idea of the interest taken by Englishmen in the works of Victor Hugo during the nineteenth century and of the controversy which these works provoked at a time when the English public was passing through a period of puritanical conservatism. Modern criticism manifests little interest in Hugo. It is sometimes hazy when it operates with the notion of the giant – and the author of *Notre-Dame* was, indeed, a literary rock – but already the change in approach has set the poet, the novelist and the humanitarian free from the many mishandlings characteristic of the last century.

We usually go to great writers for broad and powerful developments of narrative, for intense emotion and for varied and imaginative expression, etcetera: Victor Hugo gives us all this. However the feeling towards him may have changed from one generation to another, there is always a hope to find at least in some of his works the expression of universality. He remains one of the most difficult writers to assess, and the all-embracing study of his life and work, a really complete and impartial, critical and psychological biography – by a new Georg Brandes, perhaps – has still to be written.

And now, after having endeavoured to trace Hugo's footsteps in England, it is necessary to point out that after all he fared no worse over here with both critics and public than he did among his own country-men – remember Gide's ambiguously nasty 'Victor Hugo, hélas!' – and there were dozens of French writers who called him a demagogue, a charlatan, a nuisance, a public menace, a precocious dotard, and what not. And if only on account of some of his misrepresentations of things English – 'L'Angleterre est égoiste: l'égoisme est une île'; 'L'Angleterre crée admirablement la richesse: elle la répartit mal. Cette solution qui n'est complète que d'un côté la mène fatalement à ces deux extrêmes: opulence monstrueuse, misère monstrueuse'; the description of London as the very cradle of misery, 'une femme qui avait dans un coin un objet depuis des jours. C'était le cadavre de son enfant mort la semaine passée, elle n'avait pas de quoi le faire enterrer' (see Mms *L'Homme qui rit* dated June 1867) – and of his defence of Pyat's abusive letter addressed to Queen Victoria (which, incidentally, precipitated the poet's expulsion from Jersey in October 1855), one can hardly be surprised at the recurrent and bewildered reluctance on this side of the Channel to take to a genius so essentially un-English.

• • •

Several young poets and critics have written to us asking whether we see a solution to the tragic impasse of the 'little review' in this country to which we alluded in our previous editorial. We thought we should have the necessary space to discuss the problem at some length. Unfortunately, we have neither the solution nor the space to dwell on the various possibilities which might arise in a more humanistic future. Meanwhile, we suggest a recipe which we consider both dignified and practical. As far as our experience goes, all that a literary monthly of 24 to 32 pages needs to keep going is to: (a) sell through the main agents a minimum of a thousand copies; (b) have an additional number of at least five hundred subscribers at £1 per annum; and (c) have four full pages of advertisements. This would enable a determined editor who believes in the continuity of his function not only to pay the printer's bill – that deadly obsession – but also to allocate a flexible sum of, say, £30-£50 each month to pay his younger and more needy contributors the rate of one guinea per poem, £3-£5 for a short story, £2-£3 for one page of reviewing.

Alas, these fairly modest conditions still appear to be quite utopian for a great many reasons. One of them is that the public libraries, which have the power to encourage the circulation of the most esoteric publi-cations, usually keep away from 'little reviews', even from those which have appeared for more than one or for several years. Newsagents, too, will simply not touch small magazines, on the disarming but unlikely plea that there is lack of interest among their vast public (in fact, millions of readers) for 'highbrow' literature. We mention this particular point, as we consider that the leading newsagents in this country could become the alternative to the vanished class of patrons and to publishers, many of whom are still distrustful of the ultimate utility of small literary publications.

What is to be done? We consider it a duty (on behalf of our fellow editorial sufferers and on our own) to appeal to you, readers and subscribers with a strong, 'unashamed' intellectual background. If you think that the launching of an emergency fund for the rescue of the half-dozen 'little reviews' still struggling through the haze of total indifference is beyond your scope, would it not be possible, if you happen to mention to your friends any of these afflicted magazines, to give full particulars about their addresses? Some of those friends, willing to help but unable to trace any such magazines, either on bookstalls or in public libraries, will thus be able to write direct to the editors. This would, in our view, turn out to be an expedient way of preserving from the present humiliating starvation and final extinction the all too few literary papers which still have the audacity to appear.

● ● ●

Owing to abundance of material, the conclusion to Mr Peter Wood's study of D. H. Lawrence will appear in our next issue. So will the note on Jean Genet.

CONTRIBUTORS

Jean-Jacques BERNARD – *La nouvelle bataille d'Hernani*
Victor HUGO – *London as seen by Victor Hugo* [poem fragment in French]
Victor BOWLEY – *English Versions of Victor Hugo's Plays*
E. M. FORSTER – *Dickens Visits Hugo [from Life of Dickens]* [short quote]
Victor HUGO – *Recent Hugo discoveries* [fragments of poems from *Pierres*]
Translations of Victor Hugo poems: R. TYERMAN; Caroline BOWLES (Mrs Southey); David
    TOLMIE; Gilbert CAMPBELL; G. W. M. REYNOLDS; 'Father PROUT' (Frank S.
    MAHONY); Andrew LANG; Edward DOWDEN; W. C. K. WILDE; Emily HICKEY
Algernon Charles SWINBURNE – *Dédicace à VH; From Victor Hugo; To Victor Hugo; Victor
    Hugo in 1877* [3 poems]
Victor HUGO – *Fragment of poem*
Miron GRINDEA – *A Chronological English Bibliography on Victor Hugo [with appendices based
    on English journals and plays founded on VH and various researchers' works]*

ADAM

INTERNATIONAL REVIEW

Edited by Miron Grindea

In this issue :

" Perhaps the world is all a joke"

2/6

GBS

Nos. 255–256, Vol. XXIV, 1956–

GBS AND FRANCE

You can classify me by my age, my height, my native language,
the colour of my eyes, the length and breadth of my head,
for these facts are ascertained and manageable;
but when the critics and biographers try to classify me as an author,
I smile.
I fit none of their pigeonholes.

Will any future exegetist ever come to grips with all the Shaws who, for nearly a century, struggled for intellectual mastery? GBS always insisted on the 'unscrupulousness' of the man of genius (and undoubtedly he was one), 'a sublime altruist in his disregard of himself, an atrocious egoist in his disregard of others'.

Always at war with society and warning his contemporaries that 'the part a man plays to perfection before the world, is never his real self: it is as different as I am from GBS', Shaw had the most complex character imaginable and enjoyed surrounding his over-involved self with constantly changing fences of paradox, flippancy and exhibitionism – a hard dialectical core to be detected through the rapier points of his invective. His torrential intelligence, the often unbearable charm of his epigrams and his odd ways of showing his goodness of heart turned all too readily to a relentless masquerading, hardened by eloquence into mulish obstinacy. In few other cases did he suffer the consequences of his unpredictable nature worse than in his relations with France and the French theatre.

Certainly, a just assessment of Shaw's plays and prefaces has yet to be made by French intellectuals and theatre-goers generally. Meanwhile, one looks forward to the new production of *Heartbreak House* which Jean-Louis Barrault has had in mind for some time ('cette pièce d'atmosphère chekhovienne', as he described it to us in Christopher's Fry's house a few months ago); this will, we hope, be done in the unforgettable pioneering tradition of Georges Pitoëff, who first produced the play at the Théâtre des Mathurins in January 1928.

The question of language and translation is one of the primary considerations when looking at Shaw from the point of view of the French theatre; thereafter follows the gamut of opposites in English and French taste and attitude towards life. During an inquiry I made into the theatrical archives of the Bibliothèque de l'Arsenal in 1951 for a 'GBS à la France exhibition',[1] I had the constant feeling that Shaw's partial failure in France was due to his perverse determination in choosing a writer totally unconnected either with literature or with the theatre as the exclusive translator of his works. The many savoury details accumulated by GBS's Boswell,[2] as well as the equally lively incidents I myself was able to piece together in conversations with Henry René Lenormand, with Jean-Jacques Bernard and especially with Ludmilla Pitoëff, have confirmed this impression. It is one of the most extraordinary stories in the whole history of modern theatre.

A Fabian Congress held in London in 1894 was the scene of Shaw's meeting with Augustin Hamon, a well-meaning French anarchist and student of social affairs who had produced some political tracts which linked up closely with Shaw's sociology (*L'agonie d'une société*', '*La psychologie du militaire professionnel*', '*Déterminisme et responsabilité*'). In January 1904, Hamon arranged for a young French student who was coming to London to improve his English to meet the dramatist and offer his services as a possible translator of *Man and Superman*. By way of introduction, the youth was to present GBS with an autographed copy of a recently published Turkish translation of Hamon's latest booklet, *Etude sur les eaux potables et le plomb*. The outcome of the visit was a typical Shavian farce, which unfortunately turned into a controversy that lasted decades and involved much ink-wrestling. Shaw blandly and unequivocally dismissed the student and instead invited Hamon to undertake the translation of all his works into French ... No one was more dismayed by this sudden and absurd proposal than Hamon himself. He protested as vehemently as he could that he knew nothing about the theatre *and precious little of English!* '... d'accord,' Hamon answered Shaw, 'pour les ouvrages sociologiques et philosophiques, mais pour les pièces de théâtre, *non*, car je ne suis pas un homme de théâtre. Puis je ne sais pas assez profondément la langue anglaise pour transposer vos comédies en la langue dramatique française. Non, cher ami, adressez-vous à des spécialistes, aux familiers des scènes parisiennes, mais pas à moi, un scientiste.' But there was no escape. Shaw would not have been Shaw had he yielded to the reluctance of this humble publicist to undertake a literary work of such gigantic proportions. Moreover, when poor Hamon began being attacked for his clumsy translations, his indomitable protector buoyed him up with yet another incredible credential: 'Don't you worry. I knew very well what I was doing. The *dramatic liveliness* of the reports you gave of some of the Socialist Congresses[3] had satisfied me to such an extent that I saw in you *the man*

to undertake the French version of my plays [our italics]. As far as an intimate knowledge of English was concerned, it was enough that your wife
possessed this.'

At long last the first Shaw play produced in French was *Candida*, presented at the Théâtre Royal du Parc in Brussels in February 1907 and
afterwards, in May 1908, at the Théâtre des Arts in Paris, with Vera
Sergine in the title part, exactly four years after being produced by
Reinhardt in Berlin.

André Antoine, France's leading producer and actor, immediately
wrote to Shaw begging him to rescue all his future plays from utter disaster and grant the translation rights to several people 'of the trade'. The
answer came via the columns of the *Athenaeum*: 'I have had assurances,'
GBS wrote, 'that the Hamon translations are unfaithful, absurd, impossible – the object being to humbug me into allowing some of the numer-
ous gentlemen, who assure me that they have influence with managers
and that they know how to adapt my plays to the requirements of "the
boulevard", to fasten themselves as collaborators on the harvest of fees
my plays are expected to sow in France. If a Frenchman says to me that
the translations of Hamon are infamous, I can evidently not contradict
him. I can read French easily. I can speak it after a barbarous fashion,
provided I am not asked to go more deeply into grammar than the present of the indicative. I can understand it when it is spoken as badly as I
speak it, that is to say, by everybody but the French. How, then, could I
venture to object if a Frenchman, a man of letters, says to me that
Hamon is totally illiterate? But when, as generally happens, the gentlemen who denounce Hamon show the most disastrous and complete
incomprehension of my works and sometimes undisguised hostility
towards them, I begin to ask myself whether Hamon has not made enemies for himself by attempting to be too faithful to me instead of turning my works into Parisian articles, like the others think they can do so
adroitly.'

These first skirmishes were only the beginning. The Paris correspondent of *The Observer*, in a cable to his paper after the premiere of
Candida, complained that, as a consequence of the Hamon translation,
much of the fine flavour and bouquet of GBS had departed by the time
it reached the audience. *The Daily Telegraph*, too, found the translation
'stilted'. Even the enthusiastic manager of the Théâtre des Arts (where
most of Shaw's plays were about to appear in the French limelight),
Vicomte d'Humières, complained that 'Monsieur Shaw is attached to his
translators like a criminal is attached to the rope which hanged him'
and that this strange attachment, however 'defiant and heroic', would in
the end prove to be 'a suicidal act on the threshold of our admiration'.
But GBS still did not seem to care. All he said in an answer to Vicomte

d'Humières was this rather puerile quip: 'Well, gentlemen, I am no doubt the greatest obstacle to my own success.'

A few years ago I had some correspondence on the same subject with Robert de Smet, the Belgian poet and critic, who, under the pen-name of Roger Sanvic, has so far made the best translations of Christopher Fry into French. M. de Smet knew both GBS and Hamon well, and this is what he wrote:

'Les hasards des années de guerre de 1914 me firent rencontrer Augustin Hamon à Birmingham, où il donnait une conférence sur Shaw (en français).[4] Je fus surpris de constater que le traducteur officiel de GBS ignorait la langue anglaise au point de ne pouvoir demander son chemin dans les rues. Au surplus, je fus fort étonné quand M. Hamon me confia qu'il avait été stupéfait aux représentations de *Candida*, d'avoir entendu le public y rire de bon cœur. "*Je ne croyais pas*," me confia-t-il, "*que cette pièce fût drôle. Elle traite de questions si sérieuses.*"'

The remarkable social theorist! Hamon realised in horror that he must have betrayed both his idol and himself (as the authorised interpreter of Shaw's ideology) when he saw Belgian and Parisian audiences bursting into laughter: 'En entendant le premier éclat de rire de l'auditoire, je m'écriai: "Mon Dieu, on rit! *Tout est perdu! Ma maladresse a ruiné Shaw.*"'

Hamon's candour reaches its climax with this *cri de cœur:* 'J'avais été si absorbé par la sociologie et la psychologie de la pièce, que je n'en avais perçu l'intense comique! Au foyer, les félicitations de mes amis me semblèrent des politesses de commisération. Cependant, à la remarque de ma femme, "Mais tu ris toi-même" mes yeux se dessillèrent et je compris que j'avais le pouvoir de *faire rire* les gens aussi bien que les faire penser.'

And so the Hamons went on with their enormous task. Quite often they would hit upon a more flexible style, valid as theatrical language, but in most cases producers and actors waited until the dress rehearsal had passed and then introduced all sorts of changes and stage tricks. If one of the charming but obstinate partners happened to be in the audience and protested most vehemently against their re-translation, the producer would invariably answer that the changes must have been made without his knowledge and would make a show of telling the actors off ... As Professor Archibald Henderson tells us in his *magnum opus* on Shaw, the qualifications to which the Hamons owed this arduous and – at the beginning – far from lucrative task 'were their complete and incorruptible integrity as interpreters of Shaw's own revolutionary opinions, and their utter innocence of the arts by which any experienced French *homme de théâtre* would have striven to adapt Shaw's technical innovations to the tastes and stage superstitions and caprices of the boulevard. Augustin Hamon's touch was that of the political essayist and of the agitator rather than that of the playwright, but he understood the Shavian propaganda and revelled in it. And his and his wife's translations were, indeed, like no one else's. Unfortunately, this was far from being an advantage in dealing with theatre managers, who could not understand a play that was not exactly like all the other plays; and so it was no wonder that the Hamons brought upon GBS most of the ostracism which so many third- and fourth-rate playwrights usually escape.'

Here again, M. de Smet's version of Shaw's devotion to his *traduttore-tradittore* adds hitherto unknown details about the GBS-Hamon ménage. In a second letter, which I received in February 1951, the Belgian author wrote to me: 'Plus tard, quand il m'advint de voir jouer du Shaw en français, l'accent gris et neutre des traductions me désola et je me souviens que je joignais ma voix à celles qui s'élevaient dans la presse française pour déplorer que la verve du grand Irlandais eût tant perdu en traversant la Manche. Lorsque, vers 1930, je commençai de suivre assidûment le Festival qu'à Malvern Sir Barry Jackson avait organisé à la gloire de GBS, je fus mis en présence du redoutable écrivain et je lui parlai avec enthousiasme du grand effort que faisaient les Pitoëff pour imposer son théâtre en France, mais je crus pouvoir faire quelques réserves sur la qualité des traductions offertes au public: "J'approuve tout ce que les Hamon ont fait de mon théâtre," me répliqua GBS avec vivacité. "Monsieur Augustin Hamon *partage toutes mes idées politiques. Il ne saurait donc me trahir*". Exemple typique du paradoxe shavien. Bernard Shaw estimait d'autre part que les Pitoëff, auxquels il devait tant en France, avaient mis dans son théâtre une sentimentalité qui n'y était pas et qui avait provoqué entre le public et lui un malentendu.' But about Shaw's clashes with the Pitoëffs we shall have more to say later.

We are back in 1904, when the hardworking couple embark on their fierce crusade aimed at introducing the Shavian gospel into France and Belgium. Augustin persuaded the Sorbonne to let him hold a series of lectures, the outcome of which was a commendable book entitled *Le Molière du XXe siècle*. Meanwhile, some of the Hamon translations began to be taken into account by students of English literature and even by men of letters. No less an essayist than Rémy de Gourmont, in an article published in the *Mercure de France*, gave the Hamons an unexpected accolade: '*Trois pièces déplaisantes*, si curieuses, n'ont pas l'air d'être traduites, tant le style français parait naturel. Shaw est un génie dramatique et son théâtre est le seul théâtre qui traduise une vie un peu élevée et une vie profondément originale.' Oddly enough, one of the first critics trying to demolish GBS as a playwright was Maurice Dekobra, who, long before becoming the novelist of sleeping-car *belles*, wrote at some length in the *Revue des Revues* (March 1910) that 'Les pièces de Shaw sont dépourvues de toute valeur dramatique'. Louis Gillet, the future expert on Joyce, in the *Revue des Deux Mondes*, was worried as to how French audiences would in the long run react to Shaw's 'horreur de la sensualité et de l'éducation sentimentale, son dédain de l'amour'. Gabriel Marcel instead, in the *Nouvelle Revue Française*, expressed his open enthusiasm for Shaw's message and verve. Emile Faguet could no longer afford to ignore Shaw, whom he considered to be 'Un Ibsen doué d'humour', although, he added, as a playwright he might never gain a serious following in France, as Frenchmen are always suspicious of parody. Henri Bidou, Henri Bordeaux, Henri Davray, Robert de Flers, Henri de Régnier, Firmin Roz, Valéry Larbaud and Denis Saurat contradicted each other with relish in their reactions to GBS's theatrical ambushes and explosive strategy when attacking critics and audiences alike.

When, in February 1912, the Théâtre des Arts risked its very existence by producing *La profession de Mme Warren*, Shaw thought it proper to mock the Parisians by sending this note to be inserted in the programme: 'Paris is always the last city in the world to discover an author or composer of international reputation, London is twenty-five years behind the times and Paris is ten years behind London. Paris is a marvellous city, but Parisians have not yet discovered Paris. It is not surprising then that they have not yet discovered me.' This rather pointless and obtuse comment made Léon Daudet jump to his feet and call Shaw a fool. Gide's reaction (*Journal*, p. 370) was more subtle: 'J'arrivais à la première tout hérissé, indisposé d'avance par l'insupportable immodestie de l'auteur. Et les premières scènes ont dépassé mon attente; on n'imagine rien de plus revêche, de plus sec, de plus abstrait. Mais, au second acte, je me suis laissé séduire sans plus songer à la résistance. Je me suis ressaisi vers la fin du troisième acte. Il est fâcheux que le quatrième soit si mauvais. Quel art grimaçant et quelles grinçantes pensées! Pas pu m'endormir avant l'aube'.[5] The premiere in 1913 of *You Never Can Tell* (ineptly translated as *On ne peut jamais dire*) attracts the attention of Jean Schlumberger, who writes an intelligent note in the *NRF*. After the first world war, Firmin Gémier was the first great man of the French theatre to call Shaw a genius, and he produced *Arms and the Man* at the Comédie des Champs Elysées and the Odéon.

But it was the privilege of two foreign actors to conquer Paris for GBS. The fact that Shaw quite often treated Ludmilla and Georges Pitoëff with scorn and ingratitude is a different matter altogether. Georges Pitoëff was a young Armenian born at Tiflis, an actor and producer of implacable fire, and his production of *Sainte-Jeanne* in 1925 took Paris by storm. 'Georges et Ludmilla Pitoëff,' wrote Lenormand, 'découvrirent le chef d'oeuvre de Shaw avec un enthousiasme sans réserve, pour autant que son texte original était en cause. Mais l'examen de la traduction leur apporta un profond malaise. L'émotion vraie qui marque le rôle, la chaleur envahissante au contact de la Sainte, le cœur glacé de l'ironiste professionnel, aucun de ces miracles n'était discernable dans l'épaisse matière verbale dont les Hamon avaient barbouillé l'original. Le texte anglais d'une main et la traduction de l'autre, Ludmilla déclarait en hochant obstinément la tête: – Non, et non, et non, je ne dirai pas ces mots-là.' Lenormand then gives us a few delightful details as to the way a plot was to be hatched in order to distract the translator's attention: 'Les Pitoëff me demandèrent de récrire en secret le rôle de Jeanne. Les traducteurs se seraient gravement formalisés d'une pareille atteinte portée à leur droit de trahison, mais comme ils ne devaient assister qu'aux dernières répétitions, Georges se faisait fort d'escamoter la refonte du dialogue. Si, par malheur, les Hamon, jaloux de leurs néfastes prérogatives, suivaient, livre en main, il prendrait sur lui les altérations trop voyantes et prétendrait que des nécessités de mise en scène les avaient motivé. Je me mis donc au travail avec Ludmilla. Le rôle commençait à l'habiter. Elle recueillait avec une touchante gratitude les miettes de sainteté dont elle se sentait gratifiée. Bernard Shaw qui fut, comme tant d'auteurs, un juge aberrant de ses interprètes, a proclamé la satisfaction que lui donnait le jeu de Sybil Thorndyke. J'ai vu cette dame se mesurer avec le personnage. Des forces elle en avait. La noble fille, en son infinie bonne volonté, donnait l'impression de s'être chargée, outre ce qu'exigeait le personnage d'un devoir domestique, faire le ménage du roi de France. Tandis que la fragilité de Ludmilla démentait cette conception ancillaire de l'héroïne. La robuste paysanne, la cavalière émérite étaient remplacées par une enfant inspirée, dont le bon sens, la stratégie et les réponses prenaient une force surhumaine, grâce justement à cette faible voix, à ce visage de gamine illuminé par la foi radieuse et distendue, par la peur du bûcher. Ici, le génie de Ludmilla, éclatant contre le personnage, lui donnait sa vérité profonde. Certaines puissances de l'âme, une fois libérées à propos d'un rôle, d'une situation, d'une pièce, les dépasse. C'est peut-être ce dépassement, dont Shaw prit conscience, quand il vit Ludmilla jouer *Sainte-Jeanne* à Londres, qui lui inspira, envers les Pitoëff, l'attitude réservée, presque hostile, dont ils eurent à souffrir. Comment croire qu'un tel artiste ait pu rester insensible à l'interprétation de Ludmilla? Croyons plutôt à une espèce de gêne du créateur, de rivalité poétique en face de la comédienne outrepassant sa mission et conduisant l'oeuvre là où il ne savait pas lui-même qu'elle pût aller. Les lettres de Bernard Shaw froissèrent et peinèrent gravement les Pitoëff. Ils n'admettaient pas que le seul succès durable et incontestable que l'Irlandais eût remporté en

France leur valût ces missives irritées.[6] Il va sans dire que les Hamon, de leurs poumons remplis d'air breton, soufflaient sur le feu. Le secret de ma participation dans la refonte du texte s'était, comme tous les secrets du théâtre, aussitôt ébruité. Shaw, mis au courant du sacrilège, avait fulminé. Peu lui importait qu'au lendemain de la générale, la presse parisienne se fut abstenue, pour la première fois, de dauber sur la traduction. Il chérissait d'un même amour ses traducteurs, leur contre-sens et cette étrange pâte à reluire, avec laquelle ils fourbissaient, dans leur honnêteté de tâcherons littéraires, les trésors commis à leurs soins. D'Angleterre arrivaient des lettres mordantes où Shaw me remerciait ironiquement d'avoir pris soin de sa gloire et souhaitait à mes prochaines pièces autant de succès qu'aux siennes. Je m'abstins de répondre, car je ne pouvais ni prétendre sans mentir n'avoir pas "retapé" le texte de Jeanne, ni le reconnaître, sans placer les Pitoëff dans une situation embarrassante. D'ailleurs le triomphe de la pièce et l'interprétation balayèrent tous les miasmes.' I have quoted Lenormand's comment at such length, not only because it comes from one of France's leading dramatists but also because it reveals the perpetual conflict between creator and interpreter.

After Firmin Gémier invited the Cassons to play *Saint Joan* at the International Festival at Théâtre Albert 1er in June 1927, the late Sir Charles Cochran saw fit to return the compliment by inviting the Pitoëffs to the Globe in June 1930. It was then that Shaw saw them play for the first time. He did not like them. 'You are no good for me,' he told Georges Pitoëff. 'Why, maître?' humbly asked the admiring actor-producer. 'Because you are too intelligent. Your production is excessively clever throughout: what I want is idiots to do exactly what I tell them.' And to Ludmilla: 'Madame, I am disappointed with your Joan, too. You put too much sex in the part. Look at the English Joan' – pointing towards Dame Sybil, who was present at the reception given by Cochran – 'she hasn't got an inch of sex.'

When, in 1951, I spoke to Mme Pitoëff at her house at Malmaison, she was recovering from one of the violent heart attacks from which she was to die shortly afterwards; yet she spoke with bitter-gentle affection of the ordeals she and her late husband had been through in their dealings with GBS and especially with his translators. (Mme Hamon, on the other hand, although she treated me with sincere cordiality, as soon as I introduced the name of Ludmilla could not help bursting out: 'Ah, cette femme!'). Ludmilla Pitoëff gave me a few more details – unfortunately too libellous for print; yet, when copying out the three letters addressed to her husband and herself in a surprisingly fluent French, I made a point of drawing her attention to the fact that, after all, Shaw could occasionally indulge in kind letter-writing.

I myself had the misfortune to praise Ludmilla's poetical performance when I first met GBS at Whitehall Court in November 1935.[7]
Usually calm and courteous, Shaw was truly annoyed and told me so.
'No, Monsieur, Mme Pitoëff will never be my idea of Joan. I wanted her
to be a tough and rough peasant girl, and she is a *pauvre petite mystique*.'
That was the unfortunate note on which ended an unforgettable two-
hour conversation with the great man.

The first French production of *Saint Joan* took place at the Theâtre
des Arts on April 17, 1925, but the world premiere had been given at the
Garrick Theatre, New York, in December 1923. It then provoked a bitter attack on Shaw by the American correspondent of the paper
Commoedia, Louis Thomas. A fanatical Roman Catholic, Thomas
accused Shaw of having insulted the French Maid in a most boorish and
ungallant way. At the same time, Luigi Pirandello, who also attended the
New York production, recorded a quite different opinion: 'Had a play as
powerful as *Saint Joan*,' he wrote, 'been produced on any of the numer-
ous Italian stages, all the people present would have jumped to their feet
to start a frenzied applause.' However, a fierce polemic ensued in which
the author was appealed to for a final authoritative word. It came, alas,
with yet another characteristic diatribe against Paris: 'It seems to me,'
Shaw answered in a letter to Gabriel Boissy, editor of *Commoedia*, 'that
the theatre in France addresses itself less and less to an intelligent public. The public is in fact so stupid that an explanation of the play must
be printed in the programme to help the spectators to understand what
they see. It is pitiful, because an appreciation of my plays has become a
proof of civilisation, and up to the present France is almost at the bottom of the form.[8] Nothing however can be done.' Then came GBS's
histrionic whip: 'I have educated London, I have educated New York,
Moscow and Stockholm are at my feet, but I am too old to educate Paris.
It is too far behind and I am too far ahead. Besides, my method of education is to teach people how to laugh at themselves, and the pride of
Paris is so prodigious that it has beaten all its professors from Molière
to Anatole France, and might even beat me ...'

François Mauriac was amongst the first French writers to take Shaw
to task for this absurd attack: 'Monsieur Shaw,' he wrote in the *NRF*
(Vol. XXIV, 1925), 'nous donne l'illusion qu'il est le seul dans son bon
sens et que le reste du monde extravague.' As to *Sainte-Jeanne* itself,
Mauriac considered it a complete muddle. 'Nul doute,' he wrote, 'que
pour déguiser en protestante la petite Lorraine, il a fallu que l'Irlandais
dépensât plus d'esprit qu'il ne lui en a coûté pour grimer Cauchon en
honnête homme.'

The shock effect of GBS's vituperation had begun to subside, and
critics were about to forget all about it, when Shaw produced yet anoth-

er argument, although this time in a more serious vein: 'My plays are mixtures of seventeenth century rhetoric, of modern thought and of that barbarous English humour which shocked Voltaire in Shakespeare. They are full of politics, religion, biology and all sorts of terrestrial things except adultery. They contain no traitors, no duels, no misunderstandings nor dramatic plots. And when the question of passion between the two sexes arises, it is the real thing, not the convention which holds its stead on your modest boulevards. The material which serves French gifted playwrights for the construction of a whole play would not last me thirty seconds. The old-fashioned dénouements are mere phrases in my plays, at half a dozen a page.'

Here we reach the crux of Shaw's failure to be taken seriously by the majority of French critics. He professed an absolute admiration for Molière and often accused the French of neglecting their greatest dramatist for the benefit of the empty *boulevard* products. His disdain for the *'pièce bien faite'* in which the French usually excel led him even to the coinage of a name, *sardoodledom*, and brought him into open conflict with a number of Shaftesbury Avenue-minded theatrical managers in Paris. Yet, to his great surprise, Robert de Flers proclaimed *Saint Joan* a masterpiece, and even *Commoedia*, two years only after its bitter attack on Shaw's sacrilegious treatment of the holy girl, changed its mind and, under the signature of Robert de Beauplan, accepted GBS's *protestant* approach unreservedly.

He had a great personal attachment to Tristan Bernard. The latter's son, Jean-Jacques Bernard, also a distinguished and well-known dramatist, gave me these details in a letter dated January 29th, 1951: 'Le jour où Shaw a été nommé Sociétaire de la Société des Auteurs et Compositeurs Dramatiques il a désigné comme parrains Tristan Bernard et moi. Mon père et moi-même avons été très touchés de cette marque de sympathie. Personnellement j'avais gardé un souvenir ému de ma rencontre avec Shaw lors de la création à la Stage Society de *The Unquiet Spirit* (*L'Ame en peine*), et j'avais la plus grande admiration pour lui.'

In fairness, we must admit that Frenchmen could not and still cannot help being baffled by Shaw's explosive and enigmatic intellect. However broadminded, what could a French man of letters or benevolent reader make out of such *pronunciamientos* as these: 'I am not an ordinary playwright. I am a specialist in immoral and heretical plays. I am speaking to the Universe'; or, in a letter to Lugné Poe: 'I am no poor or obscure genius, but a shark ready to devour the French artists and the French theatres, as I have already devoured the English, American, Russian and Scandinavian artists and theatres.' Surely the French would never have tolerated a 'foreigner' to live and prosper in their midst and to mock them for three quarters of a century as Shaw did, living intolerantly among the tolerant English. 'What characterises the English public,' GBS said, 'is their common nonsense, their power of dealing acquisitively and successfully with facts, while keeping them, like disaffected slaves, rigidly in their proper place, that is, outside the moral consciousness.'

A simple quarrel with a courtier was enough to send Voltaire to the Bastille. Shortly afterwards, as a special favour, he was allowed to go into exile, and he chose refuge in this country (1726–1729). It is inconceivable, however, that our twentieth-century Voltaire would have been able to bait two generations of Zolas, Brunetières, Gides or Sartres.

As one might have expected, among the few prominent contemporaries capable of matching Shaw's irreverences, was Anatole France. The two men met during a sight-seeing morning at the Sistine Chapel in the Vatican in 1910. GBS, usually wildly shy when meeting new people, went, however, straight to France and greeted him with a 'Bonjour, Monsieur, moi aussi je suis un génie.' 'Tiens!' France retorted coyly. 'Je suis enchanté, non seulement d'avoir rencontré un génie, mais d'apprendre en même temps que j'en suis un.' Two years later France was addressing a Fabian meeting in London with GBS in the chair. The latter, unaware of what true Gallic exuberance was like, had the shock of his life and blushed like an innocent young girl when the French writer suddenly kissed him on both cheeks ... In a letter to Frank Harris dated May 26th, 1926, GBS talks of France's *Vie de Jeanne d'Arc* compassionately: 'Even a long-story man of genius, Anatole France, was beaten by the Maid: his *Vie* was the absurdest *gaffe* in modern literature.'

Shaw wrote many disparaging things about France and Frenchmen in the prefaces to his plays, in the plays themselves, in his dramatic criticisms and in *What I really wrote about the War*. But he had an unbounded admiration for Berlioz, whom as a music critic he considered to be equal to ... GBS; he also thought well of Gounod, chiefly because the composer of *Faust* worshipped Mozart, and as early as 1892 singled out André Messager's subtlety of texture. He did also admire Montaigne, Descartes, Voltaire, Beaumarchais, Maupassant, Zola (*Fécondité*, for instance, was considered equal to *War and Peace*), and finally, Rodin was a hero to him, yet he was capable of making this wilful and erratic judgment: 'The French would be a very tolerable nation if only they would let art alone. It is the one thing for which they have no sort of capacity; and their perpetual affectation of it is in them what hypocrisy is in the English, an all-pervading falsehood which puts one out of patience with them in spite of their realities and efficiencies.'

With the same gleeful rapidity with which he usually jumped from one idea to another, Shaw told Rainer Maria Rilke, when he once invited him to lunch in Paris in 1912: 'In a biography of Rodin, by the name "Shaw" will appear an asterisk with the footnote, "A model whom Rodin considered worthy of a bust".' There is ample evidence that GBS did everything he could to induce Rodin to ... accept Mrs Shaw's commission for his bust. He even saw to it that four copies of the original were left to posterity: one at the Musée Rodin, another at his Ayot St Lawrence home, a third one facing his disreputable forerunner, Shakespeare, in the hall of the Royal Academy of Dramatic Art in London, and the fourth at the Royal Academy of Arts in his native city.

Rodin had never heard of Shaw before, but Rilke, who was acting as the artist's secretary, saw to it that GBS was received at the master's studio at Meudon as a great contemporary. In a letter addressed to Sir William Rothenstein, in April 1910, Rilke wrote: 'Le buste de Shaw s'avance merveilleusement déjà, vibrant de vie et de caractère; ce que ne serait point accessible, si Mr Shaw n'était pas ce modèle extraordinaire qui pose avec la même énergie et sincérité qui font sa gloire d'écrivain. M. et Mme Shaw viennent tous les jours à Meudon, puisque Rodin évite autant que possible Paris et son atelier froid et humide dans ces temps-ci.'

Another interesting fact arising indirectly from the Shaw–Rodin relationship. *Il n'y a pas de grand homme pour son valet de chambre* – in our case, no writer or artist is great enough, or at least always great, for his secretary. *Anatole France en pantoufles*, as seen by his last secretary, Jean-Jacques Brousson, appeared in a truly slippery light; Miss Blanche Patch, who honours this issue with her valuable contribution and who was GBS's secretary until the author's death, also had many an opportunity to see the 'other' side of the man. What struck us during our Shaw research was to find, at last, the cause of the brutal dismissal of Rilke by his employer and idol. Sir William Rothenstein's last book of Memoirs is, as far as we know, a source hitherto unexplored by Rilke's biographers and contains an interesting document covering the very month when Rodin was doing Shaw's bust. Rilke was then in his early twenties, still unknown as a poet but a brilliant writer of letters. Just because he took the liberty of writing a personal letter to Sir William Rothenstein (a man of extraordinary charm, a great lover of France, a friend of Verlaine, Edmond de Goncourt, Zola and Mallarmé), Rodin gave him the sack: 'Rodin was a difficult person to deal with,' Sir WR writes in his *Memoirs*. 'He could not allow that his secretary should enter into personal relations with his friends.' As to the poet himself, he sent his master this genteel farewell note: 'La lettre de M. Rothenstein était la réponse à une lettre purement personnelle que je lui ai adressée; c'était (je dois vous rappeler) comme votre ami que vous m'avez présenté à M. Rothenstein, et je n'ai pu voir aucun inconvénient à accepter la petite relation personnelle qui s'établit entre votre ami et moi à travers nos conversations, d'autant plus que des amis très chers nous étaient communs.'[9] From Rilke's zealous self-defence, it appears that Rodin resented the young man doing anything else but attend to his secretarial duties; with the result, as poor Rilke confesses: 'Me voilà chassé comme un domestique voleur.'

•   •   •

The end of the Second World War saw a wider and slightly more felicitous interest in Shaw's theatre. The culminating point was reached this year, when GBS's centenary was celebrated at the Saint-Malo Festival under the enthusiastic direction of Claude Planson, who decided to supervise yearly Shaw productions. Paris can be superficial at times, but its net of hospitalities ranges extremely wide. (The best proof is the history-making venture of the Théâtre des Nations at the Sarah Bernhardt.) Times have changed since Antoine's battle for Ibsen and Pitoëff's pioneering for Pirandello and Shaw. At a time when the most significant experimental theatre in Paris is provided by Samuel Beckett (another Irishman) and the Roumanian Eugene Ionesco, it is surely fair to assume that there is an audience for something other than only the passionate and '*bien fait*' type of theatre. In such a city there must be room for GBS theatre as well ...

The fact that many contradictory things may still be said about Shaw is in itself less important than the realisation that no comprehensive book on him has yet appeared in French. The Frenchman who comes to Shaw will have to remember that his time extended from the Victorian era right into the atomic age. Many great contemporaries (some of whom he truly admired and respected) dealt with something or somebody, whereas GBS tilted with everything and everybody. And even after achieving this he would not let the weapons down. 'I have solved practically all the pressing problems of our time, but ... they keep on being propounded as insoluble, just as if I had never existed.'

Shaw's importance as a critic is still unknown to Frenchmen. GBS did nothing perfunctory; on the contrary, he outpoured brilliant and provocative observations on practically everything concerning music, drama, painting and craftsmanship. When translated by a scholarly artist, these ideals will indeed reveal a fascinating legacy of thought on most varied themes. The *Prefaces*, too, are untranslated; consequently Shaw's basic criticisms remain unrecognised.

His future avatars in France may but repeat the fierce resistance he encountered at one stage or another of his fantastic career in his country of adoption. With the difference that in England he finished by becoming a national institution, whereas in a country with the intellectual rigourism of France, most of his written trumpeteering and blustering may still run the risk of being taken literally. In England, a wit like the late Sir Max Beerbohm could pay him this extraordinary tribute: 'I was always distracted between two emotions about him: (1) a wish that he had never been born, (2) a hope that he would never die. The first of those two wishes I retract. To the second one I warmly adhere. Certainly he will live for ever in the consciousness of future ages.'

I know from people who had been close to GBS that he did not care when Ezra Pound inanely called him 'an intellectual cheesemite and a ninth-rate artist'. He rather enjoyed having the following titles conferred upon him: 'the unspeakable Irishman' (Henry James), 'a barbarian at the barricades' (Yeats), 'the potent ju-ju of the Life Force' (Eliot). He was, moreover, particularly amused when shown an article written by W. H. Auden in 1942 and entitled 'The Fabian Figaro'. Nothing could have pleased him more than his name and work being related to music, the art which he considered superior even to God; therefore, when Auden found that 'Shaw's writing has an effect nearer to that of music than the work of the so-called pure writers', GBS the iconoclast felt as much elated as when Einstein compared him to the Almighty.

As for the necessity of establishing Shaw's work in France, it was comforting to see that, in a recent book by M. Henri Perruchot, *La haine des masques* (La Table Ronde, 1955), a serious and penetrating effort was being made to assess Shaw's theoretical work in close relation with his activity as a militant critic of society. Perruchot presents Shaw as a magnificent example of humanity. 'Il eût pu, comme tant d'autres,' writes Perruchot, 'se scléroser dans son passé, il ne regardait que l'avenir. Il est à ce titre le vrai contemporain d'un Montherlant ou d'un Camus. Le public français connaît en général fort mal l'œuvre de Shaw. Avec un entrain endiablé il encourage les hommes à rompre avec un passé mort et à s'engager dans des voies nouvelles. Moins artiste que Montherlant, moins actuel que Camus, Shaw a lui aussi recherché passionnément l'authenticité, critiqué à sa façon âpre faux-semblants et abstractions, et s'est efforcé tout au long de sa vie de ruiner les formalismes vides pour atteindre à la réalité même de la vie, en épouser l'élan.'

A thorough survey of Shaw's relations with France up to 1933 is provided by Mina Moore's *Bernard Shaw et la France* (Librairie Honoré Champion, Paris 1933), in which due weight is given to the influence of Bergson's *élan vital* on GBS's evolutionary doctrines – though it is not to be expected that the magpie-minded Irish genius would gather more than a few straws from any systematic philosophy to equip his tangled nest. ('Whenever I feel,' GBS wrote with his inimitable bias, 'that my great command of the sublime threatens to introduce solemnity in my audience, I at once introduce a joke and knock the solemn people from their perch!')

Miss Blanche Patch provides our readers with the invaluable text of a hitherto unpublished letter sent by Tolstoy to GBS. It is the answer to a letter which made the Russian prophet jump in indignation and in which Shaw puckishly said: 'Perhaps the world is all a joke – but even so, it is evidently our job to make it a good joke!' Yet one of the most reliable impersonations of GBS for centuries to come will most definitely remain the Shaw who wrote: 'My way of joking is to tell the truth; it is the funniest joke in the world.'

Bernard Shaw may have been in many ways a genial buffoon, but his snatches of penetrating insight continue to dominate the stage of twentieth-century literature with a still-unsurpassed witty and limpid prose. As to his gift for making people all the better for laughing at themselves, this will continue to overturn many recurrent conventions and values. And there is no doubt that, sooner or later, France will adopt GBS, perhaps as a *mystique malgré lui* or a tub-thumping Diogenes endearingly cursing the world for not accepting his light. No better recipe could be prescribed in this respect than the one with which André Maurois ended his essay on Shaw in his book, *Magiciens et logiciens*: 'Il serait sain, pour lIa plupart des hommes, de relire chaque année le théâtre de Shaw, afin de se décrasser de toute hypocrisie. Après ce bain de cynisme, l'esprit, lavé, serait plus digne d'accueillir les sentiments vrais.'

CONTRIBUTORS

G. B. SHAW – *Shaw writing to the Pitoëffs* [3 hitherto-unpublished letters]
Walter ROBERTS – *The Iconclast* [poem]
Henry ADLER – *The Artist Philosopher*
Blanche PATCH – *Trying to Understand Shaw*
Henry ADLER – *Theatre: Barry Stavis's* Lamp at Midnight *at the Bristol Old Vic*

NOTES

1. Held at the Institut Français, London, and opened by Sir Kenneth Barnes in the summer of 1951.
2. Professor Archibald Henderson, in an article originally written for the Shaw exhibition organised by *ADAM* but which, owing to unforeseen circumstances, could not appear in our magazine. It was published later on in the *Caroline Quarterly*, 1954. Professor Henderson, who will celebrate his eightieth birthday in June 1957, is equally distinguished as a mathematician and analyst of world theatre. As early as 1904, and with the specific purpose of finding out why Shaw had quickly become popular in Germany and Austria 'but was almost completely unrecognised in France', he wrote to five distinguished French and Belgian authors. Emile Faguet and Maeterlinck confessed that they had never heard of Shaw (the latter adding: 'Je l'avoue avec une profonde confusion') – *Le Socialisme et le Congrès de Londres*, Paris, 1897.
3. *Le Socialisme et le Congrès de Londres*, Paris, 1897.
4. The Hamon family spent almost three years near Ayot St. Lawrence during World War I and saw a great deal of the Shaws. In 1918, GBS and his wife paid the Hamons an unexpected visit at their house at Port Blanc en Penvenau in Brittany. The house is called *Ty au*

Diaoul (Maison du Diable). I myself went to Port Blanc, hoping to see Mme Hamon, but in the meantime she had moved to Paris. She received me several times in her tiny flat somewhere near Montparnasse and showed me great kindness. In one of her albums I saw a delightful postcard sent by GBS immediately after the liberation of Paris: *'Moi je suis veuf – et vous?'*. Augustin Hamon died during the last world war.

5. Ten years later, another entry in his *Diary* (July 1922) shows Gide reading to Ivan Bunin *The Devil's Disciple* 'avec ravissement. Quantité <u>d'English poetry</u>' (underlined by Gide).

6. And yet GBS loved the Pitoëffs, even if in his own way. In this respect it is perhaps appropriate to draw our readers' attention to the three hitherto unpublished letters of GBS to Georges and Ludmilla Pitoëff, which we reproduce on pages 14-15 [of this issue]. They show that, despite the great man's daily doses of self-contradiction, he was after all aware of the actors' merits.

7. I happened to be the youngest delegate at the Congress of European Music Critics held in London in the autumn of 1935. The then President of the Critics' Circle was St John Irvine, author of the first complete life of GBS (*Bernard Shaw, His Life, Work and Friends*, Constable, 1956, 50s). St John Irvine naturally invited Corno di Bassetto to take part in the debates, but, as was to be expected, Shaw refused. When asking the President why Shaw failed to turn up, he told me with an enigmatic grin: 'You'd better ask him yourself.' 'I wish I could.' And before I could even express my wish, StJI went into a telephone box, only to come out smiling: 'GBS will see you tomorrow morning. You may talk as much music as you like with him.' Needless to say, I availed myself most greedily of the opportunity. It was a very sunny morning, and Shaw was in a delightful mood. When asked why he would not meet the music critics, he answered in a most picturesque French: 'Because I was afraid I might be tempted to say what I thought of English music.' I was at the time too ignorant of Shaw's delight in jumping from one extreme to the other and saying with equal aplomb the most glaring absurdities. He first sat down at his upright piano and accompanied his raucous voice in an aria from *Don Giovanni*, indulging afterwards in a few phrases from *Siegfriedidyll*. Finally he got up, walked to the window overlooking the Horse Guards in Whitehall and came towards me with an astonishing leap over the piano stool. Had I not mentioned 'cette femme', it is most likely that the musical and gymnastic treat would have lasted longer. As regards his contempt for English music, he most movingly refuted it when he addressed a Malvern audience with these inspired words: 'Although I am rather a conceited man, I am quite sincerely and genuinely humble in the presence of Sir Edward Elgar. I recognise a greater art than my own, and a greater man than I can ever hope to be.'

8. Shaw was completely wrong. He would not see that, unlike the idiotic programmes sold in most English theatres – ashamed, as it were, of giving a synopsis of the play and a biographical note on the author – the programmes sold in Parisian theatres are real brochures, offering a number of intelligent and documented articles and a graceful layout. It was a pity that, with his pernicious pen, he never 'had a go' at attacking the scandalous mental laziness of our theatrical catering firms.

9. Mr and Mrs Shaw.

A LITERARY MONTHLY IN ENGLISH AND FRENCH : YEAR XXVII : No. 276-277 : 1959

ADAM

INTERNATIONAL REVIEW

edited by Miron Grindea

Schiller Bicentennial

1
7
5
9

*

1
9
5
9

This hitherto unknown miniature, possibly the earliest surviving Schiller portrait, is attributed to Nicolas Guibal de Luneville. One of the most precious possessions of King's College, London. Reproduced by kind permission of the Principal.

4/6

SCHILLER BICENTENNIAL
Nos. 276–277, Vol. XXVII, 1959–

This introductory note can be regarded as a mere enumeration (and an insufficient one at that) of only a few countries where Schiller's poetry, as well as his dramatic and philosophical works, have for more than one hundred and fifty years enjoyed an enormous popularity. Nowadays the position is strikingly different. 'To be universally accepted; to be damned by the praise that quenches all desire to read the book; to be afflicted by the imputation of virtues which excite the least pleasure and to be read only by historians and antiquarians – this is the most perfect conspiracy of approval' – how cruelly do these opening words in Mr T. S. Eliot's moving verdict on Ben Jonson apply also to Friedrich Schiller, whose birth bicentenary is celebrated [*sic*] throughout the world. Indeed, ceremonies are now taking place for widely opposed reasons, according to the different political-aesthetic attitudes which characterise our modern society. The poet is overpraised but, alas, unread ... His reputation, not only in England and France but also in the USA and especially in the USSR, is still remarkably high; but more often as a name to overawe students or to satisfy official propagandists, than to inspire true lovers of literature who delight in Goethe, Hölderlin, Heine and Rilke.

Schiller's whole life was a revolt. One cannot overlook the fact that the imprisoned student at Duke Karl Eugen's Military Academy (*Sklaven-plantage*) in Castle Solitude near Stuttgart began his literary career with the anonymous publication (and at the author's expense) of *Die Rauber* and ended with *Wilhelm Tell* – both equally galvanising denunciations of tyranny, in family as well as in public life.

The indifference to his work, especially in Western Europe, is most unjust and unexpected, for his language is still both powerful and exquisite, his stagecraft still invigorating and modern and his personality still a rich source for critical comment. In a recent almost exhaustive study of comparative literature, *Schiller's Wirkungsgeschichte im Ausland* by Kurt Wais (Walter de Gruyter, Berlin, 1958), one is amazed to find that Schiller's influence upon European literature during the last two centuries has been as great as, if not greater than, that of Goethe.

Characteristically enough, it was the emotional and 'sentimental' element in Schiller's dramatic works – an element largely derived from Rousseau – that first appealed to, and was subsequently imitated by, many West European writers. In this country it was Henry Mackenzie, 'the historian of feeling', as Walter Scott called him, who first discovered Schiller and delivered a lecture on him at the Royal Society in Edinburgh (April 21st, 1788). The equally lachrymose Sébastien Mercier, a disciple of Diderot, was Schiller's first French follower: he hurried to Germany to attend the first performance of *Die Rauber* and partook of the bountiful overflow of tears shed by the first-night audience at the Mannheim Hoftheater! Admirers, translators, adapters and plagiarists followed in a vertiginous tempo; for, apart from the immediate following of Schiller's revolutionary ideas, there was a propitious climate for sentimental literature just waiting for its great inspirer. Many French and Italian writers found an expression of their own emotions and aspirations in the young rebel, who, shortly after freeing himself from the chains of Duke Karl Eugen's 'Metressenwirtschaft', wrote *Kabale und Liebe.* Another of Schiller's characteristics (sarcastically criticised by Dorothea Schlegel), his idealisation of women, had an equally sudden effect upon foreign writers. Echoes of Amalia's virtue and courage (*Die Rauber*) are heard in some of Alfred de Musset's poems, and in Victor Hugo's Dona Sol, Karl Moor's 'Sie verzeiht mir, sie liebt mich' is unavoidably identified in Hernani's 'Elle m'a pardonné, elle m'aime', which shows that young Hugo borrowed generously ... Thekla's noble pride (*Wallenstein*) and Joan's pure love (*Jungfrau von Orleans*) appear respectively in Manzoni's drama, *Conte di Carmagnola*, and in Silvio Pellico's abortive play, *Matilde. Maria Stuart* sent countless poets in search of a noble historical heroine at grips with the slings and arrows of fate from which the monumentally melodramatic Act V releases her in heroic death. (See K. Kippa's *Maria Stuart im Auslande*, Studien zur vergleichenden Literaturgeschichte, Berlin, 1905.)

The same confusion that goes on in the ideological feud which divides Germany today can be traced in the first symptoms of Schiller's impact abroad. His conception of liberty, at first based on Rousseau's conflict between nature and society or between freedom and convention, was as enthusiastically received – and often grossly misinterpreted – by revolutionaries everywhere, as at other times it was heartily condemned by 'the other side', which promptly placed the author on the blacklist. A typical example is Schiller's French honorary citizenship. On October 10th 1792, *l'an premier de la République Françoise*, the poet received the following solemn address:

'J'ai l'honneur de vous adresser ci-joint, Monsieur, un imprimé revêtu du sceau de l'Etat, de la Loi du 26 Août dernier, qui confère le titre de Citoyens Français [*sic?*] à plusieurs Etrangers. Vous y lirez que la Nation vous a placé au nombre des amis de l'humanité et de la société, auxquels elle a déféré ce titre.

'L'Assemblée Nationale, par un Decret du 9 Septembre, a chargé le Pouvoir Exécutif de vous adresser cette Loi; j'y obéis, en vous priant d'être convaincu de la satisfaction que j'éprouve d'être, dans cette circonstance, le Ministre de la Nation, et de pouvoir joindre mes sentiments particuliers à ceux que vous témoigne un grand People [*sic?*] dans l'enthousiasme des premiers jours de sa liberté.

'Je vous prie de m'accuser la réception de ma lettre, afin que la Nation soit assurée que la Loi vous est parvenue, et que vous comptez également les François [*sic?*] parmi vos Frères.

'*Le Ministre de L'Intérieur*
de la République Françoise'

How *Monsieur Gille, Publiciste Allemand*, reacted to this 'red' unction (which, in any case, reached him only six years later, as the revolutionary committee ignored not only his proper name but also his address) can be surmised from the delightful details given by Monsieur Robert Minder on page fourteen [of this issue]. What is more interesting to retain from a European point of view is the fact that Schiller's consecration led to further perversions of his thought and to a total misapprehension of his art, even among his fellow-countrymen. (Wordsworth, who made an extensive use of *Die Rauber* when writing his drama, *The Borderers* (1795–96), described to Coleridge a visit he had paid to Klopstock. The already senile author of *Der Messias* told young Wordsworth that he could not stand any of Schiller's dramas and that anyway his exasperating reputation will soon vanish ... *Biographia Literaria, III.*) On the other hand, Schiller's fragmentary novel, *Der Geisterseher*, written in 1794 and published in England only a few months later, exerted a considerable influence upon English writers, although perhaps for the wrong reason ... They concentrated all their attention on a Protestant's fight, oppressed by a Jesuit priest, for his spiritual freedom. Coleridge wrote *The Ancient Mariner* under the impress of the *Geisterseher* – which brought him a devastating comment from Southey: '*The Ancient Mariner* is, I think, the clumsiest attempt at German sublimity I ever saw' (Letter to William Taylor, September 5th, 1798). The *Ghost-Seer* also influenced Ann Radcliffe, who read German quite fluently and thus succeeded in acquainting herself with Schiller's story while she was working on *The Mysteries of Udolpho* (1795). Yet another of her 'thrillers', *The Italian*, as well as Lewis's *The Monk* (which also appeared in 1795), were much indebted to Schiller's short novel.

It is perhaps appropriate to point out how often literary history is perverted by insufficient information. In 1794, while still a student at Göttingen, Coleridge dedicated an exalted sonnet to Schiller. On his return from Germany, Longmans entrusted him with the difficult task of translating *Wallenstein* from the original manuscript. The undertaking proved utterly boring to the poet, leaving him with 'a sense of weariness and disgust which unfitted me for anything but sleeping or immediate society' (Letter to Southey, February 28th, 1800). Yet when the translation came out, and Coleridge grumbled about the poor fee of fifty pounds ('Heaven knows! for a thick octavo volume of blank verse'), his *Wallenstein* was hailed on the Continent as a major literary event. It emboldened Benjamin Constant to attempt a French version of the same play, which appeared in 1809, and also led to Zhukovsky's translation of *Die Jungfrau von Orleans*, to Adam Mickiewicz's freedom drama *Konrad Wallenrod* and to Kudivka's translation of *Wilhelm Tell* in Lithuania. Schiller's intellectual itinerary took him from Rousseau's conflict to an ideal of harmony which was to transform the semi-historical drama *à thèse* of Voltaire and Mercier into the romantic historical drama of the nineteenth century, with freedom and patriotism, humanism and nationalism at last reconciled. Oehlenschlager brought Schiller to Denmark, Tegner brought him to Sweden, and in the early dramas of Ibsen, and even Bjørnson, Schiller's influence is clearly felt. Although he once said that he did not regard 'the national' as the highest aim of men, there can be no doubt that he is the father of nineteenth-century national-historical drama.

His ideal of harmony found a purely stylistic interpretation when he attempted to unite elements of Shakespeare with elements of Racine, thus reconciling two styles hitherto considered as diametrically opposed: the classical and the romantic. In *Das Lied von der Glocke*, Schiller went one step further by introducing imagery both realistic – almost technical – and abstract. The daring *genre mixte* was well received by Lamartine, who, like Vigny in *Le bal*, imitated the German master in *Jocelyn*. (This is how Lamartine, in his *Cours familier de littérature*, greeted Xavier Marmier's translation of *Die Glocke*: 'Un poème lyrique sans égal dans la poésie de toutes les langues modernes … le poème lyrique de Friedrich Schiller est digne de tinter éternellement dans l'oreille des hommes. Nous n'avons rien de pareil en France.')

Jean Paul's criticism of Schiller's compromises – a mixture of Corneille and Crébillon to which Paul attributed the poet's popularity in France – was not shared by posterity. On November 10th, 1859, at a fabulous celebration concert given at the Crystal Palace for the hundredth anniversary of the poet's birth, a choir of a thousand voices sang a setting by Romberg of *The Song of the Bell*, with *The Athenaeum* proclaiming that: 'If a choice must be made between the two great men' (the other being Goethe), 'England's sympathies would possibly, as regards the majority, be for Schiller, because of his fire, his wondrously picturesque imagination, his direct and intelligible style.' Later still, from across the Atlantic, came Longfellow's *The Building of the Ship*, which owes much to the *Bell*. As fastidious a critic as Henry James also recognised the indebtedness to Schiller of two other great American writers, Emerson and Thoreau (*The American Scene*, 1907).

Nevertheless, however wide and important Schiller's influence may have been in the West of Europe, it appears feeble by comparison with the depth of its impact in Russia, particularly on Dostoevsky. West Europeans like Carlyle, Madame de Staël and Goethe recognised Schiller's unique purity, his nobility and a sort of saintliness which Goethe coined as 'Christ-quality'. Carlyle in his *Life of Schiller*, which he wrote between 1823 and 1824 and which was translated into German by Goethe himself, even recognised in Schiller's works a 'heavenly fire', but it was left to the Russian writer to understand the full meaning of Schiller's flame. To the West, Schiller was chiefly the father of historical drama, the man who raised tragedy to lofty heights; he was a fine, even great poet, whereas to Dostoevsky he was a profound experience, an experience which no other Russian writer since has shared with such intensity. Kafka is perhaps the only modern writer to follow the Schiller-Dostoevsky idea of the worm in the dew drop and the angel at the Maker's throne, both creations of God. Modern Schiller scholars place their author diversely – with Shakespeare, with Racine, with Dante, Calderón and Milton. With the last group, Schiller certainly shares the experience of the nothingness of life on earth; but, lest we forget the other experience, the *Brothers Karamazov* will always remind us that

> *Wollust ward dem Wurm gegeben*
> *Und der Cherub steht vor Gott.*

Every centenary celebration of a creative mind usually helps towards reassessment and further research. 1959 has brought about new discoveries in the field of Schilleriana, not only in the divided parts of Germany itself but also in the USA and in Europe, especially in France, where he is treated as *le poète de la grandeur*. As regards Schiller's impact on nineteenth-century Russia, a touching new detail has not long ago come to light: in 1854, a 26-year old Russian officer in the Imperial Army was passing through Bucharest to join his regiment in the Crimean War. On that very night, *Kabale und Liebe* was given its first performance at the National Theatre, and the officer, who was no other than Lev Tolstoy, wrote in his *Diary* how deeply moved he was by Schiller's drama (the first he had ever seen). As Roumanian was Greek to him, Tolstoy began looking for any French translation of Schiller to keep him company for the rest of his journey – to the Crimea ...

Schiller's adulation by the emancipated Jews in Central Europe was another phenomenon of considerable proportions. Significantly, while the writings of their great coreligionist and reformer, Moses Mendelssohn, were still widely banned by orthodox Jewry, Schiller, with his inflammatory tirades, became the 'Liebling der gebildeten Juden'. Many an exalted proselyte would pride himself on having just read *Die Glocke* – though he could not quite remember the author: was it Schiller von Goethern or Goethe von Schillern ...? *Maria Stuart* became emphatically *Miriam* Stuart in the Hebrew translation of a progressive-minded Rabbi, and six different versions of *Die Glocke* appeared in Hebrew journals between 1820 and 1859. In his charming novelette, *Die Juden in Baranow*, Karl Emil Franzos gave an unforgettable description of his Schillerian ecstasy among that greedy intellectual elite, still injured by ghetto chains.

The distinguished film director and art historian Pierre Rouve may soon find the necessary leisure to write a paper on an equally impressive set of circumstances regarding 'Schiller worship' in a small country like Bulgaria, where Dimitri Svevsky's translations read as memorably as Zhukovsky's renderings into Russian.

Schiller has so often been accused of lack of humour (the caustic Alfred Kerr attacked him in 1928: 'Schiller es geht nicht') that he ended by admitting it himself ... In a letter to his friend Christian Gottfried Körner, dated July 2nd 1786, the poet makes this candid confession: 'Seriously, I am more and more fed up to find myself in my own company. One cannot say of me that I am a joker or, as our good ladies would say, an agreeable companion in society.' Yet the same overworked, pipe-smoking Schiller, weakened by years of tuberculosis, indigestion and abdominal pains, would often relax by poking fun, not only at himself but at his friends and enemies as well. The drawing reproduced on the next page [of this issue] is one of the thirteen truly humorous sketches painted by Schiller in delightful colours for the thirtieth birthday of his friend Körner. The originals have disappeared, but luckily the Deutsche Verlangstalt, Stuttgart, found it possible to reproduce a facsimile of the original posthumous edition which appeared in Leipzig in 1862 under the title *Avanturen [sic?] des neun Telemachs von Hogarth (Friedrich von Schiller)*. Which shows that Schiller was familiar with the work of his great English contemporary. The same 'humourless Schiller' left a playlet, *Ich habe mich rasieren lassen – Ein dramatischer Scherz*, which may still be worth translating into English. Our greatest wish, however, would be to see a reprint of *The Correspondence between Schiller and Goethe*, endearingly translated into English by Dora Schmitz, and 'The pleasures of travelling' – a drawing by Schiller published by George Bell in 1879. There were nine hundred and ninety-nine letters which the two great men exchanged between 1794 and 1805 (the last one by Goethe only a few days before Schiller's tragic death at the age of forty-five). 'You gave me a second youth and made me a poet again,' the proud, grumbling patrician wrote to Schiller, and this was no exaggeration, for it was due to the electrifying influence of the younger playwright that Goethe completed his *Faust*.

● ● ●

In this country, several important contributions have recently been added to Schillerian scholarship. Professor E. M. Garland, of Exeter University, published a concise but stimulating *Schiller Revisited* (Grant and Cutler, 5s), focussing our attention on totally forgotten aspects of the poet's tumultuous career. Professor William Witte, of the University of Aberdeen, under the title *Schiller and Burns* (Blackwell's, 15s), has collected a number of engaging essays, among which is one of particular interest, devoted to the theories of social-realist criticism and attempting to re-interpret Schiller both as a *petit bourgeois* and as an ideological forerunner of modern revolutions.

As with many special issues of *ADAM* in the past, our tribute to Schiller also had its share of adventure and excitement. While having lunch with Professor William Rose, author of a remarkable book on Heine, we learned that King's College, London possessed a hitherto unidentified portrait of the poet (a legacy included in the Mond bequest). By special permission of the Chancellor we took the valuable original out of the building (under the energetic supervision, it is true, of the secretary of the German Department, Mrs Tiresias), and within one hour it was photographed and restored to its lovely frame. While Professor Frederick Norman took the portrait to be studied at the Schiller Institute in Marbach, a reproduction of it could appear on our cover [of this issue].

Two of our contributions came from France. Both authors wrote directly in German, a *tour de force* and an unheard-of courtesy. Who would have thought, ten years ago, that such a thing would be possible? Whenever we feel inclined to mourn the disappearance of the common intellectual language – Latin – in the free exchange of ideas through the centuries of humanistic commerce, we should remember that the bicentenary of a German poet was celebrated in his own language by a member of the Académie Française and by a professor at the Collège de France. We could not possibly spoil this extraordinary gesture by translating the text of a French Academician from German into ... French, but we took this liberty with Professor Minder's text. We sincerely hope that he will accept the symbolic meaning of our editorial initiative. One of the younger French *germanistes*, Professor André Drijard, also sent us a contribution in German, but it was too late to translate it into English. Grateful acknowledgments to Dr Nelly Wilson for her invaluable editorial assistance; to Dr Eugen Guerster, the well-known Bavarian playwright and essayist for his many encouragements; to Dr Pafford, Chief Librarian of London University; Dr Schiel, Librarian of the German Institute, London; Dr R. Klein, the world authority on Andersen; and especially to the Schiller Museum in Marbach, E. Schreiber Verlag, Stuttgart, and the Editor of *Leben*, Stuttgart, for their generous loan of Schiller portraits.

CONTRIBUTORS

SCHILLER – *Quotation in English on Poetry*
André FRANÇOIS-PONCET – *Our Fellow-Citizen* [translated]
Robert MINDER – *Schiller et la Révolution Française*
SCHILLER – *Elegy (from Nanie, 1799)* [translated]
Alan PRYCE-JONES – *The Playwright*
Martin COOPER – *Schiller and Music*
Elizabeth M. WILKINSON – *The Great Contemporary*
Ilse APPELBAUM-GRAHAM – *Schiller's Aesthetic Temper*
Miron GRINDEA – *To a Distant Admirer* [sales pitch for The Guardian ...]
Janko LAVRIN – *A Note on Schiller and Russia*
Hans Christian ANDERSEN – *The Old Church Bell (written for the Schiller Album)* [an imaginative review of Schiller's life]

Views and Reviews: Miron GRINDEA, *A New Heine in English* and *Modern German Theatre*

INTERNATIONAL REVIEW

Edited by MIRON GRINDEA

A LITERARY MONTHLY IN ENGLISH AND FRENCH : YEAR XXIX : Nos. 291 - 292 - 293 : 1961

THE GRAVE
IS IN THE
CHERRY ORCHARD

Arnold Daghani

Twenty-four reproductions of
water-colours and drawings by
the author

10/6

THE GRAVE IS IN THE CHERRY ORCHARD –
ARNOLD DAGHANI

Nos. 291–293, Vol. XXIX, 1961–

'TOO FEW ATROCITIES'

There is a danger of a new type of literature being established which literary history might one day classify as 'atrocity writing'. The recent spate of psychoanalytical journalese and statistics on Eichmann, most of them contradicting one another, has appealed to readers for mixed motives, to say the least of it. Even works of poetical restraint and nobility of feeling such as, for instance, *The Diary of Anne Frank* have been mercilessly exploited for commercial or political reasons. Perhaps it is one of the conditions of our half-demented society that great human documents cannot be left to speak for themselves. Thus, much creative writing, like any other object of modern entertainment, soon becomes subject to publicity fashion.

We do hope that the poems written in the extermination camps, sometimes only a few hours before their authors passed the threshold of the gas chambers, will be rescued from oblivion and translated into as many European languages as possible.

Das Lied vom oisgehargeten yidishen Volk (The Song of the Murdered Jewish People), that appallingly beautiful poem by Itzhol Katzenelsohn, which André Schwarzhart quoted in *Le Dernier des Justes*, is still waiting for a brave, great poet to translate it into English. (In the meantime, thanks are due to Mr Jacob Sonntagg, who has coped with a few dozen of the poem's nine hundred lines.) On the other hand, the Parisian painter Mane Katz is at the present moment working on a number of engravings to illustrate the French edition of this modern Jeremiah. The Yad Washem Museum on the Mount of Remembrance in Jerusalem is collecting all available evidence regarding the greatest holocaust of all time.

The majority of the original water-colours and drawings reproduced in this issue are also to be found at Yad Washem, together with the works of many other artists who have unfortunately perished at Auschwitz, Theresienstadt, Warsaw and Maidanek. When Daghani's manuscript was submitted in 1946 to a number of London publishers, the author was told – invariably – that nobody would be interested in reading yet one more book about such unpleasant experiences. War memories were too recent, and the wounds on the public mind were too raw, to be enhanced by further writing in that vein. Perhaps having a right sense of values is to be unpredictable in our approach to life. Indeed, as recently as last year Daghani's manuscript was submitted to an important literary agent: her comment was – to quote exactly – 'Good, but too few atrocities!' Some time later the same manuscript came into the hands of a high-society lady who reigns supreme over the Parisian literary scene. While instructing one of her maids to zip up her gown, this unmistakably distinguished *femme de lettres* told her secretary in horror that she could never touch a tale of 'such atrocities'. Here we are.

Since that time, *The Grave is in the Cherry Orchard*, which the author wrote directly in English, has appeared in a German translation under the title *Lasst mich leben* (Weg und Ziel Verlag, Tel Aviv, 1960) and is now about to appear in a few other European languages. Arnold Daghani (born in 1909 at Suceava, Bukovina, a fragment of the now legendary Austro-Hungarian Kaizerdom, which afterwards became part of Roumania and is now Russian territory) has also become a remarkable painter, and his art, ever since he emigrated to Israel in 1958, has grown in deftness and colouristic excitement.

The publication of Daghani's *Diary* in a full issue of *ADAM* is not prompted by the orgy of Eichmanniana to which we have already alluded. In 1946 we printed Daghani's first piece of writing in English, *So This is the End*, which showed pronounced literary talent and aroused wide interest in the writer. We feel that *The Grave is in the Cherry Orchard* is not only a haunting document of our time but also a work of literature in its own right. Written with a flaring gift for dense observation, it captures a rich mixture of poetry and squalor, of cruelty and goodness, which makes these memoirs both wryly diverting and superbly tragic. The striking coinage of words, imperfect as it may sound from a purist's point of view, brings out the essential contribution made by Daghani to a language which he had taught himself out of sheer indebtedness to English culture.

The story of how one of the inmates succeeded in getting 'preferential treatment' by painting portraits of his torturers and of their mistresses is as fascinating as the circumstances in which the author and his wife (also an artist) had the nerve to take the works away. While crossing the river Bug almost naked, they carried the bundle containing the watercolours and drawings on their heads, and whenever the treacherous full moon came out of the clouds they risked being shot by the Roumanian sentries who were patrolling along the banks. During a second getaway, the works were tucked all round Anishoara Daghani's body under an enormous peasant cloak. As to the actual description of the main escape from Gaissin, we consider this to be one of the most accomplished passages in post-war writing. The *Diary* ends on an overwhelmingly cheerful note:

the ordeal seems to have been almost forgotten, and a vision of goodness emerges as the author's only passionate ambition. The policeman whose duty it was to take Daghani and his wife to the train of human cattle soon to be started off into the wilds of Transistria suddenly saw a painter's tools in the miserable room. 'Take them with you,' the improvised henchman said, 'they will save your life.' This was a sign of humanity on a night of total beastliness. The time for cruelty is over, the author tries to suggest – we are perhaps at the dawn of the age of mercy.

Loaded with artistic humility and still blinded by the munificence of Palestinean landscapes, which he considers to be the most beautiful in the world, Daghani is now on his first visit to this country. The present issue is *ADAM*'s welcome to an artist of great integrity of purpose and whose impact may soon be recognised as important.

CONTRIBUTORS

Arnold DAGHANI – *The Grave is in the Cherry Orchard*
Arnold DAGHANI – *La fin (Le 10 décembre 1945 le Camp … fut exterminé …)*
  [translated into French]

ADAM

INTERNATIONAL REVIEW

Editor: Miron Grindea

NOBEL 1966

Pen Drawings of S. Y. Agnon
and Nelly Sachs by Moshe Gat
and Chana Orloff

Ten Shillings and Sixpence

NOBEL 1966

Nos. 307–309, Vol. XXXI, 1966–

NOBEL DICE

The Nobel awards for literature have always been a subject of universal and sometimes violent contention. Some of the reproaches showered on the harassed Swedish academicians during the last sixty years were, no doubt, justified: *why* not Strindberg, the embittered genius who, in 1905, told Gordon Craig that he had 'not a single friend in the city of my birth'; and *why* not Tolstoy, Gorky, Wells? On the other hand, detractors forget that, on so many other occasions, the ten Swedish 'immortals' have chosen well. Romain Rolland, in the midst of the first world war, when the author of *Jean Christophe* was defying militarism *au-dessus de la mêlée*, Anatole France, Hamsun, Yeats, Thomas Mann, Pirandello, GBS, Hermann Hesse, Camus. One must envy the literary historian who will one day unravel the intricacies which made it possible for so many giants of this century to be overlooked. The task is absurdly difficult, and one of the most exciting and at the same time infuriating exercises is to speculate, year after year, on that supreme Swedish game of literary chess: who will be next? 'A mystery wrapped in an enigma', to quote the rhetoric of yet another mysterious Nobel choice ... Let us in the meantime dream of Malraux, Robert Graves, Graham Greene, Auden, Beckett, Aragon among the probables. However, seldom has there been such a felicitous choice as this year's joint award to Agnon, the greatest writer in the renascent language of the Bible, and to a unique poet who has had the temerity to approach the Nazi Holocaust as perhaps only Goethe or Heine would have done. Granted the element of unpredictability in any such decision, this time one had the feeling that telepathy had played some part in it.

I first met Agnon at Christmas 1951, when two different British passports were already necessary if one wished to visit both halves of barbed-wired Jerusalem. It was the time of the first reactions to the new horizons opened up by the Dead Sea Scrolls – dynamite for so many obscurantist developments along the centuries in both Judaism and Christianity. The veteran historian Joseph Klausner (whose pioneering work on the historicity of Jesus had been translated into English by the Oxford scholar, the Reverend Danby) took me to see his colleague, Professor Sukenik, the archaeologist who was then engaged in the deciphering of the first scrolls. 'I am as dry as dust,' he said, 'but, if you would like to spend a poetical evening, go up the mountain and speak to Agnon.' All I knew of S. Y. Agnon's work was a short novel, *Das krumme wird ja gerade*, which I had read as a student thirty years before.

Agnon was occupying a house on the very top of the Jerusalem hills. Klausner and I found him immersed in the study of the Talmud (his daily routine has always been praying at dawn, writing the whole morning and studying the Scriptures in the afternoon). He had already become a legend, although the younger writers were afraid of being contaminated by his hermetic and, for us in the West, untranslatable language. It was only in the autumn of 1957, during a second encounter, that I ventured to ask the Master whether he would allow a group of European critics to put his name forward for the Nobel Prize. 'You are joking, mein lieber Herr,' he said and walked away from the gate. Again, at Christmas two years ago, I spent a rich evening in his study drinking vodka and savouring the home-made honey cakes made by the self-effacing Mrs Agnon. The subject of the Nobel Award was raised once more. 'Too late, my man, too late,' were his words; 'I am ready for the grave.' Towards midnight he walked with me to the bus. As we waited for nearly half an hour under the glorious moonshine covering the still-separated Holy City, two groups of ebullient young tourists from West Germany passed by, chanting and strumming their guitars, on their way to a kibbutz situated close to no man's land. The old man bit his lip, wanted to say something but abstained. I have not seen him since. As this issue comes out just a few days before the official ceremony in Stockholm, it is still uncertain whether Agnon will be able to attend. Since he heard about the award, his tired heart has played havoc, but the man is of tough fibre, and he may, we all hope, make the happy journey.

• • •

He will meet in Sweden a tiny, frail refugee, who, by a touching coincidence, will be seventy-five on 10 December, the very day King Gustav presents the awards.[1] She is Nelly Sachs. A discreet writer in pre-Hitler Germany, she was destined for one of the main concentration camps. She chanced a letter of agony to Selma Lagerlöf, herself a Nobel Prize laureate and author of two unforgettable novels, *Gösta Berlings saga* and *Jerusalem*. The Swedish authoress obtained an audience with her King and persuaded the Royal Palace personally to intervene for the rescue of this unknown poet. Within days Nelly Sachs crossed the border to safety – but, much to her despair, Selma Lagerlöf died soon afterwards. The German refugee felt compelled to express her gratitude in poetry; she therefore began studying the language of her new country and was soon able to translate most of the modern Swedish poets. It was only after

Hitler's world crumbled that she had the courage to write her own poems in her native tongue – 'Flowers planted on the graves of the Jews, the Phoenix risen from their ashes,' as a critic described them. By that time, details of the most unthinkable slaughter in history had become available. No Dante was at hand for this unnarratable epic, and most probably no poet of the future will come to grips with the canvas. Even Picasso had no longer the strength to visualise anything on the lines of *Guernica.* Only his friend Ossip Zadkine has come near by the casting of his Monument in Rotterdam, whose grandeur is sung in our current issue by the Belgian poet Philippe Jones.

Nelly Sachs is no Dante; nonetheless, she is a poet of stature. Her work has appeared in print only during the last decade.[2] It casts well into English, as readers will appreciate from the renderings made for us by Georg Rapp and Karen Gershon (two German-born poets now resident in this country).

Gordon Craig we met only in his 92nd year, at his bungalow in Vence. He could be as charming as intolerable. His conversation sparkled, and his huge, indomitable body was an extraordinary sight as he lankily pursued and tried to hug *n'importe quelle jeune fille* in the street. To amuse me, he seized one of his cats and performed a rickety pirouette. This did not prevent him next day from refusing to see me. 'That is father,' his saintly daughter Nelly said resignedly. My last attempt to speak to him was early this year, when he was already inclined to sleep more and more. This revered visionary of the theatre has had an impressive number of children, some of them more or less legitimate. Edward Craig, the artist and stage designer who contributes to this number, is one born within wedlock. The biography of his great father, on which he is now at work, is awaited with impatience.

CONTRIBUTORS

Gunnar EKELÖF – *The Swan (for Nelly Sachs)* [translated poem]
Anne GOOSSENS – *Poem Four*
Marcella SALZER – *Communication* [poem]
David PATTERSON – *The Writer and the Legend*
S. Y. AGNON – *Me'oyev Le'ohev – From Foe to Friend* [translated story]
Stuart FRIEBERT – *Kinderlied (for Nelly Sachs)* [poem]
Leah GOLDBERG – *On Agnon's 'Metamorphosis'*
Arnold BAND – *The Evolving Masks of S. Y. Agnon*
Nelly SACHS – *O the chimneys; Who emptied the sand from your shoes?; Chorus of the survivors; Chorus of the wanderers; Chorus of things invisible; That the hunted do not turn into the hunters* [6 translated poems]
Erich FRIED – *Zeile um zeile (Eine Montage für Nelly Sachs)* [poem]
Nelly SACHS – *Eli, a mystery play* [scenes from, translated]
Edward CRAIG – *Gordon Craig at Home*
Ariana HARAN – *Quand on a partagé le monde* [poem translated from Hebrew]
Philippe JONES – *Dialogue pour une ville détruite* [prose-poem]

Views and Reviews: David LUTYENS, *How to capture a sigh (Tarjei Vesaas's Is-slottet]*

NOTES

1. Since by yet another coincidence, a sinister one, the Nobel award concurs with the happy revival of Neo-Nazism in Germany (so it is unlikely that the toast for Nelly Sachs on 10 December will find any echo in the famous München Bierhalle, where, in 1922 ...), it is possible that her work may well light a path for the younger people in search of a conscience.

2. *Eli: Ein Mysterienspiel vom Leiden Israels,* written in 1943 but published only in 1951 in a private edition by another German exile in Sweden, the eminent literary historian Walter Berendsohn; *In den Wohnungen des Todes* (In the Abodes of Death, 1947); *Sternverdunkelung* (Eclipse of the Stars, 1949); *Und niemand weiss weiter* (And no one knows where to turn, 1955); *Flucht und Verwandlung* (Flight and Transformation, 1959); *Fahrt ins Staublose* (Journey into Dustlessness, comprising the Collected Poems, 1961); and *Späte Gedichte* (Late Poems, 1965). The anthology of lines (p. 44 [of this issue]) prodigiously compiled by the Austrian poet Erich Fried, resident in this country since 1938, reads like yet another poem by Nelly Sachs – and this we consider the noblest tribute as from one great poet to another.

ADAM

INTERNATIONAL REVIEW

Editor: Miron Grindea

PROUST...
après
Painter

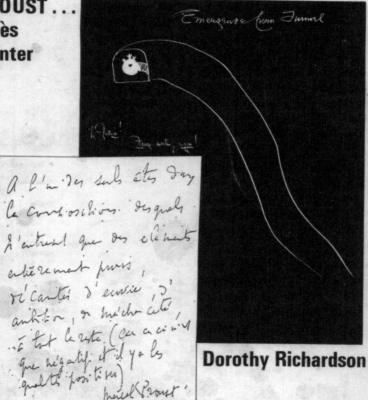

Dorothy Richardson

10/6

PROUST ... APRÈS PAINTER

Nos. 310–312, Vol. XXXI, 1966–

The volume of Proustian research and discovery continues to grow so rapidly that it is hardly possible to keep pace with it. The occasion for this third issue of *ADAM* devoted to Proust is, of course, the publication of George Painter's monumental biography (vol. I, 1959, vol. II, 1965, Chatto & Windus, London). If we find it difficult to be entirely detached in its appraisal, it is because we have witnessed the agonising obstacles the author has encountered over the past few years. At one time he was no longer sure whether his publishers, in view of circumstances still mysterious to us, would ever bring out the concluding volume; we therefore have particular reason to rejoice in the triumphant completion of the work. To fellow-Proustians throughout the world, this biography must provide a most reassuring shaft of light on their ever-puzzling, ever-exasperating idol. (Incidentally, will the noun *proustolatrie* and the verb *proustifier* ever be included in a future *Littré*?)

As usual, London is either too lazy or simply incapable of waging sustained literary warfare. There was a brief polemic in the *TLS* aiming at stabbing Painter with a cardboard *poignard*, the victim survived and, to everybody's surprise, announced that he was embarking on a life of Chateaubriand ...

What a cheering sight, on the other hand, across the Channel! How Marcel Proust would have enjoyed the salvoes fired back and forth from the Rive Droite salons so familiar to him; or a Paris divided into two violently opposed factions, the *pour-Paintère* and the *contre-Paintère*. How he would have revelled in that truly aristocratic outburst attributed by a literary weekly to the Vicomtesse Marie-Laure de Noailles: 'Ce Monsieur Painter devrait être fusillé; il a mal parlé de ma tante, Mme de Chevigné; quel droit a *cet anglais* de parler de Proust?' Saint-Germain may never get over the fact that a simple *fonctionnaire* in the Printed Books Department of the British Museum has had the effrontery to touch one of the most sacred cows of French literature – an act of *lèse-majesté*.[1]

To turn to the contents of our own present number: *A la recherche du temps posthume*, which we are privileged to publish in John Jolliffe's translation under the title *Time after Death*, first appeared in 1957 (Collection *Libelles*, Fasquelle Editeurs). How one longs for another novelist or playwright as perceptive and subtle as Monsieur Jean-Louis

Curtis to capture the uproar and chaos caused by the translation of Painter's work: *Les Années de Jeunesse*, 1959, and *Les Années de Maturité*, 1966, translated by Georges Cattaui and R. P. Vial (Mercure de France). In an elegantly phrased introduction, Monsieur Cattaui (who has himself often thought of writing a life of Proust) has admitted Painter's rare gifts by pointing out 'ce don du récit et de la mise en scène que les Anglais semblent seuls posséder à un si éminent degré'. However, not even this noble acknowledgement seems to have been of any avail, for the battle continues unabated. A thrilling compensation for all the misery came from no other than the still-redoubtable Amazon of Letters, ninety-year-old Natalie Clifford Barney.

Judging the state of affairs from the pinnacle of her accumulated wisdom, she wrote to us to say that she considered Painter's biography one of the most thrilling experiences of her whole literary career. Miss Barney, who usually takes pleasure in making her friends believe that she finds intensive reading tiresome (she has concentrated the best of her mind onto the art of the *conversation à deux*), had read the two Painter volumes from cover to cover and, as we were able to witness ourselves, asked for some of the pages to be read to her more than once.

●　●　●

The worst sin committed by this hitherto-unknown Englishman was that he based all his discoveries and interpretations only on published materials. Although he went to Paris four times, in 1949, 1950, 1951 and 1960 (plus a bicycle trip to Illiers-Combray), he paid no visits to any salon, nor did he in any way gratify the vanity of those few contemporaries of Proust still alive – he did demurely agree, though, to accompany us on a visit to Violet Schiff some seven years ago.

One hardly dares imagine how Marcel Proust himself would have reacted to the merciless accumulation of facts achieved by his eccentric biographer. Would he have written, one wonders, to Mr Raymond Mortimer, begging him not to forget to enumerate in his next Sunday *feuilleton* the scandalous number of misprints?[2] Would he have telephoned the French Ambassador at the Court of St James to inquire whether there was any chance of extraditing 'ce sacré anglais' to be tried in France? Or else, by some miraculous feat of artistic objectivity, and without this time tearing a hat to pieces, would the by-now respectable member of the French Academy, and no doubt also a veteran of the Nobel Prize, have fallen, too, under the spell of so many extraordinary facts related to his tragic nocturnal existence? (When Dorothy Bussy, the author of *Olivia*, once told her friend André Gide that Painter was presenting *Paludes* as the major key to his works, Gide gave this gratified reply: 'Dites à ce jeune homme qu'il est dans le vrai!')

To our mind, the episode which best illustrates the present division of France is the elation which a very fine novelist, renowned for his piety, is alleged to have shown recently while preparing an article in praise of 'Monsieur Paintère' – not so much because he found the book *hallucinant* as because his appreciation was bound to infuriate a certain power in the enemy camp!

Meanwhile, George Painter's work – pride of a generation – advances along the tricky furrows of literary history, but – alas – even this great achievement is far from being the last word on the subject. The stand taken in this number by the novelist Elizabeth Warington-Smyth shows how many more potential visions of the Proustian world are in store. No sooner has vol. II of the biography come out than several dozen new books on Proust have mushroomed, both in the USA and in Europe. The frontierless map of Proustiana will go on being examined and re-examined as long as there are universities to hatch doctoral theses and as long as Joyceans and Kafkologists alike are allowed to practise their own game unpunished. After all, *ADAM* itself is part of the racket and can hardly plead innocence. One cannot do anything about it other than suggest the formation of a Proust Council, consisting of no more than half a dozen experts such as Germaine Brée, André Ferré, Philip Kolb, Georges Cattaui, Anthony Pugh, Kynichiro Inoué, together with a General Secretary sufficiently tactful to keep the warriors at bay and, if possible, with M. André Maurois, Pamela Hansford Johnson and Cyril Connolly as alternating chairmen.

At this juncture one is tempted to suggest that a few more baits are cast into the unquiet rivers of Proustian paddling. One of them is a study of Proust's peculiar anti-semitism, with a thorough scrutiny of his tragic dichotomy: the occasional attraction to Jewish traditions symbolised by his mother, and the occasional need to take revenge in the way he depicted the Comte de Montesquiou and most of the anti-dreyfusard aristocracy – yet these so often offset by his own outbursts of an aberrant form of *Judenhass*, which one also finds in the works of Karl Marx and Otto Weininger. In a series of articles and essays published in the thirties in *Palestine, Menorah* and in his own brilliant *Revue Juive*, Georges Cattaui has broached this obsessive subject, but this was before the Nazi holocaust; now there is room for an entirely new and fuller analysis.

One would also wish to see, among the many potential anthologies which are bound to be inspired by Proust's work, a selection of the *bêtises* written on it. H. G. Wells's *Exploration in Autobiography* (vol. I, pp. 462–3) offers a superb entry: 'We belonged to different schools. [My wife's] admiration for Katherine Mansfield, for instance, was unbounded, while my appreciation was tempered by a sense of that young woman's limitations; and she had a leaning towards Virginia Woolf, whose lucubrations I have always regarded with a lack-lustre eye. My wife liked delicate fantasy after the manner of Edith Sitwell, to whom I am as appreciatively indifferent as I am to the quaint pattern of old chintzes or the charm of nursery rhymes. Again, she found great interest in Proust, who for me *is far less documented and entertaining* [our italics] than, let us say, Messrs Stoolbred's *Catalogue* of twenty years ago or an old local newspaper which is truer and leaves the comments to me.' Wells's odd persiflage is surpassed, though, by a 'review' of *Swann* written by André Chaumeix, a member of the Académie Française: 'C'est écrit comme par un cochon, comme par un Allemand.'

Louis le Sidaner, the artist's son (who, incidentally, in *Sodome et Gomorrhe* was described as 'un homme exquis; vous verrez que ses tableaux vous enchanteront') has assembled in his *J'ai relu Proust* (Bibliothèque de l'Aristocratie, Paris, 1949) an amusing list of lexical curios, which we think could be expanded; such words as 'aménageuse', 'transvertébration', 'bienveillamment' surely would have aroused Littré's wrath, but they might one day be adopted by a more broad-minded lexicographer ...

• • •

Another theme worth perhaps considering in the light of recent research is that of Proust, *homme d'affaires*. Years ago, M. André Maurois convinced most of us that, had he not been the greatest French novelist of the century, Proust would probably have become France's greatest critic. Now comes Professor Philip Kolb, with two new offerings of Proust's endless correspondence: *Choix de Lettres* and *Lettres Retrouvées* (Plon, 1965 and 1966), written between 1886 and 1922. Some of these letters were addressed to a variety of merchant bankers, bank managers (including 'MM. les Directeurs de la London County et Westminster Bank') and stockbrokers. Proust's business sense appears to have been unusually acute, so much so that one can safely surmise that, had he not been the novelist he was, he might have become known as the most cunning businessman in the literary world ... GBS was famous for his ruthless negotiatory abilities. Another striking example was that of the late Lucien Fabre (1889–1952), author of the now sadly neglected novel, *Rabevel, ou le mal des ardents*, which won the Prix Goncourt in 1923; between the wars, Fabre earned his living as a broker at the Bucharest Stock Exchange. Dr Paul Einzig, the economist, was for many years fascinated by T. S. Eliot's skilful business letters (one of his superiors, Crofton of Lloyds Bank, always boasted of the author of *Prufrock* as one of his most talented clerks whenever a difficult point had to be made in current banking correspondence).

But what one discovers in Proust's way of purchasing and selling his shares is something even more remarkable – the instinct of a born financier. As Dr. Einzig once pointed out: 'Proust seems to have been guided by the classical principles of the Rothschilds – never to ring the bell while the shares were rising.' Writing to the banker Leon Neuburger in November 1908, Proust informed him in self-congratulation: 'J'ai vendu mes Rio au-dessous des grands cours qu'ils ont atteint, mais je crois que c'est une bonne hygiène de ne pas toujours vendre "au plus haut", car alors on risque d'atteindre … le plus bas.' What is so extraordinary about this correspondence is that the ailing Proust always found the energy to instruct his *agents de change* about the most complicated transactions, interspersing his orders with unexpected beads of imagery. (He would compare, for instance, stocks and shares with mistresses of long standing – 'bien que les valeurs soient généralement commes les vieilles maîtresses, et qu'on les aime précisément en raison des embêtements qu'elles nous ont causés, espérant toujours qu'un jour meilleur se lèvera'; while keeping a tooth embedded in some unpredictable mine shares (*Doubavaia Balka*), he prepares himself for a new attack: 'Je ne leur demande que de monter tant que je suis vendeur, après quoi la baisse la plus sensible assouvira ma vengeance et éteindra mes regrets.'

But returning to *Lettres Retrouvées*: we were surprised to read a footnote on page 27 in which neither the controversial book *Le Secret de Marcel Proust* nor its much-maligned author was referred to by name ('le livre d'un homme qui, profitant de ses rapports avec la magistrature française, a éludé la loi pourtant formelle sur les droits d'auteur'). Surely Professor Kolb is too much of a scholar to leave us in the dark for too long. We wish he could tell us why he had to avoid any mention of the 'offender's' name, if indeed it was a case of a deliberate offence. As far as we can judge, Charles Briand was an inveterate bookworm who loved his Proust with the desperate, jaundiced irritability of any other addict incapable of coming to terms with the creator of *La recherche*. Just as the late Jocelyn Brooke made his 'case for the prosecution' in *Proust and Joyce* (*ADAM*, nos 297-8), so Briand too felt like debunking certain myths. Who can distrust a confession of this fervour: 'A Zürich, à Londres, à Bruxelles, à Rome, à Barcelone, où que je me trouve, chez les bouquinistes, comme dans les bibliothèques: la quête, vaine souvent, une fois ou deux miraculeuse du livre rare, de la lettre inédite, de ce qui, ici ou là, imprimé ou manuscrit, a été écrit sur Proust ou à propos de Proust. Les notes, les fiches, les copies, s'accumulent, bourrent chemises sur chemises, dossiers sur dossiers. Ce Proust *avec lequel je vis depuis des années, rythme ma vie profonde et secrète* [our italics], est-ce que je le connais? Est-ce que je le connaîtrai jamais? Qu'était, en lui-même, l'être secret et profond?' (*Le Disque Vert*, Paris–Brussels, December 1952.)

This leads to a new maze of situations, from which only a scholar could rescue us. In a shaky, hand-written letter, dated 3 December 1964, Charles Briand (whom we never met) informed us that he had translated into French 'une brochure achetée à Soho, *A Tribute to the Memory of a Friend*, signée "Alec Ralph Hobson", consacrée à un ancien protégé de Proust et contenant une quarantaine de pages de lettres, de notes ou de poèmes de celui-ci. Dès mon retour à Paris, je m'occuperai de les faire éditer.' In another letter he revealed that he had come across a number of *inédits* containing 'd'utiles détails sur la situation de fortune de Proust et montrant en lui la compétence et une pratique des opérations boursières que seules deux ou trois de ses autres lettres publiées par la Maison Plon permettaient jusqu'ici de supposer'. There followed two very sad letters from his daughter describing Briand's depth of physical misery:

'Mon père a été frappé, à la fin du mois de mai [1965] de deux attaques d'hémiplégie qui l'ont laissé paralysé et aphasique. Mon père m'a fait comprendre par signes qu'il était tout à fait d'accord pour que vous publiiez sa traduction de la brochure d'Alec Ralph Hobson, et qu'il souhaitait que je vous écrive et vous transmette ses regrets de ne pouvoir faire votre connaissance en septembre.' In a letter dated 25 September 1965, Mlle Briand added: 'Il ne souffre pas, mais c'est une vie très diminuée. Aussi je pense qu'il vaut mieux envisager franchement le fait que, compte tenu de son état de santé et aussi de son âge, il ne pourra écrire le deuxième volume auquel il avait pensé sur Proust et qui n'était encore qu'à l'état de projet (quelques notes au crayon). De toutes façons, lorsqu'il a écrit *Le secret de Marcel Proust*, il y a maintenant plus de vingt ans, il le considérait comme un tout en soi.' Finally, we received an article entitled *Un aspect inconnu de Marcel Proust*, which appears posthumously, for poor Charles Briand died earlier this year.[3]

Hobson's brochure (64 pages, with an inside title-page bearing the imprint *The House of Life*, inspired by one of Dante Gabriel Rossetti's poems), was mentioned in Briand's bibliography as having appeared in London in 1925. For more than forty years it has been a true *livre-fantôme*, unavailable even in the British Museum – until, by an almost undeserved stroke of luck and as we were about to go to press, we had the book in our hands. Both the contents and the excessive number of printing errors were enough to bring one to utter confusion and despair. The introduction first: the friend in whose memory the pamphlet was published was a certain Michael L., 'a stranger to the Jewish religion that was his parents", attracted by Christianity and yet rebellious to its discipline. German in birth by his father, English by his mother, he had followed his parents to Paris, then to Gand and back to Paris; finally, they had all come to London. There, the final separation of his parents left him at fourteen without any other resource than his intelligence, which was luckily exceptional, and his arms, which were unfortunately rather feeble.

Back in Paris between 1920 and 1921, Michael is believed to have insinuated himself into Proust's flat in rue Hamelin, presumably through the help of Henri Rochat, at that time Proust's secretary and one of the many models for Albertine. 'This 'secretary" – Hobson continues his cryptic description – 'brags to Michael of a new universe: the world of pleasure. With Marcel Proust, he catches a glimpse of another world – Society. Just at that time, a friend of Proust's, a gentleman of considerable wealth, noticed the young man, became interested in him and proposed to give him an ill-defined but profitable post. The vagabond who had tramped the docks of London and slept under the Paris bridges wore a dinner jacket and tails.' But Michael hated the sort of existence he was forced to lead and, in a moment of revulsion, decided to resume his vagrant life in Whitechapel. He then signed on in a ship as coal-trimmer and reached New York, where, after a short time, he died of pneumonia.

The circumstances in which a number of texts came to appear in English were, we thought, a gift of a riddle for Proustians. Michael L. left a *Diary* in which he marked how, on several occasions, Proust had allowed him to help himself to his waste-paper basket and to copy out a number of *'brouillons'* or actual letters, many of which the author often decided not to post, either because he had second thoughts about their contents or, more likely, because he considered some passages might be of future value for his novel. As far as *ADAM*'s own adventure goes, no sooner had we had our brief but breath-taking access to the one complete Hobson pamphlet than Philip Kolb delivered one of his expert blows by telling us: 'You need worry no more about Alec Ralph Hobson, because *I am reasonably certain* [our italics] he never existed. The whole thing was a rather childish hoax designed to evade copyright laws. What you surmise about my having access to the originals is not far from the truth.' *O rage, o désespoir!* Why should this particular brochure, which had caused us so much excitement, be nothing but a hoax? Just as Cyril Connolly, in 1959, spoke for us all when he voiced his impatience at having to wait for Painter's vol. II, so is *ADAM* now voicing its readers' anxiety at having to wait for this mystery to be solved. Who knows: perhaps we shall be forced to accept the theory that the pamphlet was concocted and printed by ... Charles Briand himself? Until proof to the contrary is available, one is still free to believe that, long before Proustian dating began (some time in the Thirties), Briand must have had access to a great many of Proust's letters, which he reproduced in good faith. Later on, the same letters were considered to be authentic, so much so that a writer of George Painter's insight made good use of them in his biography; finally, like many other similar documents, they were acquired by the University of Illinois, and this sealed their scientific fate.

In the meantime we shall have no alternative but to continue to nag ourselves in a vain endeavour to answer the question: how did these letters walk out of Proust's flat or else fall from a collector's portfolio ...? Fortunately, no scholar on earth can possibly find all the answers required by his own generation. Professor Kolb himself, returning from his latest planetary combing of sources, had the honesty to admit, in the recent edition of 'rediscovered letters', that he found them much too important to hold back until a more detailed knowledge of their origins had been reached – 'jusqu'au jour où j'aurai pu *résoudre tous les problèmes qu'elles posent*' [our italics].

The contents of the present issue show how many more riches may still come to the surface even *after* Painter's masterly excavations. The posthumous memoirs of the Vicomtesse de Nantois, which appear on page 51 [of this issue], were offered to us by Mrs Wooster, whose first husband was Eugène Fould, at one time a close friend of Proust. Their documentary interest is beyond doubt: among other things, they add St Moritz to the list of places where Marcel used to go during the early stages of his *mondain* life – at last *Présence réelle*, the 22nd 'rêverie' in *Les plaisirs et les jours*, makes some sense: 'Nous nous sommes aimés dans un village perdu d'Engadine au nom deux fois doux – le rêve des sonorités allemandes s'y mourait dans la volupté des syllabes italiennes'; surely this must have been Sils Maria, the place which enchanted Nietzsche and Cocteau. It was during his promenades around Saint-Moritz that the young Proust discovered the lake of Poschiavo, Samaden, Celerina and Val de Viol.

To persuade Count Gautier-Vignal that writing his reminiscences of Proust was imperative was quite an operation: but now the text is almost ready to appear in book form. Monsieur Louis Gautier-Vignal is one of the last celebrated representatives of 'la belle époque'; his memory is superbly lucid and his sense of loyalty to friends ferociously fresh and stimulating.

Finally, an event typical of things still to come: a few months ago we were passing through Paris when the well-known Librairie Nizet published a 700-page book entitled *Avec Marcel Proust, Causeries-Souvenirs sur Cabourg et le Boulevard Haussmann*. The author, M. Plantevignes, is a retired hatter, who has been waiting for nearly fifty years to divulge that it was he, Proust's junior by ten years, who suggested the title 'A l'ombre des jeunes filles en fleurs' (a series of titles coming from a youth not yet twenty: 'A l'abri des jeunes filles et de leurs confidences fleuries', 'A l'abri des confidences fleuries des jeunes filles', finally, 'A l'ombre des jeunes filles et de leurs confidences fleuries'). 'Ce ne fut que plusieurs années plus tard, vers 1911, que Proust me demanda soudain un soir si je ne verrais pas d'inconvénient à ce qu'il donnât de titre à un petit chapitre sur Balbec. – Ah, le titre de feuilleton pour midinettes, m'exclamai-je. – Oui, mais seulement pour un petit chapitre tout à fait secondaire … On sait ce qu'il en advint, comment le petit chapitre devint un gros volume – et comment le titre fut conservé et resta le titre fameux d'un Prix Goncourt.' At that time, during the summers of 1908 and 1909, 'Proust était encore assez vaillant et assez désireux de voir du monde pour descendre l'après-midi dans l'hôtel et au Casino.' Everybody was 'comme magnetisé par cette voix orientale en mélopée chantante qui semblait ne viser qu'à charmer ou qu'à inhiber une victime d'observations.'

But young Plantevignes played an even more important role in the writer's life: 'C'est moi qui avait fait connaître Agostinelli à Proust, absolument par hasard – en ce sens qu'un jour à Cabourg, comme il désirait un taxi, je lui dis qu'il y en avait maintenant un en permanence sur la place devant le Grand Hôtel, et que c'était un taxi de Paris, dont le chauffeur avait eu l'idée de venir faire la saison à Cabourg – que ce taxi était une voiture très bien tenue, en très bon état, et dont le chauffeur paraissait fort gentil et très arrangeant pour les longues promenades et excursions. Proust fut enchanté de ce renseignement, il prit l'habitude de le faire demander, s'en trouva fort content … Agostinelli, de son côté, prit l'habitude de ne pas se laisser employer pour une longue course ou pour une randonnée en dehors de Cabourg, sans d'abord avoir fait demander à Proust s'il n'avait pas besoin de ses services – ils firent ainsi peu à peu connaissance et finirent par devenir de véritables amis.'

Monsieur Plantevignes occupies a very large and somehow weird apartment overlooking the Champ de Mars; he looks almost as tall as the nearby Tour Eiffel and has an endearing conversational habit of emphasising his points in a sudden and prolonged falsetto. He showed and lent us his small collection of Proustian relics, the most important of which are two unique copies of the *Cabourg-Gazette*, one, dated August 17 1910, mentioning *M. Proust* among the distinguished holiday-makers who sent wedding presents to Mlle Anita Nahmias, sister of Albert Nahmias, the young stockbroker described by Marcel walking along the promenade dressed like a girl 'tout de fanfreluches habillé'; another issue of the same gossip paper, dated September 1910, published on the front page a portrait of young Plantevignes practising most of the 'sports mondains': 'Il monte à cheval, il joue au golf et, entre ses repas, fait encore de la marche sur la digue.' Moreover, this belated messenger of the Proustian Gospel, whom the Master used to call 'mon cher Chevalier Fantaisie', had also quite a reputation for his flirtatious exercises with the opposite sex. Our conversation centred round his proud claim that all his life he had been 'un homme à femmes', and that he had only been fascinated by Proust's literary *genius*. 'J'ai connu Proust intimement,' he writes, 'je l'ai connu dans ses meilleures journées de confiance totale – mais je l'ai connu aussi dans ses moments indéchiffrables; essayer de forcer les portes, eût été vain, l'on se fût brouillé avec lui et fait rapidement congédier – je restai donc sur le seuil, et m'en trouvai bien.' Monsieur Plantevignes tells his rare visitors, as he has already pointed out in his book, how sorry he is for not being able to throw any light on the identity of Albertine: 'Car autant à Cabourg qu'à Paris, je ne lui avais jamais entendu citer un nom de femme aimée qui lui eût laissé un chagrin, et jamais aucune Albertine n'était venue traverser ses propos. De même je n'ai jamais constaté dans mes si nombreuses visites au boulevard Haussmann la présence visible ou secrète d'un prisonnier ou d'une prisonnière.' The explanation? 'Proust était un très grand fantaisiste qui ne s'avouait pas toujours et qui en profitait pour se mouvoir à l'aise dans le monde de la fiction et de la semi-fiction, et en empiétant aussi même parfois sur les domaines de la dissimulation, du mensonge léger, et en tout cas du travesti.'

A NEGLECTED PIONEER

By opening our new number on Proust with a series of articles on Dorothy Richardson, we wanted to stress the significance of the re-issue by J. M. Dent of an augmented edition of *Pilgrimage* (a hitherto unpublished section, *March Moonlight*, has now been added to the original 12-volume 'roman-fleuve'). It is an event which reaffirms the pioneering achievement of one of the earliest experimenters in modern English fiction. Miss Pamela Hansford Johnson has evoked for us yet another neglected practitioner of the 'interior monologue' – Edouard Dujardin (1861–1949) – whose *les Lauriers sont coupés* appeared as early as 1887 and was almost totally ignored until an Irish exile, touring the Loire valley in 1903, bought a copy at a railway bookstall. The stranger was the future author of *Ulysses*, who now took every available opportunity to proclaim his indebtedness to Dujardin's short novel (available also in Stuart Gilbert's English version, *We'll to the Woods no More*, New Directions, 1938).[4] Dujardin was so overwhelmed by the tribute paid by Joyce that he wrote a whole book on it: *Le monologue intérieur, son apparition, ses origines, sa place dans l'œuvre de James Joyce* (Messein, 1931) – a vast confession of faith encouraged by Joyce's 'générosité sans exemple dans l'histoire des lettres'. While Mallarmé merely spoke of 'une de ces trouvailles', and Huysmans mumbled, 'C'est curieux, c'est curieux', yet another imaginative Irishman, George Moore, was more generous in his appreciation. Writing to Dujardin from London on 17 May 1887, he said how impressed he was by 'la petite vie de l'âme dévoilée pour la première fois – une musique étonnante de points-et-virgules – en tout cas *c'est neuf*'. And, a few days later, Moore discovered in Dujardin's short novel 'la forme la plus originale de notre temps'.

Unfortunately, Dujardin (who knew as little English as Proust) mentioned among his disciples only those (Virginia Woolf and Aldous Huxley) whose works were available in French translation. Dorothy Richardson was first translated into French in 1965 (*Toits pointus*, translated by Marcelle Sibon, Mercure de France), and Raymond Las Vergnas was among the first to recognize her originality: 'Si la saga de Dorothy Richardson fait penser à *La Recherche du Temps Perdu*, elle s'en sépare en ce que la romancière anglaise ne s'efforce pas, comme Proust, de tracer par l'émanation de soi-même le portrait d'une société. Elle vise bien plus à se servir des reflets qui viennent frapper le miroir qu'est sa Miriam pour pénétrer plus avant en celle-ci et rendre plus pleinement ses complexités inépuisables.' As to her future status, Las Vergnas believes that 'Elle va peu à peu, dépassant le purgatoire de la renommée, bénéficier d'une adhésion de plus en plus chaleureuse et s'affirmer durablement parmi les personnalités de tout premier ordre de la littérature: les créateurs, les originaux, les vrais écrivains.'

Literary historians are now debating whether Joyce ought not to have acknowledged Dorothy Richardson in the same breath as he acknowledged Dujardin. Dr Gloria Glikin went to great lengths of research to show that DR's first novel, *Pointed Roofs*, appeared in *The Little Review* shortly after Joyce's *A Portrait of the Artist as a Young Man*, which led a number of critics 'to link the two novelists as experimenters in kind' (*James Joyce Quarterly*, 1964). Following the blast of the first instalment of *Ulysses*, Margaret Anderson's magazine published a brief essay by May Sinclair entitled 'The Novels of Dorothy Richardson', in which the history-making expression *stream-of-consciousness* was used for the very first time.[5] The same author was to follow up the idea in one of her own novels, *Far End*, 1923: 'I'm trying to do something different this time, something that as far as I know hasn't been done before. Eliminating yourself. How do you manage that? You make things happen. Only as things happen in the character's *consciousness* [our italics]. I don't stand outside, I write from the inside out. I don't see an inch farther than the character sees. I don't display a superior understanding … There's nothing but the stream of Peter's consciousness; it's life going on and on.'

Meanwhile, '*the most abominable contemporary writer*', as Ford Madox Ford described Dorothy Richardson, is still awaiting a reassessment of her position in modern English literature. While Katherine Mansfield was at her unkindest, complaining of the 'clear shadowless country of her [DR's] mind', Rebecca West hailed *Pilgrimage* as one of the real achievements of the time, 'a miracle of performance'. The fact now that next year no less than three books on Dorothy Richardson are due to appear in the USA alone is full of promise: the first full-length biography by Gloria Glikin, a study by Horace Gregory and a monograph by Professor Thomas Staley. Finally, a Canadian scholar, Dr Shirley Rose, is engaged on a vast PhD thesis entitled 'The social and aesthetic views of Dorothy Richardson'. The summing up was made by Miss Elizabeth Bowen: 'Until Dorothy Richardson has been given her proper place, there will be a great gap in our sense of the growth of the English novel.'

As in the case of our latest additions to Proustiana, fortune once again favoured us while we were planning the contents ... Mr P. B. Wadsworth, a charming Kensingtonian retired from journalism, literally came our way to reveal, among many unrecorded episodes of the Twenties, that it was he who introduced Dorothy Richardson to the work of her great contemporary, Marcel Proust. After reading *Swann* in English, her enthusiasm for Proust never wavered. With her wide knowledge of French, she read the *Recherche* several times in the original and was tireless in marking the errors in both the Scott-Moncrieff and Stephen Hudson versions. Her understanding of Proust was wide and original, as is evident in her review of Clive Bell's study written for *The New Adelphi* (February 1929): 'If Proust could return to read it all, would he rejoice in the hullabaloo? Would the tender-hearted Marcel and the hard-hearted Proust cherish this essay as the work of a man *anglais* and yet *sensible, anglais* and nevertheless *esprit fort et clair*, who on the whole feels and thinks about life and about art very much as he did himself?' Using a rapier of irony, she warned readers that 'It is possible to be a most ardent Proustian without seeing life in Proustian terms'. To Dorothy Richardson, Proust appeared as a 'giver of life', an 'unprecedented exacter of conscious and unconscious collaboration from the reader'; nevertheless, 'Before swallowing his findings, *we have the right to know a great deal about him*' [our italics].

With more insight, perhaps, than Virginia Woolf or Aldous Huxley, Dorothy Richardson encompassed the complexities of the creative process, and, taking Proust as a justification of her own problems, she insisted on the eroding changes in time and space. 'Which of us,' she asked, 'is capable of estimating the enormous changes that have been preparing during the years of Proust's tremendous hold-up?' Again, long before specialised critics, she also pointed out that 'Proust did not deceive himself', that he did actually regard humanity as worthless except as material for art; although 'His arraignment of life is but the pathetic revelation of a psychic deficiency that was never compensated.' Dorothy Richardson originally appointed Mr Wadsworth as her literary executor, but the latter, frightened at the idea that his continuous nomad life would not allow him to cope with so great a responsibility, passed the honour on to Mrs Rose Isserlis Odle, the author's sister-in-law and herself a writer of distinction. It was she who traced for us the hitherto unpublished essay on old age and the very rare photographs of DR.

Our indebtedness to Mrs Isserlis Odle is very great indeed. We also thank Messrs Holt, Rinehart and Winston, the New York publishers, for permission to reproduce an excerpt from Mr Horace Gregory's forthcoming study, *An Adventure in Self-Discovery*; to the New York Public Library for material belonging to the Berg Collection; to M. Jean-Louis Curtis and to Editions Fasquelle for their immense kindness in allowing us to translate the whole of *A la recherche du temps posthume*. For her generous efforts in trying to obtain Proust copyright material, Mme Yvonne Israel, Conseiller Juridique, Paris, also deserves our grateful acknowledgement.

THREE *ADAM* PRIZES

With the object of encouraging new talent, *ADAM* announces the creation of three literary prizes of £100, each of which will be conferred at six-monthly intervals over the next two years.

The first award will be for a first Short Novel (40,000–45,000 words); the second, for a group of three to six Poems, preferably by someone who has not yet appeared in volume form; the third, for a first Play not yet performed or published.

Manuscripts for the Novel must reach us not later than 1st January 1968, and the decision of the Panel will be announced in the National Press in June 1968. The winning text will be featured in an issue of our magazine. Competitors for the Poetry Prize must not send in MSS before February 1968; the award will be announced six months later, and the winning text will appear in the *ADAM Poets* series. Plays should be forwarded any time between April and September 1968; the award will be announced, it is hoped, before the New Year, 1969.

Conditions:

(a) *ADAM*'s Editorial Board will select six works in each category for submission to a distinguished panel, whose decision will be final. No correspondence can be entered into.

(b) Should no entry meet the standards considered by the panel to justify the award, it may either give no prize or divide it between the two most meritorious applicants. In such circumstances, *ADAM* does not undertake to publish either of the submissions.

(c) All entries must be typewritten, in English or in French.

Intending competitors are invited to send in, together with their MS, their name, address, age, occupation and details about published works, if any, or literary awards previously won.

HAS LITERATURE A FUTURE?

At the time of going to Press, we have sent out the following question-naire to a number of writers all over the world, and we will publish their replies in a forthcoming issue of *ADAM*:

1. Have you thought in recent years whether literature as a printed process has a future? Do you fear that the new mass media (TV, newsreels, wall newspapers, Son et Lumière, etc) might in the end replace people's need for books altogether?
2. Will the present vogue of 'poésie concrète' and 'sound' poetry replace five thousand years of poetry mostly based on normal intel-ligibility? Or do you feel this to be merely another stage in the col-lapse of so many semantic values?
3. If any literary form survives, what do you think it will be – the poem, the epic, the novel, the drama, live or filmed, or some new, perhaps still unsuspected, form? And based on what values?

CONTRIBUTORS

Howard MOSS and Adrian HENRI – *Quotes on Proust*
Richard CHURCH; Storm JAMESON; Pamela HANSFORD JOHNSON – *More on DR*
Dorothy RICHARDSON – *Old Age*
Rose Isserlis ODLE – *Dorothy and Alan*
P. Beaumont WADSWORTH – *My Friendship with DR*
Gloria GLIKIN – *The 'I' and the 'She'*
Horace GREGORY – *An Adventure in Self-Discovery (DR)*
Thomas STALEY – *A Strange Anachronism (DR)*
Elisabeth FOULD – *Marcel in my Youth* [in French]
Louis GAUTIER-VIGNAL – *The Proust I Knew* [translated]
Jean-Louis CURTIS – *Time after Death (a 'brief Proustian evocation')* [translated]
Guido ALMANSI – *The 'Italian Proust'*
Pamela HANSFORD JOHNSON – *George D. Painter*
Angus WILSON – *George*
Charles BRIAND – *Proust: homme d'affaires*
George D. PAINTER – *The Sunlight of Balbec*

Views and Reviews: E. WARINGTON-SMYTH, *The Preface and Chapter Thirteen [of* Recherche*]* – L. P. HARTLEY, *Lady Aberconway's 'A Wiser Woman – A Book* of *Memories'* – Jonathan POL-LITZER, *Mary Wignam's 'The Language of Dance'*

NOTES

1. What most of these blue-stockinged 'authorities' ignore is that George Painter wrote a remarkable critical biography of André Gide (Home and van Thal, Barkers, 1931) and is also the author of a volume of verse, *The Road to Sinodun* (Rupert Hart-Davis, 1931), part of which was included in George MacBeth's *Penguin Book of Sick Verse* (1963), together with poems by Keats, Coleridge and Hardy. Was he a prophet when he lamented in his poem 'King's Langley': 'All my worldly task is done, / I have angered everyone. / Now my golden waking's past, / Silver comes at last'. Another detail which might surprise France is that Painter is the co-discoverer, together with R. A. Skelton and T. E. Marston, of the Vingate Map (*The Vinland Map and the Tartar Relation*, Yale University Press, 1965). It is a late medieval map of the world executed within a year or two of AD 1440, including a unique outline of the north-west Atlantic, with Greenland and the American coast as discovered, c. AD 1000, by the Norsemen from Greenland. This is the first and only map showing America before the voyages of Columbus and the only known example of medieval Norse cartography. Together with it is a hitherto-unknown Latin text, *Tartar Relation*, on the history and sociology of the Mongols in the mid-thirteenth century. Painter is also one of the world authorities on incunabula, held in much respect by French bibliophiles and by the Bibliothèque Nationale.

2. Actually, the present Duc de Gramont has spotted a few dozen 'erreurs' in vols I and II and has graciously sent a list to M. Cattaui in order that he may remedy the mistakes in future editions. Here are a few examples: 'Vallière, ne prend pas d'S; on aperçoit "le clocher" et non "a tour" de Senlis'; also the bronze plaque on Dr Adrien Proust's tomb at Père Lachaise, which Marcel made his mother commission from Mlle Nordlinger, 'a aujourd'hui disparu'; 'Proust demandait depuis longtemps à Guiche d'obtenir pour lui une photo de Mme Greffuhle (il n'était pas admis alors qu'il fût convenable à une dame d'en donner une à un homme); Proust dit à la comtesse que Guiche avait envisagé son mariage avec Mlle Greffuhle comme une possibilité d'obtenir pour Proust cette fameuse photo' (Painter on p. 27, vol. II, wrote: 'It's my candid opinion that Guiche married your daughter in the hope of getting your photograph'); apropos of Princesse Hélène de Chimay, the well-informed duke thinks that 'La princesse de Chimay ne pouvait être à cette époque que Clara Ward, de qui le prince était divorcé depuis 1897.' Also, 'Le titre de marquis (et de duc) ne doit jamais être suivi d'un prénom. Dire ici "le marquis d'Eyragues" et not Marquis Charles d'Eyragues (p. 90); two pages further on, Helleu did not take "a hundred sketches of the Comtesse Greffuhle" – Helleu fit 64 dessins au petit Château appelé Les Bouleaux, dont Ia comtesse se servait pour loger des artistes et jouer le rôle de Petit Trianon de Bois-Boudran'; p. 104 – could Boni de Castellane have said, 'If it please your Majesty'? 'On ne doit jamais dire – et Boni ne l'a certainement pas fait – "Majesté" à un souverain, mais "Sire" ou "Madame". On a beaucoup reproché à Mlle Maille, sans que son péché fut beaucoup plus grave, d'avoir répondu au Pape, "Oh oui, Saint-Siège"'. p. 538: '"showing the stereoscope" – il ne s'agissait pas d'un stéreoscope, mais d'une lanterne magique.' Same page: '"with views of their travels in Egypt" – le comte ni la comtesse Greffuhle n'étant jamais allés en Egypte, d'où, justement, le "Est-ce ressemblant?"' p. 254: '"It is said that he (Comte Greffuhle) left her (Mme de la Béraudière) too much money in his will" – ceci est inexact: le Comte Greffuhle est mort sans laisser de testament. Mme de la B produisit alors un papier qu'elle disait en être un, où le comte exprimait notamment le souhait d'avoir un enfant de Mystère... "Ma mort sera la preuve de la vérité" Mme de la Béraudière fit alors un procès aux héritiers du Comte Greffuhle qu'elle perdit, avec des attendus trés déplaisants pour son honorabilité. Elle fit appel, et le Duc de Gramont lui fit alors remettre 500.000 frs pour prix de son désistement.' There are many more corrections which cannot be enumerated owing to lack of space. However, in future editions of the biography, which are on the way, one will have to write Louis, marquis d'Albufera, and not marquis Louis d'Albufera, likewise Adélaïde, marquise de Blocqueville, Doasan Jacques, baron ('on supprime le prénom, bien inutile ici'), Charles, marquis d'Eyragues, Agénor, duc de Guiche, and Mary de Rothschild, duchesse de Gramont, Elaine Greffuhle, duchesse de Guiche, Corisande de Gramont ('et non Guiche') and many more etceteras.

3. He was born in 1881 in Algiers, the son of a pharmacist; spent years of poverty in Paris while studying law; became editor of *Rappel* before the first world war, then was called to the bar; joined the radical-socialist party, but after an unsuccessful candidature for the

National Assembly he joined the magistrature in 1930. Briand wrote three novels, *Comme à Paris*, *Le Sang*, *Aliaga* and a one-act comedy, *Phynance*.
4. There also exists a dramatised version of Dujardin's novel by Rayner Heppenstall, which was broadcast on the Third Programme.
5. Characteristically, DR rejected the label, 'devised to meet the exigencies of literary critism, isolated by *its perfect imbecility* [our italics]' – so that's that ... Ed.

DESCRIPTIONIBVS A BENED ARIA MONTANO OBSE

JERUSALEM

A literary chronicle of 3000 years

JERUSALEM

Nos. 325–327, Vol. XXXIII, 1968–

INTRODUCTION

September 1941–September 1968: the first Anglo-French edition of *ADAM* appeared in London during the Blitz, when as yet no outcome could be foreseen of the struggle against the forces of darkness. The present issue is a new beginning – we are now affiliated to a seat of learning, the University of Rochester, New York.

This does not mean that we are removing our furniture and hopes to another corner of the usually stony, awkward and rather unseraphic Paradise of Letters: *ADAM* will still be issued from London, with its editorial policy unaffected. The only difference will be that, while the first issue appeared in 24 pages and the latest in 240, in future we shall be able to bring out enlarged tables of contents, with additional features on various aspects of contemporary art. We shall also rely on the advice of three distinguished associate editors: Jules Brody, author of *Boileau and Longinus* (Droz, Geneva, 1958) and co-editor of the *Critical Bibliography of French Literature*; Anthony Hecht, the latest winner of the Pulitzer Prize for Poetry; and Bernard Schilling, well known for his work on Dickens, Balzac, Zangwill and Thomas Mann.

Literary dreams should not be presented in 'digest': future issues may well prove the happy consequences of our new association.

CITY OF GRIEF AND HOPE

To the memory of my parents –
who dreamed of Jerusalem

The idea of this anthology came to us one Christmas Day, when, in blazing sunshine, we first saw Jerusalem. Only the night before, in Rome in a downpour, we were among many thousands gathered for Midnight Mass at St Peter's. Soon afterwards, in a storm-tossed, angry aircraft, we had accomplished in less than six hours the physical link between the two shrines: a journey that in former times took pilgrims months, sometimes years, of travel on foot, horseback or in small boats over hostile seas and mountains, until Sion the dream became Zion the incredible sight.

When we arrived, there were still bullets whistling above and throughout the place, in the name of the recent 'unholy war'; a brooding desolation and an exhausted tension prevailed where the Holy City had been grotesquely and ruthlessly cut in two. It was not a sense of premonition, nor any particular prophetic anticipation, and certainly not a desire to make literary use of contemporary tragedy, that forced this particular subject upon us. It sprang rather from an emotional experience: finding ourselves in the *Civitas Dei*, which, throughout the ages, has been a radiant and inexhaustible inspiration to writers, poets and mystics.

From time to time, history seems to ridicule mankind, though in the case of Jerusalem it took thousands of years to fulfil the whole cycle of irony. Amidst the inevitable scholarly controversies as to the *precise* date, Jerusalem released, a few years ago, an unusual invitation throughout the world to a celebration unique in history: the three-thousandth anniversary of God's City – not of its mysterious birth, lost in legendary antiquity, but of the event that made it the metropolis of monotheistic religion – King David's conquest of Mount Zion.

The long, dramatic sweep of history that lies between this event and the international disputes raging round the centre of three world religions may perhaps be glimpsed in our selection of prose and poetry. The image of the past is ever present with the various civilisations which have in turn settled there, mingling together against a fantastic background of downfalls and rebuilding. Never at rest – in constant contradiction to the traditional interpretations of its name: *peace*. The city falls, only to rise again after scores of destructions, each with its accompaniment of pestilence and famine. Assyrians, Babylonians, Egyptians, Romans, Moslems, Crusaders, modern armies have battered its gates, in defiance of Israel's claim: 'We will not fear, though the earth be removed, and though the mountains be carried into the heart of the sea. God is in the midst of this city, she shall not be shaken.' During centuries of warfare and strife, the level of the streets has risen higher and higher, to the despair of archaeologists trying to achieve concordance between the Biblical narrative and the findings of the spade.

The Holy City has been the subject of innumerable books of pious learning, as well as of inflammatory argument. It was natural that a literary record such as ours should try to avoid paraphrasing these serious feats of scholarship, skirt the traps of theological controversy and turn away from the deep involvements of religious dogma. Ours has been the more modest yet fascinating aim of tracing and assembling some of the most significant passages in literature, from Biblical times to the present day, when the Holy City has once more become a pawn in the universal game of political chess. There can, of course, be no illusions about the shortcomings and omissions of so vast an undertaking. To treat adequately a subject at once so noble and so contentious would require a lifetime of research and far greater space. Several selections of Hebrew texts relating to Jerusalem have been published during the last fifty years or so, but of Christian and Arabic texts many have remained isolated or, for the most part, inaccessible in manuscripts or ancient editions. With all its limitations and omissions, it may be claimed that this is the first Jerusalem anthology drawn from world literature.

It is surprising that, even in England and the United States, love for the Holy Land and for Jerusalem in particular has, with few exceptions, been subordinated either to theology or, in the last hundred years, to history and archaeology. The present selection may bring into brighter focus how travellers, poets and visionaries have reacted to the image of the heavenly and earthly capital of the spirit: the 'rock of ages' which has endured by virtue of its dramatic surroundings and the faith of those who have built and rebuilt it.

While refraining from taking sides in any of the controversies that hedge the subject, we have had the joy of travelling through innumerable avenues of poetry and prose, sacred and profane, magnificent or frivolous, eccentric or commonplace. Nothing has of course been so revealing as the journey through the Bible, which in the context of our exploration has been regarded, first and foremost, as literature of the highest order and whose light, in Cardinal Newman's words, is 'like the body of Heaven in its clearness; its variants like the bottom of the sea; its variety like the scenes of nature'. However, we have assumed the Bible to be a thoroughly explored territory, hence the relatively small number of Biblical quotations. Our aim has been rather to concentrate on other sources, some well known but most of them relatively obscure. The limits of this anthology allowed little room for comment; it is hoped, though, that the introductory notes and the bibliography will further the interests of all those involved in literary history.

The extracts are arranged in ten sections, as they bear upon the varied history, the landscape and the spirit of Jerusalem. In each of these sections, the strict chronological order has often been interrupted to make room for what we consider to be of greater interest in the sequence of episodes recorded by ancient and modern writers. Many of the prose extracts and even some of the poems have had to be abridged. Similarly, the notes preceding each section present no more than a summary introduction to one particular aspect of this intensely human story, still fraught with violent arguments.

Through this maze of antagonisms we have tried our best to steer a course as non-partisan as possible, except in the unavoidably 'heretic' partisanship that is implied when doing a work in which personal choice is both required and justified. This is a literary portrait of the holiest and most blood-stained city on earth – the 'city of the world's tears' – perhaps a key to the sublime idea of a future Jerusalem. The voyage has been richly rewarding in itself, and for the spoils with which it has enabled us to return.

THE IMAGE OF JERUSALEM
– a literary chronicle of 3000 years

Edited with Introductory Notes by Miron Grindea

PART ONE: The Story of Jerusalem

PART TWO: The Image of Jerusalem

ADAM

INTERNATIONAL REVIEW

Editor: Miron Grindea

Baudelaire

Berlioz

10/6
$1 50

BAUDELAIRE – BERLIOZ
Nos. 331–333, Vol. XXXIV, 1969–

THE MISJUDGEMENT OF PARIS

En musique, il y a deux colosses: le penseur Beethoven,
et Berlioz, le plus que penseur.

Moussorgsky

Berlioz n'est pas du tout musicien.

Debussy

If for no other reason than that of simply catching by the tail what fate brings into one's editorial net, running a literary magazine would still be a rewarding way of life. More often than not one has to leap from one precipice to another, move the odd mountain, cross swords with many, cajole others sadistically reluctant to give even a thimbleful of information, accept refusals, even humiliations, as if they were acts of grace. There are *times*, though – and this is one – when things seem to just happen. Within less than a fortnight events and meetings, clues and documents simply floated our way. The Berlioz Year, which in England was given, probably uniquely, the status of a daily calendar of events, plunged us into Berlioziana.

It all began with trying to find out whether the Berlioz centennial orgy in this country was being emulated by any comparable festival in France and the United States. It was not. On the other hand, the first thing that fell into our hands upon arrival at Rochester was a shy-looking bundle containing *fifty-one* autograph letters by Berlioz ... The city was celebrating its annual week of lilac blossom and at the same time bewailing the peril of extinction threatening its excellent Philharmonic Orchestra.

Space ought to be found some time to describe in detail how Hiram Sibley made use of the funds accumulated by the Western Cable Company to endow the Eastman School of Music with one of the most exciting collections of music manuscripts in the USA. During the late Twenties he pledged 50,000 dollars for the purchase of scores and MSS and so led to the foundation of the Sibley Music Library – which contains Debussy's *La Mer*, itself a big enough bait for any music pilgrim. The Berlioz treasure was acquired gradually by the late librarian, Barbara Duncan, from the Heinrich Rosenthal Antiquariat in Lucerne and Sotheby's, then by the present Music Librarian, Dr Wanatabe, from the Pougin Collection. To her and to her zealous assistant, Charles Lindahl, our gratitude before the typewriter fails to spell it out ...

Since adventure seems to remain the safety valve of this journal, news also reached us that at Cambridge, Mass., there was a notable assortment of unpublished Berlioz letters. Within hours, contact was established, and the cultured and generous owner, Mrs Sarah Fenderson, offered to send across the Ocean more spoil than even the greediest editor would ever dare to dream of. What a consolation for Boston (the city where Poe was born) to be able now to claim a Berliozian store of such value, after that city, on innumerable occasions, had rejected Berlioz's music. 'It needs no gift of prophecy to predict that he will be utterly unknown a hundred years hence to everybody but the antiquarians,' wrote the *Boston Daily Advertiser* on 29 October 1874. Another Bostonian gem appeared in the *Musical Record* of 21 February 1881: 'The *Symphonie Fantastique* may be called delirium tremens set to music – a monstrosity.' As to the *Damnation of Faust* – in Boston's *Home Journal* for 15 May 1880: 'If all bedlam were about to be let loose on earth, it does not seem as though any preparatory shock or foreboding could be more stupendous.' Among the many sorrows that darkened Berlioz's volcanic life was also the regret that he never went to the United States – 'Je voudrais voir l'Amérique,' he wrote to his sister Adèle, 'la grande nature à catastrophes ...' A good thing he didn't, for the *New York World* might have greeted his *Requiem* in similar terms to those that appeared on 20 November 1885 – 'An embodiment of the pomp and circumstance befitting death – the torchlight is there, the catafalque, and all the flummery.'

This same New York gave us the opportunity of meeting Jacques Barzun – in the precincts of Columbia University.[1] This was the place to search for more details about the diarist George Templeton Strong, who, while describing Berlioz's *Roi Lear* as 'mere rubbish', warned music lovers against 'galvanized anthropoid Parisians [who] are becoming a nuisance' (entry for 17 December 1864). It was also he who compared the *Carnaval Romain* to 'nothing but the caperings and gibberings of a big baboon, over-excited by a dose of alcoholic stimulus' (15 December 1886). (Strong (1820–75) was an amateur organist, who at one time became not only President of Columbia but also Chairman of the New York Philharmonic.) However, our afternoon there was sunny and free of any sign of student warfare except a leaflet floating a Kantian morsel – 'Undisciplined men are apt to follow every caprice' – and that big question, 'Why are you taking exams?' Young couples were hugging each other, as they should more often do, on the steps of the Philosophy Hall. In the same seductive surroundings we then had to rub our eyes at the sight of ... nine hundred unpublished letters addressed by Gide to

Dorothy Bussy (Olivia), which will, one day, be classified by M. Jean Lambert – but that's another story!

Whenever one encounters an essential contribution to a better understanding of French cultural values, one inevitably asks, is this also known in France? Barzun (possibly the most respected Frenchman in America next to Henri Peyre) has devoted nearly twenty years of his life to producing the first full-length study of Berlioz in any language. If he seems to be philosophical about his opus – *Berlioz and the Romantic Century*, 2 vols, 1950, ignored in his native country – *ADAM*, still dreaming of a more eloquent bridge between the cultural values of the English-speaking world and those of France, is less amused by such strange negligence. It is hard to understand why Barzun's name is not – even in the first critical edition of Berlioz's literary writings so competently annotated by M. Léon Guichard (*Les Soirées de l'Orchestre*, Librairie Gründ, Centre National de la Recherche Scientifique, 1968) – mentioned among the translators of this work.

There are times when we prefer to think that such lack of interest and cordiality among many erudite Frenchmen may be due, not so much to competitiveness or professional jealousy (which after all flourish everywhere on earth) as to the irritation provoked by the extensive bibliographies and indexes that accompany almost every serious work in English. Men of learning, and even more their publishers, give the impression of intensely disliking this 'foreign' tradition; and, even when they suffer the ordeal of preparing such tiresome 'trifles', many of the items are printed without page numbers – something like 000 ... Maurois once devoted an essay to justifying the resistance to this type of un-French intellectual discipline, but he must soon have realised that he had been mistaken, for he recanted graciously in his swansong, *Prométhée, ou la Vie de Balzac*. The subject is a nagging one, and it should remain so, for it requires sustained and detailed reappraisal. Even if there are signs that today many more Frenchmen speak fluent, imaginative English than Englishmen or Americans speak good French, the amount of research on French literature, the visual arts and music in the United States and in Britain is often conducted with more enthusiasm and thoroughness than in France itself. None of the clichés surrounding the *mésentente cordiale* should prevent the genuine scholar from admitting openly this unequal balance of exchange.

• • •

Lorsqu'un poète connaît dans un pays étranger une renommée particulière, c'est en général pour la plus grande stupéfaction de ses propres compatriotes.

Georges Pompidou

It was by browsing in a great many indexes during the early research for the current issue that the Baudelaire–Berlioz association took shape. There was no anecdotal temptation, nor a mere accident of alphabet, that caused us to seek a connection between the B's; it was only a fascinated curiosity to find out whether two of the greatest innovators of the nineteenth century, whose work has been mocked and disregarded in equal measure by their fellow-countrymen,[2] ever recognized each other's achievement.

In fairness to Baudelaire (twenty years the younger), it must be stated that, although he did not grant Berlioz what he granted Delacroix – the merit of having opened 'de profondes avenues à l'imagination la plus voyageuse' – he at least mentioned him several times in his famous essay, *Richard Wagner et Tannhäuser* (*Revue Européenne*, April 1861), chiefly to reproach the often waspish composer for ignoring the Wagnerian gospel: 'M. Berlioz, qui montra cependant beaucoup moins de chaleur qu'on n'aurait pu attendre de sa part,' wrote the disillusioned poet. Baudelaire resented Berlioz's ambiguous and, in the end, venomous attitude towards his greatest contemporary in music, particularly as Wagner had once saluted his genius. ('I felt almost like a little schoolboy by the side of Berlioz' – Wagner, in *My Life*, vol. 1). On the other hand, Baudelaire also must have been aware of what Berlioz meant to his small circle of admirers in France; indeed, in his anonymous letter on the *Anniversaire de la naissance de Shakespeare*, printed in *Le Figaro*, 14 April 1864, he did not forget to speak of the 'auteur d'un *Roméo et Juliette*'.

What about Berlioz? One cannot, of course, invent literary byways for the mere purpose of satisfying one's inquisitiveness. Our self-inflicting query sprang from our admiration for Berlioz the man of letters. He was a born writer, whose literary works, when properly edited and annotated, will reveal, to quote the French composer Henry Barraud, 'une des personnalités les plus marquantes de la littérature romantique, un écrivain de race'. The author of *Les grotesques de la musique* was almost as much an artist as the composer of the *Requiem*. As voluminous a letter writer and as skilled a strategist perhaps as Proust, he seems to have been somehow more sincere – each of his letters revealing a different and genuine aspect of his unhappy life rather than an adopted mask, as was often the case with Proust. At one time or another he was associated with the most prominent exponents of the romantic movement. He courted Hugo, although he ridiculed his indifference to music – 'Hugo juge la musique comme tous les poètes, c'est-à-dire que le sens de cet art lui manque complètement' (letter to his mother, January 1836). Nevertheless, he set to music Hugo's poem *La Captive* and was pleased when the poet sent him a dithyramb on 3 August 1837: 'Tout ce qui m'entoure vous aime.' Gautier, whose *Nuits d'été* inspired some of the most beautiful melodies ever written, was not only a friend and champion of Berlioz at the time when the Establishment and the public ignored his new idiom ('Il tient dans son art,' he wrote, 'la place qu'occupent Hugo et Delacroix dans la poésie et la peinture'); he was also the dedicatee of *Les Fleurs du Mal*. These shattering poems were tried in a Court of Justice in the same year, 1857, that *Madame Bovary* was also branded as immoral; Flaubert admired the two Bs with equal favour. So did Alfred de Vigny, whom, anticipating a favourite Coctelian image, Berlioz used to call 'cher poète invisible'. Balzac, who hated music and confessed that 'Un orchestre n'a jamais été pour moi qu'un rassemblement mal entendu' *(Correspondance,* vol. III, p. 292), was nonetheless a witness of the times; he not only dedicated *Ferragus* to the composer, but also lent him his majestic fur coat when Berlioz embarked on his first journey to freezing Russia, and 'advised' him on how to speculate financially and make 150,000 francs in six months – just as Balzac himself expected to make! Nadar tried his inspired hand at taking photographs of both artists.

How, then, should one account for the fact that the over-impressionable Berlioz – 'Il lisait si bien aux beaux endroits, les larmes lui coulaient le long des joues, mais il continuait à lire, essuyant à la hâte les larmes, pour ne pas interrompre la lecture …' – never seems to have so much as noticed the poet who first expressed the solitude of his age? Was the element of spleen prevalent before Baudelaire invoked *'l'esprit gémissant en proie aux longs ennuis'*? A revealing passage in Berlioz's *Mémoires*: 'Ce fut vers le temps de ma vie académique que je ressentis de nouveau les atteintes d'une cruelle maladie (morale, nerveuse, imaginaire, tout ce qu'on voudra), que j'appellerai *le mal de l'isolement*. Cet état n'est pas le *spleen* [our italics], mais il l'amène plus tard; c'est l'ébullition, l'évaporation du cœur, des sens, du cerveau, du fluide nerveux. *Le spleen, c'est la congélation de tout cela'* [our italics].

To return to Baudelaire's indictment:

> Rien n'égale en longueur les boiteuses journées,
> Quand sous les lourds flocons des neigeuses années,
> L'Ennui, fruit de la morne incuriosité,
> Prend les proportions de l'immortalité.

One more bypath down which Berlioz himself turned. 'Il y a d'ailleurs deux espèces de spleen,' he wrote. 'L'un est ironique, railleur, emporté, violent, haineux; l'autre, taciturne et sombre, ne demande que l'inaction, le silence, la solitude et le sommeil. A l'être qui en est possédé *tout devient indifférent; la ruine d'un monde saurait à peine l'émouvoir*. Je voudrais alors que la terre fût une bombe remplie de poudre, et j'y mettrais le feu pour m'amuser' [our italics]. How close to:

Quand le ciel bas et lourd pèse comme un couvercle
Sur l'esprit gémissant en proie aux longs ennuis,
Et que de l'horizon embrassant tout le cercle
Il nous verse un jour noir plus triste que les nuits.

Has this parallel ever been followed by a *comparatiste*? Admitting that, during one's feverish pursuit, one assumes points of contact that loom larger than evidence would allow, the vaguest references nonetheless make one's heart beat with anticipation. The game is conceivably worth playing as one of the more cheering exercises in literary history, for which 'nothing' or 'never' are after all only relative terms! The introductions in this journal (even when disproportionately longer and more onerous perhaps than in other publications) should therefore not be taken as pretexts for ostentatious knowledge: we simply rejoice whenever we stumble upon anything that may lead to unexplored literary territory and imagine that this scrabbling may provoke the true men of learning to embark on their own special subjects, which *ADAM* has neither the time nor the qualifications to tackle.

● ● ●

In this context, our old readers should perhaps once again accept the thought that, an obsession being by its very nature obsessive, we simply cannot help hoping, however absurdly, that among the many hundreds of letters of Berlioz, still unpublished and waiting for their editor,[3] there may be some mention of Baudelaire – just as we hope that yet another bait for restless Berliozians might stay safely on the hook – Dickens! Indeed, in the Prologue to *Les Soirées de l'Orchestre*, Berlioz describes an orchestral player who, instead of counting the bars, is 'fort souvent acquis tout entier aux merveilleuses scènes de Balzac (et) aux charmants tableaux de mœurs de Dickens'. Pray, room for further speculation? Pauline Garcia Viardot, Malibran's sister, was adored concurrently by Berlioz, Dickens and Turgenev (in fact she became the mistress of the last). Did the first two wooers ever meet? We know that Dickens heard Viardot sing in a performance of Gluck's *Orphée* in November 1862, under Berlioz. As we queried this with Mrs House, the new editor of *Dickens' Letters* (which supersedes the None Such 1938 edition), we were given access to a hitherto unknown letter addressed from 27 rue du Faubourg St Honoré (17 November 1862) to *My dear Madame Viardot*: 'I am delighted to have your letter, for I can most honestly assure you – though on second thoughts I believe you know it already – that your wonderful powers as a great and true artist make you one of the most interesting people in the world to me.' We also know, at any rate, from a letter written to his friend Auguste Morel (12

February 1848), that Berlioz met Dickens' father-in-law, George Hogarth (1783–1870), an amateur cellist and composer, who was also writing music criticism for the *Daily News*. In an article published in that paper on 13 February 1848, Hogarth was deploring the fact that 'Berlioz's music cannot be said till now to have come before the public at all'.

• • •

And as we are anyway engulfed in speculation and legitimate fantasies, why leave out another nineteenth-century giant? Your guess is as good as ours. Unlike Dumas, who, according to Berlioz, could not endure 'even bad music', Stendhal found in it 'the strongest and undoubtedly the most expressive passion of my life'. Did *he* react to Berlioz's revolutionary language? Or did he only come across this nasty description in Berlioz's *Mémoires* (vol. I): 'Et ce petit homme au ventre arrondi, au sourire malicieux, qui veut avoir l'air grave? – C'est un homme d'esprit qui écrit sur les arts d'imagination, c'est le consul de Civita-Vecchia: il médite en ce moment quelque nouveau chapitre pour son roman de *Rouge et Noir.*' How perspicacious he was when, in a moment of truth, Berlioz described himself as 'méchant comme un dogue à la chaîne' (*Mémoires*, p. 224). Still, what matters for us is that he knew about, and was irritated by, Stendhal.

Who next? Of course, there was Nietzsche, choosing Wagner as his *bête noire*. Anything at hand during his prolonged, relentless demolition campaign was used with superb vehemence and *méchanceté*. Thus, in *Ecce Homo* (p. 1091): 'Wer war der erste *intelligente* Anhanger Wagners überhaupt? Charles Baudelaire, derselbe, der zuerst Delacroix verstand, jener typische *décadent*; in dem sich ein ganzes Geschlecht von Artisten wiedererkannt hat – er war vielleicht auch der letzte ...' Baudelaire was also, together with Schopenhauer, responsible for the 'Fluch auf die Wollust' ('The curse of sensual pleasure,' in *Aus dem Nachlass der Achtzigerjahre*, p. 431). In a letter to Peter Gast, written from Nice on 26 February 1888, Baudelaire has become 'jener bizarre Dreiviertel-Narr' ('that bizarre three-quarters madman'), also a libertine, mystical, satanic, but above all Wagnerian. More important still was Nietzsche's description of Wagner as a product of the 'französische Spät-Romantik, jene hochfliegende und doch emporreissende Art von Künstler wie Delacroix, wie Berlioz, lauter Fanatiker des *Ausdrucks*, Virtuosen durch und durch ...' ('that lofty and yet exalting type of artists such as Delacroix or Berlioz, all fanatics of *expression*, virtuosi through and through', in *Jenseits von Gut und Böse*, II, p. 724). Curiously enough, after having at first shown unlimited enthusiasm over the appearance of Berlioz – he played, for instance, the piano versions of

Benvenuto and *L'Enfance du Christ* and even tried his hand at an orchestral work of his own, *The Mystery of Saint Sylvester*, in imitation of Berlioz's religious style and being twitted by his friends about his passion for his great 'Hector' (Barzun), finally greeting Bizet with a 'Hurray, a genuine French talent, not at all led astray by Wagner, a true *pupil of Berlioz*' [our italics] – the unpredictable philosopher ridiculed him as being the exponent of the 'sogenannte Zukunftmusik' ('the so-called music of the future') in *Autobiographisches aus den Jahren*, 1856 bis 1869, p. 34.[4]

If some of the Baudelairians we consulted took *ADAM*'s query in their most highly ... negative stride, Professor T. W. Bandy, the director of the Centre d'Etudes Baudelairiennes at Nashsville, Tennessee, was less discouraging; moreover, he condensed a great deal of his knowledge into a survey befitting 1969. In the meantime, M. Marcel Ruff, who has edited a magnificent edition of Baudelaire's *Œuvres Complètes* in one volume (Collection L'Intégrale, Editions du Seuil, 1968), cast out one of the most intriguing biographical shadows by giving unmistakable evidence that Baudelaire was the son of a defrocked priest ('Son père aurait porté la soutane avant de porter le bonnet rouge'). Which corroborates the poet's own casual confessions, 'Moi, fils d'un prêtre', or 'Mes conversations avec Dieu'.

As to our latest bouquet of translations, it should be taken as yet another proof of Baudelaire's contemporaneity. Baudelaire has echoed most widely in translation.[5] '*Les parfums, les couleurs et les sons se répondent*': thus, the rare powers of evocation of his prosody defy the many unsuccessful attempts at 'wrestling in despair with the entire angel of the original' (Jackson Mathews) and keep poets like Robert Lowell or Richard Wilbur well on the alert. We share Professor Mathews' belief that P. F. Sturm was one of the best English translators. His *Poems of Charles Baudelaire* first appeared in the Canterbury Series, London, 1906 – which did not prevent Brentano's from issuing in 1919 an American edition *without* the translator's name! (As this edition was prefaced by Huneker, everybody, including even Mr James Laver, who edited that remarkable 1942 edition for bibliophiles, thought that Huneker was also the translator.) As a tribute to this obscure but genuine artist, here is his version of *Parfum Exotique*:

> When with closed eyes in autumn's eyes of gold
> I break the burning odours of your breast,
> Before my eyes the hills of happy rest
> Bathed in the sin's monotonous fires, unfold.
> Islands of Lethe where exotic boughs
> Bend with their burden of strange fruit bowed down,

Where men are upright, maids have never frown
Unkind, but bear a light upon their brows.
Led by that perfume to these lands of ease,
I see a port where many ships have flown
With sails outwearied of the wandering seas;
While the faint odours from green tamarisks blown,
Float to my soul and in my senses throng,
And mingle vaguely with the sailor's song.

There is no need for unnecessary anecdotage – life being even stranger than an editor's fiction. If, for Roy Campbell, *Les Fleurs* suggested *Flowers of Sickness*, of *Anguish*, of *Pain* rather than of *Evil*, ADAM has now the indescribable privilege of presenting Baudelairians with the latest interpretation of the haunting title: it has become *Vegetables of Evil!*

Bernard Schilling's essay on 'This Harsh World' has a place of its own. It introduces the second volume of a trilogy which will put the inexhaustible fascination of Balzac and Dickens into a fresh perspective. The first volume, *The Here as Failure: Balzac and the Rubempré Cycle*, has already come out (Chicago University Press, 1968). It will be followed by *The Ambiguous Hero: Dickens and the Shame of Pip* while the third volume will be devoted to *The Hero in Triumph (Mann and the Return of Joseph)*.

* * *

We were ready to let this issue rest when Mr Richard MacNutt, another world-famous authority on Berlioz, found it proper to entice us, from Tunbridge Wells, Kent, with more temptations. Out of a tantalising embarrassment of riches only one single document, too irresistible for words, has to be included here, even if out of context: yet another unpublished letter, addressed to the violinist Heinrich Ernst, undated and sprinkled with various asides to a number of London and Parisian friends and admirers:

Mon cher Hallé

Vous m'avez fait une charmante surprise avec votre lettre, et (aye!) je voudrais bien (aye! aye!), je voudrais bien (oh! ah! sacré point de côté!), je voudrais bien vous ... (Pas moyen! Tonnerre de dieu! quelle douleur!). Je voudrais bien vous dire ... (impossible! superimpossible!) addio, un altra volta.

H Berlioz

(à Heller)[6]

Oh! to blow! to blow! What a profound satisfaction! But alas! to blow is not for me.
My dear Heller, I am a very suffering man. Aye! and I cannot to be a blowing man. Don't forget me! I will be tomorrow, I shall be tomorrow, as poor Mercutio, a very grave man. I am dead, dear, receive my soul or perhaps I am not sure of it.

HB

Mille choses à Davison, qui part toujours et n'arrive jamais.
Et mille injures à Barnett qui est un bon et digne ami, qui ne répond jamais. C'est égal, on l'aime silencieux puisque c'est sa manie de ne rien dire.
N'oubliez pas mon billet à Chorley. A proposito, vous ne savez pas une chose? Donc, dis-je, vous ne savez pas une chose?... Je vous invite pour le 11 Décembre prochain, à boire chez Ernst, un vigoureux saladier de punch en mon honneur si je suis vivant, et à ma mémoire si je suis mort. Car il faut que vous sachiez que le 11 Décembre a eu l'honneur de me voir venir en ce monde. Livrez vous ce jour là a tous les jeux héroïques, Ceste (ou Boxe) course en chars (ou en cab) danse Pyrrhique (ou chahut) et autres divertissements dont vous trouverez la description dans Homère et dans Virgile.
Sur ce je vous bénis tous, et je vous prie de croire que je sais bénir de main de Lemaitre. Vous ne risquez rien de dire de moi comme dit Frédérick (le surdit Lemaitre) du baron de Worms père:
Comme ce gaillard-là bénit bien.

HB

As always, there is no end to complications and new beginnings. In the Centenary Issue of the *Musical Times* (September 1903), Charles Maclean discovered that 'Artistically, almost the chief significance of Berlioz's music lies in the fact that it was wholly free from Judaic influences.' Who will take this up? Here was one of the earliest rallying cries for a 'Judenrein' society *avant la lettre*, or somehow midway between Nietzsche, Chamberlain, Gobineau and the rest.

• • •

While going to press, two more things happened to this issue: one localised on this planet, the other opening up a new age for mankind – and possibly for literary magazines as well.

The best part of an *allocution*, pronounced by M. Georges Pompidou at the Baudelaire Symposium held at Nice in 1967, came into our hands. Except for the president-poet of Senegal – our friend Sédar Léopold-Senghor – what other living statesman cares with the same

intensity for poetry and politics? Here you find the profession of faith
made by a President of the French Republic: 'Ce n'est jamais sans émotion qu'il m'arrive de regarder ce petit volume à couverture jaunâtre,
paru en 1857 et qui s'intitule *Les Fleurs du Mal*. Là est, de toute poésie,
ce qui me touche le plus. L'angoisse devant la vie et devant la mort, le
sentiment de la faute et celui de la révolte, la poésie de la vie moderne
et celle de l'évasion. A vrai dire, il est impossible de résumer en
quelques mots une œuvre où il y a tout et qu'il faut connaître en total-
ité.' As characteristic as it is moving, then comes President Pompidou's
statement that 'Baudelaire seems to me to be a man of the twentieth
century rather than of the nineteenth, inasmuch as he ventures (out of
ignorance, indifference or genius, I wonder?) far beyond the scope of
his contemporaries who, although witnesses of the first great transfor-
mations ushering in our modern age, regarded these changes merely (I
would almost say, imperturbably) as the confirmation of their faith in
the power of reason and scientific progress. But Baudelaire, either
because he gauges the overthrow of the old beliefs or because he realis-
es the breakdown of former props – metaphysical, moral and social –
refuses to share the scientist's certainty and optimism. Driven by his
own restless misery, the poet can only gaze in agonized enquiry at the
impenetrable horizon. If he looks back, it is only to be more certain that
the past is gone for ever; that man has reached the point of no return.
This drama seems to me to hold true both for us and for our present-
day world. It is this, in my view, that makes him so completely a man
of our time.'

However insignificant man feels when confronted by the conquest of
space, he cannot refrain from dwelling on the infinite new vistas for
poetry, now that one of mankind's most mysterious symbols has become
computerised. Should one turn away from 5,000 years of imagery while
waiting for a totally different creative response? What a task – rescuing
the innumerable evocations of 'the innocent moon which nothing does
but shine' (Francis Thomson), before poets and anthologists *up there*
enter the race and return the compliment. While there is still time, one
should think of Robert Frost's 'Moon Compasses' or of Christopher
Fry's 'The moon is nothing / But a circumnambulatory aphrodisiac /
Divinely subsidised to provoke the world / Into a rising birthrate'. And
– why not? – of Mark Twain, who was convinced that 'Moontalk by a
poet who has not been in the moon is likely to be dull.'

But even an editorial must come to an end – particularly as the
Berlioz Centennial year has not yet run its course ...

CONTRIBUTORS

W. T. BANDY – *At the 'height of his glory'*
New translations from BAUDELAIRE – *Un fantôme; Invitation au voyage; Parfum exotique; Remords posthume; Spleen; Le possédé; Sed non satiata; Le vampire; Epilogue; The phial; Le revenant*
Michael HAMBURGER – *Notes on Baudelaire*
Charles BAUDELAIRE – *Obsession* [translated poem]
Michel RYBALKA – *Le 'Baudelaire' de Sartre*
Jacques BARZUN – *Berlioz in 1969 : A Fantasia for Friends Overseas*
Hugh MACDONALD – *Hector Berlioz 1969: A Centenary Assessment*
Charles BAUDELAIRE – *Spleen* [translated poem]
Hector BERLIOZ – *Sixty-one Letters (in French and English)*
John R. ELLIOTT, Jr – *Berlioz the Critic*
Charles GRANDMOUGIN – *A Hector Berlioz* [poem]
Michael WRIGHT – *Berlioz and Anglo-American Criticism*
E. HOLMES – *The Genius of Hector Berlioz*
John W. KLEIN – *Berlioz's Béatrice et Bénédict*
Bernard N. SCHILLING – *Balzac, Dickens and 'this harsh world'*

Views and Reviews: Professor Pasteur VALLERY-RADOT, *Un humaniste est mort (René Dumesnil)* – John WARRACK, *Colin Davis's Berlioz* – Miron GRINDEA, *Monica Nurnberg's 'The technical vocabulary and phraseology of music as exemplified in the writings of Hector Berlioz' (thesis, Liverpool University, to be submitted)*

NOTES

1. It was there that we learned that the recently resuscitated Berlioz Society of America was planning a chartered flight for one hundred pilgrims to come over to London to attend the premiere of *The Trojans* at Covent Garden this autumn – *Où êtes vous, Hector?* Now that Beethoven, Schubert, Liszt and Debussy are believed to dictate fresh compositions to a lady pianist at Balham, London SW, what about your descending in an ectoplasmic storm to join us on 17 September 1969? If you don't feel like communicating some music for the piano (which was never exactly your medium), give us at least a new blare of trombones outrageous enough to astonish even a Boulez, a Xenakis or a Stockhausen. And, at all costs, do not miss the psychedelic *Damnation* at Sadlers Wells!
2. 'O crapauds de Parisiens!' (the poet writing to Léon de Wailly from Brussels, 19 March 1855). 'Je suis las de la France et je désire l'oublier pendant quelque temps.' 'Il ne faut pas oublier que nous sommes à Paris, où l'on aime la musique à peu près comme chez les Sioux, les Pawnies et Pieds-noirs de l'Amérique' (Berlioz in a letter to M. de La Chapelle, 26 February1865). 'Si je vivais cent cinquante ans je finirais par arriver' (letter to Heine, 20 December 1854).
3. This great task will soon be undertaken by M. Pierre Citron, who has recently published a new two-volume edition of the *Mémoires*, Flammarion, 1968. (Ed)
4. More concerning both Baudelaire and Berlioz may be expected from the forthcoming study of Nietzsche by Professor Kurt Weinberg, a disciple of Henri Peyre. See also F. Reyna: *Nietzsche, musicien refoulé*, Revue Musicale, 1953–54. (Ed)
5. Not only Holy Russia (to take up Professor Bandy's point), but even a small country such as Roumania can claim to have translated Baudelaire three years after the poet's death; one poem alone, *L'Albatros*, has been translated in thirty-three different versions. Recently, a complete bilingual edition of *Les Fleurs du Mal* appeared in Bucharest, edited by Vladimir Streinu and Geo Dumitrescu. No less extraordinary is the feat of the poet Nicolas Moore – he has done (so far!) thirty-three different versions of *Spleen*.
6. Written in English. (Ed).

ADAM

INTERNATIONAL REVIEW

Editor: Miron Grindea

Four writers
and music

Bernard Shaw

a hitherto unpublished essay

André Gide

Samuel Beckett

David Gascoyne

10s 6d
$1·50

FOUR WRITERS AND MUSIC: BERNARD SHAW, ANDRÉ GIDE, SAMUEL BECKETT, DAVID GASCOYNE

Nos. 337–339, Vol. XXXV, 1970–

INVOLVED WITH MUSIC

Four writers whose creative lives have been deeply involved with music. With three of them, *ADAM* was fortunate in establishing personal contact through a shared predilection, even passion, for a particular composer or work. But this subjective element is only incidental to the nature of the contents.

Professor Dan Laurence of New York University, in a joint act of generosity with the Society of Authors, has offered us the first English rights of an essay by GBS.[1] Bernard Shaw may have left behind him a number of outrageous statements on European literature and music, but Corno di Bassetto undeniably exerted a stimulating influence as one of the most inspiring music critics of his time. At 95, only a few hours before the stupid accident that precipitated his death, he was playing the first movement of Beethoven's *Ninth* – his score, on public view at Ayot St Lawrence, is still open at the page where he stopped. When we first visited him at his flat in Whitehall Court in November 1935, he brought our conversation on Wagner to an abrupt end (perhaps from boredom) and chose rather to accompany himself in a few bars from *Tristan*. His unmusical secretary, Blanche Patch, reassured us that this was a sign of courteous hospitality. Some time later, in August 1941, he suggested that, if we 'deserved success for our paper', we must not 'pad it with contributions from superannuated Victorians'.

• • •

Recently, as we rejoiced at the bestowal of the Nobel Prize for Literature upon a third Irishman (the other two were Yeats (1923) and Shaw (1925)), a host of Beckettian *croque-mitaines* in Paris tried to scare us away from paying tribute to Samuel Beckett the human being, claiming that 'Sam would not like it' – as if that solitary artist could possibly care one way or the other. We mention our own experience merely to illustrate how futile it is to try to build a fence around this essentially kind and considerate personality. In 1954 he rang from a public telephone box to ask us to come to his old house in rue des Favorites near the Porte de Versailles. And a memorable afternoon it was. Instead of discussing literature, we did nothing but argue about who were the best interpreters of this sonata or that concerto. The names of Lipatti (Chopin),

Clara Haskil (Scarlatti or Beethoven's *Op 111*) and Monique Haas (Bartok's *Third Piano Concerto*) united us as if we belonged to the same Lodge! Small wonder that, throughout the years, music has become the main topic of our few but cordial long-distance telephone conversations. After listening to the *A Minor String Quartet* of Schubert, he told his nephew, the composer John Beckett: 'Schubert's music seems to me to be more nearly pure spirit than that of any other composer.' He is very fond of the piano sonatas of Haydn – a composer he mentions in his novel *Murphy*. He is often heard playing Haydn's *Sonata in E Flat (no 49)* from memory. Pointing out a passage in the first movement of Beethoven's *Seventh Symphony*, in which, after a *fortissimo*, there follow two bars of silence, Beckett asked, 'What happens during this silence?' On the other hand, he dislikes 'the inexorable purposefulness of Bach'.[2]

So this is the man who has been punished with hundreds of dissertations and monographs in the last two decades. Despair lies at the heart of his work, many of these learned studies say. We do not believe, though, that Beckett's life is 'almost totally irrelevant to an understanding and appreciation of his work', as Professor Colin Duckworth states in a recent school edition of *Godot* (Harrap). Rather than perpetuate the undeserved legend of a 'dehumanized factory of poisoned misanthropy', denounced in unmistakable terms by Harold Hobson, we would prefer to see a few intrepid researchers hurrying to Dublin to meet some of the affable people in the midst of whom the future creator of *Molloy* and *Malone* spent his childhood and adolescence. The city Shaw and Joyce both ran away from is still a valuable source of information about 'Sam', the affectionate representative of a colourful and gifted clan: 'I'd been very happy and was fond of my parents', he wrote to Professor Duckworth.

Lady Beatrice Glenavy, in her refreshing volume of reminiscences, *Today We Will Only Gossip* (Constable, 1964), has already spoken of 'the kindness of May Beckett's heart' – Sam's mother, who was not only a gifted pianist but a composer too – so beautifully evoked in the poem *Malacoda*: 'Hear she may see she see not / here she must see she must.' Lady Glenavy has also left a masterly portrait of Beckett's Aunt Cissie, who became crippled with arthritis: 'I used to go to see her in her house by the sea at Raheny, where she lived with some of her family. She often spoke of her nephew Sam Beckett with great affection, and when he came from Paris to see his mother at Foxrock he went to visit Cissie also. He would take her for a drive or a turn in her wheelchair along the sea-road. She used to say with pleasure, "Sam was here" or "Sam is coming". When I read *Endgame*, I recognised Cissie in Hamm. The play was full of allusions to things in her life, even the old telescope which Tom Casement had given me and I had passed on to her to amuse herself by watching ships in Dublin Bay or seabirds feeding on the sands when the tide was out. She used to make jokes about her tragic condition. She once asked me to "straighten up the statue" – she was leaning sideways in her chair and her arthritis had made her heavy and hard and stiff like marble. As I did what she asked I saw tears of laughter in her eyes. Cissie finished her days in a rather dreary home for old people. I gathered from her that Sam still came to see her and that his visits brought her much happiness.'

Unlike Sartre, Beckett was complaisant enough not to reject the Nobel Prize, although he accepted it by proxy and – the height of tolerance – even uttered this *cri de coeur* in an interview with John Gruen in *Vogue* during his first visit to the US last December: 'Writing,' he said, 'becomes, not easier, but more difficult for me. Every word is like an unnecessary stair in silence and nothingness.' In the same interview he admitted: 'Perhaps, like the composer Schönberg or the painter Kandinsky, I have turned towards an abstract language. Unlike them, however, I have tried not to concretise the abstraction – not to give it yet another formal context.' Significantly, the official citation of the Swedish Academy when conferring this year's prize for literature admitted that, although 'the degradation of humanity is a recurrent theme in Beckett's writing', the author nonetheless 'has a love of mankind that grows in understanding as it plumbs further into the depths of abhorrence'.

•   •   •

Gide reigned in France through the magnetism of his multiple personality, the anguish of his self-communing and his unappeasable desire for pleasure. It is not fanciful to glimpse, in one of his self-portraits, a musical sensibility: 'Son être se défait et se refait sans cesse. On croit le saisir … Il prend la forme de ce qu'il aime.' He was a passionate pianist – witness the entries in his *Journal* and in *Si le grain ne meurt* on Bach Preludes, Chopin Nocturnes, Fauré and even the rarely played *Variations sur un thème de Rameau* by Dukas. Alas, the only time *ADAM* was invited for tea to his flat in rue Vaneau, the unexpected presence of a pianist, Eve, who had asked to come along hoping to hear the Master play, seemed to annoy Gide so much that, after an awkward five minutes, the visit was cut short, *sans thé* and *sans musique* … On the other hand, Youra Guller, having been married to Jacques Schiffrin, the founder of the Pléiade collection, heard Gide play several times. It took him a long time to overcome his shyness (Mme Guller told us recently), but, once at the piano, 'Il jouait comme un vrai musicien'.

•   •   •

As for David Gascoyne, a brief comment will suffice to explain his presence in this issue. He wrote the three 'atonal' poems during a recent convalescence; he was introduced to the music of Bartok, Berg and Webern by Pierre Jean Jouve, that splendid and sadly neglected poet who wrote on *Don Giovanni* and *Wozzeck*. At the height of the Nazi terror, Gascoyne evoked the tragedy of German musicians in five of his many French poems. *ADAM* also recently persuaded him to describe how he came to music in the first place (see p. 23 [of this issue]). Let us now move on to the texts themselves – though not before drawing attention to David Gascoyne the painter and acknowledging the encouragement received from Mary Hutchinson while preparing the tribute to Beckett.

CONTRIBUTORS

Bernard SHAW – *What I Owe to German Culture*
David GASCOYNE – *Three Verbal Sonatinas* [poems]
David GASCOYNE – *How I came to music* [letter to Miron Grindea]
David GASCOYNE – *Notebook I*
Pierre DE BOISDEFFRE – *Les débuts d'un homme de lettres (1891–92)*
Cyril CONNOLLY – *Memories of André Gide*
Raymond MORTIMER – *Gide's Total Honesty*
Arnold NAVILLE – *L'ami*
Peter HOY – *Robert Harborough Sherard, Lord Alfred Douglas and Gide's* Si le grain ne meurt
Michael EDWARDS – *Gide and the Symbol*
Marcel MIHALOVICI – *Ma collaboration avec Samuel Beckett*
Jonathan M. WEISS – *The Dialectic of Movement in Beckett's* Happy Days
John CALDER – *Beckett – Man and Artist*
Michael BAKEWELL – *Working with Beckett*
Mary HUTCHINSON – *All the Livelong Way* [in French]
Raymond JOHNSON – *Waiting for Beckett*
Hugo MANNING – *A Man to Remember*

Views and Reviews: Philip O'CONNOR, *The greatest exponent of nihilism (Samuel Beckett)* – Leon S. ROUDIEZ, *In memory of Justin O'Brien* – A. K PETERS, *Gide and Cocteau* – Alan DENT, *Words are queer things (Ivor Brown's* A Rhapsody of Words)

NOTES

1. It has only once appeared, as an introduction to Vol. I of Shaw's *Dramatische Werke*, Berlin, 1911, in a translation by Siegfried Trebitsch under the title 'Was ich der Deutschen Kultur verdanke'. The original version appears here from the author's corrected typescript.
2. The most authoritative opinion concerning his 'astonishing musical intuition' comes from the composer Marcel Mihalovici, who readily unearthed for us the original French text in which he described his collaboration with Beckett on a number of musical scores. (The article was first published in an English translation in *Beckett at 60*, London, 1967, and appears here with the kind permission of John Calder, the editor and publisher of the *Festschrift*.)

ADAM

INTERNATIONAL REVIEW

Editor: Miron Grindea

BARIONA or The Son of Thunder -
a hitherto unpublished play by Sartre

Jean-Paul Sartre visiting *ADAM* in 1947: the author talking to Henri Jourdan and Miron Grindea
(Radio Times Picture Library)

10s. 6d. $1.50

SARTRE (INCLUDING 'BARIONA')
Nos. 343–345, Vol. XXXV, 1970–

VOLTAIRE 1970

This issue was planned some time ago – motivated by three events which we expected would coincide: a new study by Sartre of Flaubert, an out-of-the-ordinary bibliography by Michel Contat and Michel Rybalka and the publication of *Bariona*, Sartre's first play, written during his internment in a Nazi camp at Trèves. In the meantime, the concordance was broken: the text on Flaubert (which may prove as revealing as Sartre's book on Baudelaire) was delayed and will not be published until early 1971. On the other hand, *Les Ecrits de Sartre*, Contat's and Rybalka's monumental opus, has come out and must be acclaimed, as it represents a new opening in the field of literary history.

Committed politically more passionately than any other contemporary artist, Sartre nonetheless sought an 'unengaged' moment to express his joy at being the focus of this 800-page exegetical chronology. 'While recognising my incompetence,' he wrote to the authors, 'from a personal point of view I love your book, which acts as a Bogomoletz to my memory: not only have I rediscovered every piece of writing which I remember, but you have also brought back those I had forgotten. I am astonished and at the same time a little uneasy to find myself reunited with them. In a broader sense, your rare merit has been to humanise what, without you, could have been no more than an inventory after my death. Through your condensed analyses you have transformed the mere listing into a portrait: you have resuscitated the process by which every writer, good or bad, can objectivise himself in his works. I approach myself as a stranger, yet I cannot eject anything. Your work undoubtedly establishes my self-portrait, and if I only partly like it, this is obviously because it is true.'

As for *Bariona*, one can only share the puzzlement of Sartre's intimate friends: why did the author withhold publication for so many decades? Was it really because, as he told a Swedish critic, Thure Stenström, in 1965, he never considered it sufficiently polished? Soon after being interned at Stalag XIID in August 1940, he became very close to a number of Catholic *prêtres de banlieue* and thought that the best Christmas present he could offer them was participation in as wide a theatrical canvas as possible, in which all the inmates, believers and non-believers, would co-operate, not only as actors but also as stage designers, musicians and chorus. Did Sartre ever regret the Christian atmosphere which he, the professed atheist, created in this miracle play? As late as 1962, he found it necessary to protect himself against the slightest imputation of religious feeling by writing: 'If I took a subject from Christian mythology, this does not mean that the orientation of my thoughts changed, even for one moment, during captivity.' Like so many other controversial aspects of his personality, *Bariona* will probably attract widespread comment. As for *ADAM*, it is grateful for the exclusive privilege finally accorded to it, after a lengthy and interesting correspondence with the author, of publishing this English version open to all readers.

The addenda to the *Ecrits* show what a persistently dominating role Sartre the philosopher, the awakener, the self-denying poet, continues to play in public life. This particular world is one in which *ADAM*, compulsively suspicious of the brittle and pragmatic nature of politics, has never quite fully entered ... In the case of Sartre, however, this is an inherent touchstone which we should all by now have learned to live with.

Many of his admirers sincerely believed for some time that Sartre was seeking arrest by the authorities and that his wish was (almost perversely) disregarded by a number of influential men of letters, including the President of the French Republic. The author has emphatically denied this (see p. 97 [of this issue]). On the other hand, he recently assumed responsibility for the latest revolutionary *quinzomadaire*, *TOUT*, September 1970, and made this significant statement: 'Puisqu'on *ne m'a pas même inculpé dans les procès qui se déroulent* [our italics], je me mets à la disposition de tout journal révolutionnaire *pour obliger la classe bourgeoise ou à me faire un procès politique* [our italics], dont l'objet sera clairement, cette fois, la liberté de la presse, ou à démasquer, en ne m'inculpant pas, l'illégalité délibérée de la répression.'[1] According to François Bondy, 'Sartre is torn between commitment and critical meditation; ... his latest dramatic commitment to a Maoist newspaper in France prompts one to wonder whether his deepest attachments are not to a cause which can command his mind and heart beyond the exercise of political scepticism and intellectual self-doubt' (*The New Left*, ed. by Maurice Cranston, Bodley Head, 1970, 30s).

In its reassessment, history will no doubt relate Sartre to the more poignant ideological dilemmas of this century – just as it linked Voltaire to the 'affaires' Calas, Sirven and Lally-Tollendal. As the American critic Thomas Molnar has shown in his *Sartre, Ideologue of Our Time* (Funk and Wagnalls, NY, 1968, ingeniously translated into French as *Sartre, philosophe de la contestation*, Le Prieuré, Paris 1969), Sartre seems to have taken Voltaire's place nowadays. Ours is not an Age of Enlightenment, alas, yet still it is in desperate need of a new *Traité sur la tolérance*, or even of a new *Candide, ou l'Optimisme.*

CONTRIBUTORS

Oreste PUCCIANI – *Sartre et notre culture*
Michael EDWARDS – La Nausée, *a Symbolist Novel*
Henri JOURDAN – *Sartre à Berlin*
Michael CONANT – *Poem*
John WEIGHTMAN – *Sartre Catalogued (Les Ecrits de Sartre)*
Dominique DESANTI – *Sartre et l'engagement*
Jean-Paul SARTRE – *Quote from* Derrière le Miroir
Martin ESSLIN – *Sartre's Nativity Play* (Bariona)
Jean-Paul SARTRE – *Bariona, or, the Son of Thunder* [play, translated]
Jean-Paul SARTRE – *Moby Dick* [translated]
Judy CARR – *Fertility* [poem]
Michel CONTAT and Michel RYBALKA – *Sartre 1969–1970: Bibliographie commentée*

Views and Reviews: Gabriel JOSIPOVICI, *Sartre and the Nouveau Roman (André Puig's* L'Inachevé – Georgeta HORODINCA, *Sartre's 'comeback in strength'* – Gordon BLAIR, *Sartre in British and American Literary Criticism (plus 'select bibliography')*

NOTE

1. At the moment of going to press, the BBC has begun broadcasting *Les chemins de la liberté*, under the title *The Road to Freedom*. It is a dramatised version by David Turner, directed by Mr James Cellar Jones, in thirteen instalments – surely a Sartrean event, if there was one.

ADAM

INTERNATIONAL REVIEW

Editor: Miron Grindea

"Ah, mon Dieu! si l'on pourrait toujours écrire cette belle langue de France"—Dickens writing to Forster in 1849
(Duc de Gramont Collection)

51p. $1.50

MARGINALIA

Cycles of fame are both a mystery and a cliché. In 1920, Methuen the publishers tried hard to launch a first novel, *Voyage to Arcturus*, described by J. B. Priestley as a 'grand piece of wild imagination'. Gollancz reprinted it three times (1945, 1963, 1968) and showed further courage by republishing a second novel, *The Haunted Woman*, by the same author, which, when first printed in 1922, was ignored by most reviewers – Desmond MacCarthy, L. H. Myers, Rebecca West, Oliver Edwards and L. P. Hartley were among the very few critics to react favourably to the qualities of the author, David Lindsay (1878–1945). Both works are now circulated as paperbacks in the United States, but Lindsay – 'so different from others ... with a complete originality of mind and great intensity of feeling' (Hartley) – continues to be regarded as an irritating *undefinable*. Recently, John Baker resumed the crusade by publishing a brave 200-page plea, *The Strange Genius of David Lindsay*, in which three eulogists have joined forces with equal fervour. Colin Wilson, with the same stylistic ebullience that characterised his *Outsider* (1956), proclaims Lindsay 'the most acute psychologist since Nietzsche', a rather ambiguous parallelism, one would think; Mr J. B. Pick, a novelist and essayist of merit, put much devotion and skill in assembling the relatively few available facts for a future *Life of Lindsay 'as Man and Writer'*; but the most moving contribution is that by Mr K. H. Visiak, the only one who knew the author personally and fought relentlessly on his behalf. To him, *Voyage to Arcturus* is a 'stupendous ontological fable, a metaphysical Pilgrim's Progress to and in an imaginative Ultima Thule, inhabited by crude, emblematic beings'. The *TLS* begs to differ by calling it 'a riot of morbid fancy', although it also agrees that 'The problem remains: how to come to terms with a writer whose vision is so profound and so individual that it cannot really be talked about in the usual language of literary criticism'. The critic and poet Robert Nye, while admitting that we are confronted by 'an awkward, insufficient writer', thinks that 'No amount of neglect will put Lindsay out entirely'. To anyone interested in the process of slow literary recognition, the correspondence published in this issue is bound to reveal the virtues of a deep and noble friendship that lasted for nearly three decades. As the letters are primarily concerned with the spiritual beliefs of two writers struggling in uncompromising loneliness for their ideas, they might, we thought, stimulate a wider acquaintance, not only with Lindsay's work, but also with that of Mr Visiak, the 92-year-old poet, novelist and Miltonian scholar, whose latest poem appears on page nine.

FOOTNOTES TO CENTENARIES

The centenary of Dickens and the bicentenary of Beethoven have already suffered practically all the penalties such occasions usually impose: a succession of books bristling with specialised learning, international symposia, dramatisations and film productions, services in Abbeys, banquets presided over by Lords Mayor, with all the accompanying regalia that both artists so much despised. *ADAM* jumps on the bandwagon with the diffidence of an old commoner, yet at the same time with the immodest hope that, in addition to the intrinsic value of such contributions as those from J. B. Priestley, Angus Wilson, Mosco Carner, Margaret Mein, Sylvère Monod and Jeremy Noble, our own marginal notes might be of service to future bibliolaters reading this journal ...

Dickens' Centenary for us has brought forth several themes which, like anything else connected with an ocean-deep creative force, ceaselessly invite fresh research and unhindered exploration. One of them concerns the writer's attachment to the 'dear, old France of my affection', and here an alluring field clamours for co-ordinated sifting. His many escapades across the Channel ('I hope to make further dashes from my desk before I want them,' Dickens wrote to his daughter Mary of all people), as well as certain sprees 'to throw myself *en garçon* on the festive *diableries* de Paris' (CD's own italics!), continue to intrigue scholars. This stocktaking year should, then, not be allowed to slip away without a closer and perhaps enlarged study of the vast amount of material tucked away in *The Dickensian* of 1932, 1963 and 1966. For instance, in an article entitled 'Dickens' forgotten retreat in France', Mr W. J. Carlton seems to have made a trustworthy point as regards the controversies relating to the Staplehurst railway crash of June 9th, 1865: 'The studied vagueness of some of Dickens' references to his cross-channel expeditions and the enigmatic phrasing of others must inevitably give rise to the suspicion that he had something to hide, especially when it is remembered that from 1860 onwards he systematically destroyed all letters and papers received by him except purely business communications.'

There are not many examples of English writers in the nineteenth century who could express themselves in French with such endearing gaucherie and verve as Dickens could. The exuberance with which he handled the language was quite astonishing. According to Professor

Monod, 'Il dut apprendre un peu de français dans sa jeunesse', but sure-ly there must have been more than a passing whim in his *cris de cœur*. This is the way he wrote to Forster in 1848 and 1849 respectively: 'Je trouve que j'aime tant la république qu'il me faut renoncer ma langue et écrire seulement le langage de la République – France – langage des Dieux et des Anges, en un mot, des français' (*Life*, II, p. 74); 'La diffi-culté d'écrire l'anglais m'est extrêmement ennuyeuse. Ah, mon Dieu! si l'on pourrait toujours écrire cette belle langue de France' (ibid p. 214).

One is equally indebted to Mr Carlton for having recalled the pic-turesque features of Louis Augustin Prévost, a Frenchman who was familiar with something like thirty languages, including Hungarian, Bohemian and Wallachian, and who also catalogued Chinese books in the British Museum. He is plausibly believed to have taught Dickens more than the rudiments of French and to have served as model for the frisky little master in *Household Words* – 'who used to come in the sun-niest weather with a handleless umbrella' – as well as for Charles St Evremonde in *A Tale of Two Cities*: 'He read with young men who could find any leisure and interest for the study of a living tongue spoken all over the world ... an elegant translator who brought something to his work besides mere dictionary knowledge.'

On more than one occasion during the negotiations with Hachette for the integral translation of his works into French, Dickens would often feel the urge to use the ... language of the Republic, as in this let-ter written on December 7th, 1835, from his residence at 49 Avenue des Champs Elysées: 'Messieurs, je viens de recevoir la lettre que vous m'avez fait l'honneur de m'addresser. Permettez-moi de répondre d'abord que si vous voulez bien me faire le plaisir de m'expliquer votre projet un peu plus en détail et en pleine confiance encore par lettre, je vous serai infiniment obligé et je m'empresserai de vous entretenir ou de vous écrire franchement. A présent, je n'autorise pas aucune traduc-tion de mes livres en Français et il me parait que presque tout le monde étranger me fait l'honneur très flattante [*sic*!] de regarder mes écrits comme une espèce de propriété publique.'

The present Duc de Gramont (whose father was a friend of Proust) has most generously put at our disposal the full texts of eight letters writ-ten by Dickens in French to Count Alfred d'Orsay, that intriguing char-acter who befriended Lamartine, Disraeli, Louis Blanc, George Sand, Alfred de Vigny.[1] D'Orsay knew how to flatter his friends, and, in the case of Dickens, he naturally complimented him on his French. In a letter dated February 10th, 1847, the perennial dandy, ruthlessly scorned by Thackeray, tried to persuade Dickens that he was perfectly entitled to regard himself as an honorary Frenchman: 'Mon cher compatriote (car enfin un homme qui écrit aussi bien le français est certainement un

Parisien consommé), j'ai été charmé de recevoir votre lettre. Elle m'a confirmé dans l'idée que j'ai toujours eue, qu'un homme de génie devine même ce qu'il ne sait pas. Donc, vous avez complètement deviné ma langue et je n'assassinerai plus vos oreilles avec mon *broken English*'. This must have gone to his head, for he addressed Forster in these hyperbolical terms: 'Eh bien, mon ami, quand vous venez à Paris je me mettrai à quatre épingles et nous verrons ensemble toutes les merveilles de la cité, et vous en jugerez. Vive le roi des français, Roi de la nation la plus grande, et de la plus noble et la plus extraordinairement mer- veilleuse du monde. A bas des [*sic*] anglais. – Charles Dickens, français naturalisé, et citoyen de Paris.' A few years later, writing to Georgina Hogarth, Dickens felt entitled to take pride in his achievement: 'I walked about with Régnier for an hour and a half yesterday and received many compliments on my *angelic manner of speaking the celestial language*' [our italics].

No matter how much naïveté enters in this self-glorification, one must admit that Dickens succeeded in being vigorous, funny and emo- tional even when using what he considered to be his 'celestial' French, but this does not in the least mean that he was wrong by not giving up his mother-tongue ... For all his flamboyance and sense of drama, his attitude was rather that of an adolescent discovering the facts of life. On the other hand, his tireless francomania makes a dramatic contrast to the rather acrimonious remark by Joseph de Maistre: 'L'Angleterre et la France, ces deux aimants qui s'attirent par un côté et se fuient par l'autre, car ils sont à la fois ennemis et parents.' Be it as it may, the cor- respondence reproduced on page 24 [of this issue] makes a telling sequel to another group of letters which Dickens addressed, also in French, to the actor François Philoclès Régnier (1807–1887). As such, they are bound to receive a well-deserved annotation in one of the forthcoming volumes of the Pilgrim edition.

... And the variations on this theme are still far from having been exhausted! Among the lesser known French tributes to Dickens are one by Abbé Bremond, who, in an essay entitled *Le Triomphe de Dickens*, stressed the 'génie bouffon, une des formes de l'amour', and another by Alain, who, in his book *En lisant Dickens* (Gallimard, 1945), found one of the most spirited and poetical phrases in contemporary Dickensian appreciation: 'J'entre dans Dickens comme dans une géographie; je l'ex- plore comme une réalité. C'est le génie humain qui vous regarde de tous ses yeux.' But the most revealing addition to French appreciation of Dickens is the recent (partial) publication of Gide's *Notes de lecture*, made between 1889 and 1893. Reading one or even two books a day, Gide began from early adolescence to jot down innumerable comments which only now begin to receive proper critical comment. One is infinitely indebted to Professor Jacques Gotnam, of York University, Toronto, who has edited these salient critical strokes. Here is an example: 'Dickens plus affairé, plus grouillant encore que Balzac; les personnages sont plus près les uns des autres, et plutôt moins solitaires. Balzac est plus sérieux; il se croit plus sérieux; c'est un savant. Dickens est, et veut être, amuseur.' Also, 'Caractère affirmatif (des œuvres de Dickens) opposé au caractère interrogatif de tels autres, Tourguéniev, Ibsen, etc. Je pense qu'il est supérieur à Balzac en d'autres choses ...; il me semble que c'est plutôt par l'absence des défauts ordinaires de Balzac (insupportable pesanteur, prétentions à la pensée haute). Dickens raconte toujours ou s'exclame. Il n'eût pas écrit *Louis Lambert*. Un roman de Dickens et même le moins bon le fait connaître tout entier. Un roman de Balzac et même IIe meilleur ne fait connaître de lui qu'une partie, et qui plus est une partie nouvelle.' Gide was critical of many Dickensian characters, those in *Little Dorrit* for instance, but all in all he confesses that 'Dickens est celui dans les romans duquel j'aimerais le plus vivre, au moins un temps – pour m'amuser.'

Strange as it may seem, and however much Proustian experts would have liked to be able to establish direct links between Dickens' cosmos and that of the *Recherche*, there is no positive proof that Marcel, who was so deeply impressed by a great many English novelists – George Eliot, Hardy, Meredith in particular – ever read Dickens; but, although he is not mentioned either in his works or in the correspondence, the subject remains fascinating nonetheless. In an introduction to *Oliver Twist*, Mr Graham Greene pointed out 'the gradual transformation of that thick boggy prose into the delicate and exact poetic cadences, the music of memory, that so influenced Proust'. Another suggestive comment à propos *Oliver Twist* appeared in *Dickens and the Twentieth Century*, edited by John Gross and Gabriel Pearson, 1962: 'When Proust sets out to "overgo" the Dickensian monster with his Charlus and Françoise, the ebullience and energy are seen to proceed from a creative Centre which is meticulous, reflective and the reverse of energetic: the peculiar Victorian harmony of created and creating energy.' Also, 'Dickens' superb artistry in the echoes and overtones of memory seems (to Mr Angus Wilson) quite the artistic equal of *A la recherche*.' Finally, in the first authoritative essay on the subject, Monsieur Jacques Nathan, a lecturer at the Sorbonne, although admitting that 'Proust n'a jamais mentionné Dickens ni signalé des emprunts éventuels qu'il lui aurait faits', could not resist the temptation of establishing an analogy between two characters in *Nicholas Nickleby* – Mr and Mrs Wittiterly – and the Verdurins; but, adds the French critic, 'Ces analogies et bien d'autres auxquelles on pourrait penser, défient "analyse précise"'.[2] We had better restrain ourselves and leave speculation to others; after all, we have a full Proustian year in front of us, and the Dickens–Proust parallel begs ingenuity of treatment.

Another point in need of clarification is the extent to which Dickens, after giving up the idea of becoming a professional actor, came into close contact with the Davenport family whose members are believed to have served as models for the Crummles characters in *Nicholas Nickleby*. The late theatrical historian Malcolm Morley has left an important and hitherto unpublished monograph on 'The Miraculous Jean', but, so far as Dickens' personal connections with the actors are concerned, he admitted that he had no 'conclusive evidence'. Thomas Donald Davenport, a Scotsman born in 1792, was a lawyer before he became an actor and theatre manager. 'Strolling players both,' wrote Mr Morley, Mr and Mrs Davenport made their first London appearance at Rayner's New Subscription Theatre in the Strand on January 26th, 1832: an 'illegal' theatre since 'Drury Lane, Covent Garden and the Haymarket, each proclaimed as a Theatre Royal, were the only places in London permitted by law to give theatrical performances; but by claiming to be a subscription, or private, playhouse, and not taking money at the doors, the Strand attempted to live without, as it were, having any official existence.' Where did Dickens come into the picture, if at all? Four months after the Davenports appeared in *The Triumph of Fidelity* and *Professionals Puzzled*, they took over a building in Tothill Street, not far from the Houses of Parliament, which an undertaker called Mr Gale 'was inspired to convert into a small playhouse of sorts'. While the critic of *The Times* approved of the venture, the editor of *Figaro in London*, Gilbert Abbott à Beckett, wrote that 'So appalling a spectacle never was exhibited'. It was at that time that Dickens had become a parliamentary reporter, and, according to Mr Morley, 'His daily journey to the House would have taken him so near Tothill Street, almost a stone's throw, that Davenport's venture must have been known to the young reporter, then aged twenty. One can be sure that, with the theatrical urge strongly upon him, he visited the Westminster, seeing many of the plays there, and equally sure that in time he made the acquaintance of Thomas Donald. Boz, almost certainly, stored memories of that Subscription Theatre for future use in his writing, and perhaps here was his first glimpse of Vincent Crummles.' Plausible, undoubtedly fascinating suppositions, but unfortunately impossible for the time being to base on concrete facts. Mr Morley dismissed the suggestion, made by Harvey Darton in his book *Vincent Crummles and his Times,* that Dickens acted in Davenport's own company at Portsmouth 'in one of the blank periods of his life'; but the American actor, Charles Lander (1860–1934), in a letter published in the *Daily Telegraph* of December 3 1904, was quoting Davenport as having once told Dickens to his face that he was not much of an actor – one should only bear in mind that Lander was an adopted son of the 'miraculous Jean'!

• • •

There is no need to exceed the reasonable merely for the sake of establishing seemingly absurd links. Those familiar with the unrepentant impatience of *ADAM*'s occasional assumptions and hypotheses will perhaps also accept the threads, however tenuous, which we propose to draw between Dickens and Beethoven. As this issue was planned as a commentary equally divided between the two men of genius, it was rather sad to hear from one of the greatest authorities on Dickens that no mention whatsoever of Beethoven had been found in any of the novels or correspondence. Then what about the fact established when issuing the Baudelaire–Berlioz number [331–333], namely, that Dickens was, after all, the son-in-law of George Hogarth, who himself married the daughter of George Thomson, whose collection of Scottish and Irish songs helped Beethoven to set their texts to music? In 1835, the very year that Dickens was introduced into the Hogarth home in Chelsea, both Hogarth and himself joined the staff of *The Daily News*, the first as music critic, the second as the author of *Sketches by Boz*. Writing to his uncle, Thomas Barrow, Dickens boasted about 'my marriage with Miss Hogarth – the daughter of a gentleman who has recently distinguished himself by a celebrated work of music'. This was the *Dictionary of Music*, published in 1835, *also* the year when the *Ninth Symphony* was conducted for the first time in this country by Ignaz Moscheles, one of Beethoven's apostles in Europe (more about Moscheles later). Following this path, it was tempting (almost safe!) to assume that in his energetic and full life Dickens *may* well have found time to attend the eventful performance of the Choral Symphony. Nothing to get excited about, except the unexpected disclosure that Beethoven *does* come into his work. Indeed, Mr Morfin, one of the main characters in *Dombey and Son*, is not only an amateur cellist, meeting certain friends every week for the performance of quartets of the most tormenting and excruciating nature, but also an adroit whistler who once went 'accurately through the whole of Beethoven's *Sonata in B*'. Not a bad beginning, for, although some of Dickens' early commentators denied the existence of such a work, there is in fact a *Sonata in B flat major* for flute. Even if incorrectly quoted, another of Beethoven's works is mentioned in chapter 9 of *Sketches by Boz*, when, at the private theatrical performance at Mrs Gattleton's, a bunch of well-meaning amateurs were performing *Men of Prometheus*, though the performance ended in chaos. (Dickens meant to write about the ballet music *Die Geschöpfe des Prometheus* (1801), one of whose themes was also used to brilliant purpose in the

Finale of the *Eroica Symphony* as well as in the *Eroica Piano Variations, op. 35*.) Finally, in *Old Lamps for New* (1850), Dickens had this to say about a certain group of uncultured and illbred *fanfarons*: 'In music a retrogressive step, in which there is much hope, has been taken. The PAB, or pre-Agincourt Brotherhood, has arisen, nobly devoted to consign to oblivion Mozart, Beethoven and every other such ridiculous reputation, and to fix its Millennium (as its name implies) before the date of the first regular composition known to have been achieved in England ...; it remains to be seen whether the Royal Academy of Music will be a worthy sister of the Royal Academy of Art.'

Suddenly, at this stage there came our way no other person than Mr Eric Dickens Hawksley, the novelist's great-grandson, who spread before our incredulous eyes two genealogical trees of unexpected splendour: one projecting the descendants of Sir Henry Dickens (the author's youngest son, the only one to have made a successful career), and the other representing the progeny of Antonin Roche, a French emigré in this country who married the daughter of Ignaz Moscheles. But we had better let the reader enjoy the story which we persuaded Mr Dickens Hawksley to unfold. From here it was relatively easy to enlarge on the role music played in Dickens' life. In 1823, one year after the Academy was founded, his sister, Fanny Elizabeth, joined the RAM. As a graduate she performed in public and was presented as 'a pupil of the great Moscheles' – when, on May 29th, 1827, at a charity concert at Drury Lane, she played his *Souvenirs d'Irlande, op 69*, and *Echoes of Scotland, op 75*. Charles, who had studied both the piano and violin with little success, enjoyed singing to the accompaniment of his sister and compensated in later life for his own lack of musical education by employing a 'small but efficient orchestra' for the private performances taking place at the rear of Isis House in Tavistock Square. How different from Proust summoning a string quartet in the early hours of the morning to come and play at his bedside to help him assimilate a Beethoven quartet!

In addition to the charming evocation of the two family branches spreading over three European countries, we were the first outside the family circle to be given the privilege, not only of seeing the original manuscript of a Wedding March which Charles Gounod wrote for the marriage of Henry Dickens and Marie Roche, but also of reproducing it in this number. Little did Dickens suspect, when writing to W. C. Macready on 19th February, 1863, that the author of *Faust* would have such close connections with his family: 'Paris generally is about as wicked and extravagant as in the days of the Regency. An opera of Faust, a very sad and noble rendering of that sad and noble story ... I couldn't bear it and gave in completely.' A year before that, Dickens visited Paris with a party of friends which included Arthur Sullivan (filled with glory after the performance of his music for *The Tempest* at the Crystal Palace and much flattered when Dickens 'seized my hand with his iron grip and said "I've been listening to a very great work"') and George Grove, editor of the *Dictionary of Music*. Two more striking examples of Dickens' highly emotional reaction to music. In a letter to John Forster in November 1862: 'Last night I saw Madame Viardot do Gluck's *Orphée*. It is worth a journey to Paris to see. I was disfigured with crying ...' His daughter Mary gave a long description of Joachim (1831–1907) shortly after he gave the first performance in London of Mendelssohn's *Violin Concerto*: 'We had a visit at Gad's Hill from Joseph Joachim, "a noble fellow" as my Father wrote of him – which is never to be forgotten. The great violinist perfectly enchanted him. I never remember seeing him so wrapt and absorbed as he was then, in hearing him play; and the wonderful simplicity and unselfconsciousness of this genius went straight to my Father's heart and made a fast bond of sympathy between these two great men.'

Beethoven in France – yet another subject of inexhaustible fascination; it is also the title of a remarkable work written for the Yale University Press in 1942 by the then professor of musicology, Leo Schrade. Up to the outbreak of World War II, Beethoven was still carried in France 'upon the wings of Liberty, Equality and Fraternity. If these wings break, France is to lose her own image of Beethoven.' As things appear in 1970, Beethoven is claimed as one of theirs even by a number of serialist composers such as André Boucourechliev (who, in his introduction to a special issue of *Arc* on 'Modernité de Beethoven', reassures us that 'La métamorphose de son œuvre en nous épouse nos propres métamorphoses comme celles des générations passées, comme celles des générations à venir') and Stockhausen, whose programme notes to his *Kurzwellen* have led to a refreshing parody (see page 31).

• • •

The 'God-seeker' Bored with Himself

With the death of François Mauriac, the world has lost a novelist of great distinction and depth. Neither the Nobel Prize, nor the Honorary doctorate at Oxford, affected the simplicity of his life or his zest when fighting for justice. He had many more enemies than he deserved – they considered him 'méchant' – but most of them deliberately ignored his record of courage in his fight against Franco, as well as his active participation in the French resistance. We only met him towards the end of his life and spent a memorable afternoon at his flat in Bois de Boulogne talking mostly of *Don Giovanni*. In the drawing room hung two beautiful watercolours by his friend Raoul Dufy which were inspired by

Mozart. Mauriac, who was a reluctant traveller, said that he hoped to be able to make two pilgrimages, first to Jerusalem (he reproached us for not having asked him to write an introduction to the *ADAM* anthology [nos. 325–327] with this theme) and then to Salzburg, the birthplace of his favourite composer. A final recollection of this encounter was his unreserved enthusiasm after reading the first volume of George Painter's biography of Proust, which had then just appeared in French. He said with exquisite naughtiness that he was going to write an impassioned review of this book – 'C'est hallucinant' were his words – as he was fully aware that his praise was bound to incense many of his friends belonging to the Saint Germain establishment, at that time busily engaged in weaving a net of venomous intrigues against the English literary historian.

A 'god-seeker bored with himself', as an American critic once described him, Mauriac was worried by the many revelations of old documents related to his career as a writer. In an introduction to *Essai de bibliographie chronologique: 1908–1960*, by Keith Goesch (Nizet, 1965) he wrote with sincere passion: 'Je crains de dénombrer et de retourner ces cadavres successifs qui jalonnent mes cinquante ans de vie littéraire et qui sont moi-même.' He would have rather liked to be able to scrutinise 'sa dernière mort, la vraie, l'entrée dans la lumière qui ne s'éteindra plus, dans l'amour qui ne finira plus.' As his savoury comments on the French anti-*Peineterre* front cannot recklessly be translated into print now, even as we prepare ourselves for the Proust centenary, it is fair to hope that they will still be of interest when *ADAM*'s archives are available for uninhibited consultation.

CONTRIBUTORS

E. H. VISIAK – *A Cross at Sea* [poem]
J. B. PRIESTLEY – *Thinking about Beethoven*
Angus WILSON – *Charles Dickens Today*
Laurence LERNER – *The Potter* [poem]
Mosco CARNER – *Beethoven's Deafness (the heroic element in his music)*
Margaret MEIN – *Proust and Beethoven*
Charles DICKENS – *Eight letters to Comte D'Orsay* [in French, with English introduction]
Yehudi MENUHIN – *Two Beethoven Interpreters (Enescu and Kreisler)*
Jonathan GRIFFIN – *The Goddess* [poem]
Veronica ROBINSON – *A Changeling* [poem]
Karlheinz STOCKHAUSEN – *Kurzwellen with Beethoven*
Eric DICKENS HAWKSLEY – *Memories of Two Families*
Raymond MORTIMER – *The Fascination of Mauriac*
David PRYCE-JONES – *A White Widow* [story]
David LINDSAY and Victor GOLLANCZ – *Letters to E. H. Visiak*

Views and Reviews : Sylvère MONOD, *Dickens et les Français* – Mosco CARNER, *A Bekenntnis to Beethoven* – Jeremy NOBLE, *Post-Schönbergian (André Boucourechliev)* – Jean DUTOURD, *Jean Giono, ou le sel de la terre* – Frederick LAWS, *Title Books on Art* – Louis KAUFMAN, *Kreisler and Enescu* – Geoffrey FIRTH, *Léger*

NOTES

1. More than one hundred years after his death, D'Orsay is still in want of a reliable biography. Mme Claire-Eliane Engel, to whom we are indebted for the introduction to Dickens' letters, hopes to cope with the subject in the near future, and this will probably keep good company with yet another badly needed biography of the 'gorgeous Lady Blessington', on which the English author, Cecily Lambert, is now engaged. What a *fouillis* of material, which, when properly 'decoded' and reconstructed, will throw new light on a number of literary figures of the nineteenth century.
2. *Bulletin de la Société des Amis de Marcel Proust*, no 14.

ADAM

INTERNATIONAL REVIEW

Editor: Miron Grindea

Return to Proust

Jorge Luis Borges

The Dream of Mitzi

a poem by Patricia Doubell

Fighting for Greece

Byron Shelley Keats

51p. $1.50

RETURN TO PROUST – JORGE LUIS BORGES – PATRICIA DOUBELL

Nos. 349–351, Vol. XXXVI, 1971–

RETURN TO PROUST

Toute œuvre d'art est un beau mensonge...
Tous ceux qui ont écrit le savent bien.

Stendhal

Le mensonge est essentiel à l'humanité. Il y joue peut-être
un aussi grand rôle que la recherche du plaisir. On ment
toute sa vie, même surtout, peut-être seulement à ceux qui
nous aiment.

Proust, *La Fugitive*, p. 609

After the third issue on the subject (*Proust ... après Painter*, nos 310–12), *ADAM* promised its readers never to raise the matter again. It simply slipped our mind that there would be a Centenary, and anyway, like so many other addicts, we can never escape the lure entirely. Even if one accepts the late Jocelyn Brooke's 'Case for the Prosecution' ('One of the greatest writers of all time was also a very bad novelist'[1]), one constantly feels a personal involvement with the author. Indeed, the neurotic power of his imagination has transformed his characters as well as his own creative life into a poetic universe which continues to dominate us and from which we have no wish to be evicted. Few modern artists have provoked such uninhibited hunger for facts, and the haunting quality of the *Recherche*, as well as the mystery still surrounding the author, envelops Proustians like a procession of thickening, impatient clouds. All one can do is to hope that at some moment there may be an *éclaircie*, a clearing of the sky.

So here we are, proust-icating once more. The pleasure of living with one of the finest biographies of our generation is marred only by the strange attitude of some critics across the Channel, still unreconciled to the notion of the first true *Life of Proust* being written by an 'outsider'. We remember with sadness that, when asking André Maurois why he had attacked the first volume of Painter's work with such uncharacteristic bitterness, all he could answer was, 'Mais, mon cher ami, il n'est même pas allé consulter [*sic*] Mme ...' This rather puerile reaction from a writer of Maurois' intelligence is still prevalent in many literary circles. Among the more serious disappointments of the last decade was the bunkered view taken by so stimulating a publication as *Critique* (January 1968): all that Roger Kempf could say about Painter's introduction to his book was that it smacked of rare arrogance ('Tout cela ne vaut pas une bonne partie de cricket'). We also thought that the intention of some of the fiercer Vestals at the altar of Proustian worship to kill the English biographer was a bit of an exaggeration. Even if the graph of Proust's life still shows contradictory readings, a revised edition of Painter's work will surely correct any inaccurate details. For instance, M. Albert Fournier, in the first of the two centennial issues of *Europe*, revealed that Marcel's maternal great-uncle Louis, far from being the 'black sheep' bachelor adored by so many demi-mondaines, had in fact married a respectable, rich girl, Emilia Oppenheim, aged twenty-three, in Hamburg in 1844, when the bridegroom was twenty-eight and already a successful button manufacturer. The mystery surrounding this marriage may well have had its parallel in the secrecy shrouding Swann's. Again, says M. Fournier, Marcel could not have seen the dome of St Augustin from his room at 9 Boulevard Malesherbes but from that of his friend, Pierre Lavallée. And a tragic item: two of Proust's cousins, Adèle and Maxime Weil (Georges-Baruch and Amélie Oulman's children) perished in a Nazi camp at a time when another relative was an active 'collaborateur'.

M. Georges Cattaui's fresh exploration of Bloch's world again spotlights the painful and controversial aspect of Proust's Jewish heritage – a theme which perhaps only Painter could adequately elucidate in an enlarged biography. An American thesis by Rae Winter (University of Maryland, 1966) maintains that, whereas Maurois and Léon Pierre-Quint have minimised the Hebrew elements, a deeper scrutiny of the *Recherche* would show a quite different situation. With his unsurpassed gift for concealment and pastiche, Proust transposed the upbringing of selfless devotion in his mother's family to the outwardly more spectacular, but basically austere, Catholic atmosphere of the Prousts at Illiers. It is fair to assume that, with the lifting of the present copyright restrictions next year, not only many unpublished letters but also a variety of other documents may unravel a number of hitherto unexplored tangles in Proust's personality. The alembicated and ruthless portraiture of his fictional scapegoat – Bloch – condensed the traumas he must have suffered as a full half-Jew (a sample of infantile denial of that environment can be found in Proust's irritation when a family friend hailed him, 'Ah, you are Monsieur Weil's nephew!') and is still plunged in obscurity; the material on this subject alone appears to be as baffling as it is vast. Georges Cattaui, a romantic Jew of Catholic faith, sticks to an old theory initiated by Denis Saurat and partly sustained by Dr Winter, namely, that Proust's style can be explained by Jewish atavism. As early as 1928 this view was virulently attacked by René Groos, for many years one of the most wildly anti-Semitic lieutenants of Charles Maurras, whom Proust himself obsequiously flattered in one of his classical 'strategic' letters ('Le relèvement de la France doit s'entendre dans le sens de l'élévation, et vraiment vous détenez le record de la hauteur'). In his essay, *Marcel Proust et le judaïsme*, Groos refuted the Talmudic element singled out by Saurat ('un jeune écrivain singulièrement enclin au paradoxe') by supporting the opinion held by Gustave Kahn, founder of *vers libre*, who wrote: 'Si l'on nous dit que la preuve des origines sémitiques de Proust se trouve dans la longueur de la phrase, nous objecterons que parmi les plus belles œuvres issues de l'esprit juif, l'œuvre de Spinoza intéresse par sa forte concision, que Heine est un poète qui s'exprime par strophes brèves et que dans les œuvres françaises la phrase courte n'est pas de rigueur.' Groos himself thought that 'L'analyse de Proust affecte une autre grandeur que la ratiocination talmudique' and that Proust, 'génie de la réflexion pure, règne à cent coudées au-dessus du moraliste talmudique.' But even if Proust's involutions may not be rigorously Hebraic, the glosses and exegeses they have given rise to most certainly are ...[2]

There is room here for making a link between Heine's nostalgia for his Jewish boyhood and Proust's psychological dichotomy, before embarking on the creative purgatory of his last fifteen years. Both had an ambivalent attitude towards their fellow-Jews, presenting them as equally irritating and interesting, their awkward, *different* character explainable by centuries-long mistreatment. Did Marcel depict himself when he spoke of 'certains israélites qui présentent tour à tour les états successifs par où ont passé ceux de leur race?' (*JF*, p. 432). Heine made the point with his usual trenchant sarcasm: 'Don't talk to me of the Jewish religion. I wouldn't wish it on my worst enemies ... I am telling you, it isn't a religion at all but a misfortune' (*Die Bäder von Lucca*). Another inviting association is the interest both writers showed in the pleasures of the palate.[3] Whereas Proust evoked the 'jus de fruit comme un verger au printemps qui se laisse respirer et regarder goutte à goutte' (*G*, p. 513), Heine, obviously more sensuous and unencumbered by homosexual solitariness, gave this racy description of the return of his baptised character, Isaak Abarbanel, to Judengasse in Frankfurt: 'I saw again in my mind's eye the carp in brown raisin sauce with meat-balls floating in it so dreamily – and my soul melted like the notes of an enamoured nightingale.' Compare Marcel's sophisticated return to the madeleine with the slightly vulgar but irresistible 'dumplings in the soup': '*Worte! Worte, Keine Taten. / Niemals Fleisch, geliebte Puppe / Immer Geist und keinen Braten. / Keine Knödel in der Suppe.*' Who suffered more from 'der grosse Judenschmerz' – Heine or Proust?[4] Yet another fascinating aside of comparative literature and psycho-analytical dissection!

While on problems of identity, *ADAM* repeats its query concerning Alec Ralph Hobson. As we reproduce the inside title-page of *The House of Life*, we should naturally like to be able to tell our readers if the mysterious man ever existed who, before any organised research was set in motion, had access to so much about Proust. The only recognition even of the riddle (as we formulated it in 1966) appeared in the Bibliography to volume II of René de Chantal's *Marcel Proust, critique littéraire* (University of Montreal, 1967): 'Dans cet ouvrage Hobson publia des textes qu'un certain Michael L, ami et confident de Proust, avait recueilli en vue d'écrire un livre de souvenirs sur Proust. Cette plaquette tirée à trente-cinq exemplaires à *échappé aux commentateurs de Proust* [our italics] sauf Charles Briand.' Hobson's brochure includes a prose adaptation of a Heine poem which Mme Proust may have helped her son to translate. Here is one of the stanzas: 'Pourquoi j'aime tant les chèvrefeuilles? C'est parce que mon bien-aimé à planté un chèvrefeuille sous la fenêtre de ma chambre afin qu'à mon réveil la grisante odeur de ses fleurs me dise: toute la nuit les pensées de ton bien-aimé n'ont cessé d'exaler vers toi leurs plus doux parfum d'amour.' The tone is Heine-esque, reminiscent of *Lyrisches Intermezzo*, and the idea of Proust taking an interest in Heine is plausible, since Henry Bordeaux (one of his 'safe' sponsors, should he have put up his candidature at the Académie Française!) remembered that among the works the two shared were *Mémoires d'outre-tombe* and Heine's *Reisebilder*.

What else is there to record or to suggest? The most cherished dream of M. P. L. Larcher, the founding father of the Société des Amis de Marcel Proust, now in his nineties, has just come true: Combray is to be hyphenated with Illiers – one more example of nature imitating art! On behalf of the many English and American pilgrims who have enjoyed his jovial guidance round Tante Léonie's house, *ADAM* hopes that he will reach his century and that at least one or two of his many verse-plays on Marcel will be produced *de son vivant*. He is not the only person who views Proust as suitable for dramatisation. Gabriel Josipovici, the young Sussex novelist and critic – appropriately, the grandson of Albert Josipovici, whose debut as a novelist and also a candidate for the Prix Goncourt with *Le Livre de Goa le Simple*, took place in Paris in 1913, the same year as the appearance of *Du côté de chez Swann* – is also engaged on a full-length play based on the *Recherche*. Further afield, Luchino Visconti's plans for a film with *la* Garbo as the Queen of Naples, inevitably give rise to anxiety and speculation about the rest of the cast; perhaps Ralph Richardson as Dr Cottard, Alec Guinness as Charlus, Edith Evans as Mme Verdurin? And what about the Duchesse de Guermantes (possibly Edwige Feuillère?) or Marcel (Jean-Louis Barrault)?

Assessments and counter-assessments will continue to clash for many more decades. What matters for Proustian scavengers and casuists throughout the world today is that the farandol of inquest and dissection is still tripped with unabated zest. The amount of theses grows apace. *L'Information Littéraire* has recently devoted three issues to a passage concerning Proust's comment on a telephone conversation seventy years ago. In *Journal de Psychologie*, two doctors, Georges Matoré and Irène Mecz, analyse the frequency of curtains in the *Recherche*: rideaux métaphoriques, de théâtre, de fenêtres, rideaux violets – ninety-six in all. The University of Nancy has set up a Centre specially for cataloguing the thousands of nouns, adjectives, verbs and so forth dispersed throughout the novel.[5] As for *ADAM*, even if death should be quite close, we would still like to see this journal live a little longer, if only to meet a fellow-addict such as Cyril Connolly on the Sussex downs and review with him any fresh Proustiana that may turn up.

And a final point, if one can envisage such a thing: from Scott-Moncrieff's painstaking translation (lately enriched by Andreas Mayor's new version of *Time Regained*, a marked improvement on the one by Stephen Hudson), a number of scholars such as John Weightman, John Cocking and the poet Alan Bates have over the years collected a bouquet of misinterpretations which ought to be considered in this Centennial year. If Japan can afford two different versions of Proust's novel, surely England could consider a revised one.

• • •

It is a mistake to believe that the products of South America are always the same, revolutions, beef and coffee; for now we recognize an exchange of literary products from there also. Of this literary and artistic creativity our guest today has been a notable part and stimulus: he sowed the grain from which has grown a great tree. (From the citation in Latin of the Public Orator, who also greeted Borges as *'litterarum Latino-Americanarum antistitem'*.)

In no other seat of learning is the fascination of an honorary doctorate conferred upon a contemporary poet or artist greater than in Oxford. The quiet elegance of the Sheldonian is invariably enhanced by the multitude of crumpled gowns (no matter whether they belong to the dons themselves or are simply lent in turns by the ushers). One's anticipation has already been spurred on by the display in the bookshops of the works to be eulogised; the clock is unbearably slow in striking the half hour, but one's ears are too busy recording the civilised hush of the audience, so much so that one is taken by surprise when the doors are flung wide open, and the Public Orator exchanges mortar-board civilities with the Vice-Chancellor.

The ceremony this time – April 29th, 1971 – was not so much impressive in its pageantry as it was poignant – for the recipient, Jorge Luis Borges, was a blind poet who could enjoy nothing else but the fine Latin cadences of the salutation. Later that afternoon he told us: 'Comme j'aurais aimé que ma mère – qui a quatre-vingt quinze ans – eût pu voir tout cela.'

Just how internationally significant the Argentinian poet is can be gathered from the citation at the Fifth Jerusalem International Book Fair, when, on April 19th this year, Borges received the Biennial Prize for his 'contribution to the freedom of the individual in society'. Yet when asked about two other Latin American poets, Neruda and Paz, he told us: 'Deux éminents poètes, plutôt que moi, ce sont eux qui auraient mérité un prix international.' Not that this need be regarded as committing himself, since no poet is without honour save in his own estimation ...

To those wondering why Borges, the voracious reader, never commented at any length on Proust, here is another statement worth noting: 'I have no authority to speak of an author whose work I don't know as well as I should like to; I have read Proust only in fragments, but I still remember the spellbinding description of Baron de Charlus.' When we reminded him that he had spoken at great length of Kafka and Joyce, his quick reply was: 'Oh, but surely Proust is by far superior to both.' Unlike Proust, who found it so difficult to cope with his maternal ancestry, Borges insists on his partly Jewish origins and on his immense debt to Rafael Cansinos-Assens, the Jesuit student who converted to Judaism at the beginning of the century – he was the founder of the *ultraist* movement in the early Twenties and author of *La nueva literatura*, a totally neglected work, Borges thinks. In the same spirit, he also confessed, tongue in cheek: 'Je ne sais pas si je peux dire que j'ai lu entièrement – j'ai un peu honte – un écrivain admiré par Nietzsche. C'est Gyp, plein d'argot et d'antisémites, plein de youpins et de youpines.' (See the *Heine* symposium, 1964.)

Finally, we asked him for news of Victoria Ocampo, founding-editor of *Sur,* who did so much to make her compatriot better known in Argentina. Borges's words were: 'It is a sad reflection on all of us that this marvellous publication should often have had to content itself with one hundred readers.' He reiterated his indebtedness to Roger Caillois, recently elected to the French Academy and the man most responsible for Borges's fame everywhere. Although well attuned to English literature – his masters being Donne, Stevenson, Chesterton, Kipling, Wells and Shaw – his main influences are French, as told to Georges Charbonnier in *Entretiens avec Borges* (Gallimard, 1967). He dwelt on 'les possibilités des sciences pour l'imagination' and contrasted the intellectual plane with the poetic as a constant, almost Manichaean element in his stories. As for the technique of writing, he never tired of pointing out that one thinks incompletely because always thinking of the effect one will have on others. Description, he emphasised, should rather *suggest* something than delineate it. In the introduction to *Labyrinths* (Penguin, 1970), André Maurois described him as 'akin to Kafka, Poe, sometimes to Henry James and Wells, always to Valéry by the abrupt projection of his paradoxes in what has been called his private metaphysics'.

Borges is now translating himself into English, with the constant help of a young Harvard poet, Norman Thomas di Giovanni – a slow but worthwhile task for someone who speaks the language like a native.

• • •

Patricia Doubell, whose long poem *The Dream of Mitzi* appears in this issue, made her debut in *ADAM* in 1963. She has since become widely known as a broadcaster and reader of her work at various poetry festivals.

CONTRIBUTORS

Marcel PROUST – *Letter to Montesquiou re the French Academy*
Gabriel JOSIPOVICI – *The Proust Play: In search of lost time, lost time, lost time*
Georges CATTAUI – *Du côté de chez Bloch*
Jorge Luis BORGES – *Spinoza* [translated poem]
Richard BALES – *An Elusive Friendship [Proust and Reynaldo Hahn]*
Alan BATES – *At Père Lachaise* [poem]
Antoine ANTONINI – *Proust et les signes*
Patricia DOUBELL – *The Dream of Mitzi* [poem]
Patricio GANNON – *Jorge Luis Borges*
Jorge Luis BORGES – *The Promise* [story – first publication]
G. S. FRASER – *Memories of Borges*
Jorge Luis BORGES – *The night they hold their wake for him in the South; Houses like angels* [2 translated poems]
Hector Eduardo CIOCCHINI – *Person and Persona [of Borges]* [translated]

Views and Reviews: Jean ROUSSELOT, *Ce mort sans sépulture (Isidore Ducasse/Comte de Lautréamont's* Chants de Maldoror) – Michael EDWARDS, *A life in fiction (Pierre de Boisdeffre's* Vie d'André Gide) – Gabriel JOSIPOVICI, *Journées de lecture (Proust's Recherche)* – Cecily LAMBERT, *Fighting for Greece [Byron and Shelley]* – Jean Marie BENOIST, *Borges ou le passage* – JM and AZ, *Proust, asparagus and analysis [Jean-Paul Richard's lecture]*

NOTES

1. See *ADAM*, Nos. 297–298 (1961).
2. However great his urge to please and mislead, Proust must sometimes have felt that he was, indeed, 'fatiguant à lire, avec des phrases trop longues, trop sinueusement attachées aux méandres de la pensée.' He asked Robert Dreyfus to forgive his style – 'Je n'ose pas me relire. Je sais bien qu'il ne faudrait pas écrire au galop, mais j'ai tant à dire. Ça se presse comme des flots.' . On the other hand, he could be so totally insincere, as when writing to Lucien Daudet: 'Qu'est mon pauvre style pénible même pour moi à côté de ta lumineuse musique!'
3. In an essay on the 'Gastronomie de Proust' (*Europe* I, 1970), Colette Cosnier dipped into the many references to food in the *Recherche* – a theme which was afterwards enlarged

upon by Jean-Pierre Richard (see p. 79 of the present issue). If Balzac rightly complained that 'On n'a jamais peint les exigences de la gueule', Proust treated the theme with imperishable succulence.

4. What can one make of the Duchesse de Clermont Tonnerre's description of Marcel as 'tendre et poisseux' or of the young aristocrats 'qui adoraient passer une soirée chez Marcel comme chez une cocotte très inaccessible' (*Robert de Montesquiou et Marcel Proust*, Flammarion, 1925)? This only two years after she wrote about 'son coupage de sang israélite [qui] ajoute à sa colossale intelligence ce je ne sais quoi d'universel qui est le propre de la race juive'. See also *The Politics of Assimilation* by Michael Marrus (Oxford University Press, 1971): 'Proust wrote with unmatched sensitivity about the identity problems of highly assimilated Jews ... whose Jewishness was built deeply into their nature' (pp. 19–20).

5. A more extensive work on the subject was presented by Jacqueline de Bresson (Harvard, 1967).

1. Portrait by Dorel Pascal, MG's nephew, 1957

2. Picture of MG by a young Persian artist he discovered on the New York subway, 1963

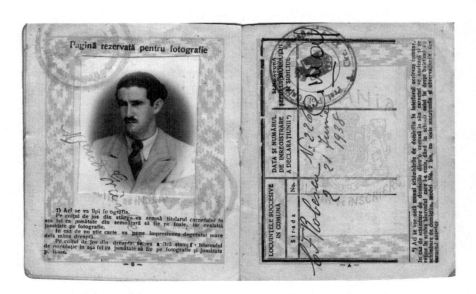

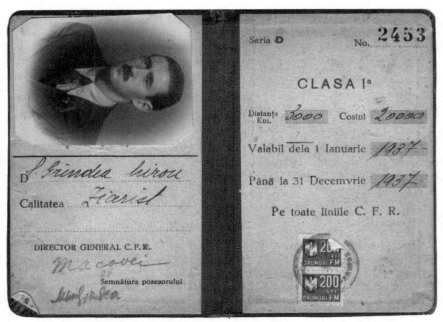

3. MG's Romanian passport and Press Association card

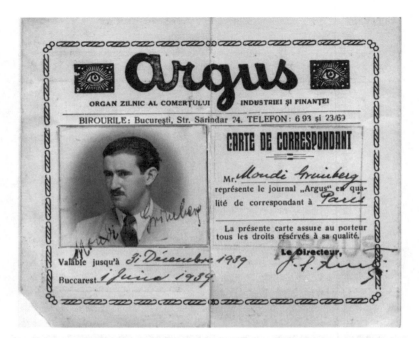

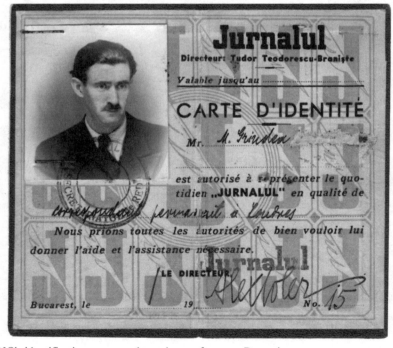

4. MG's identification papers and travel pass of pre-war Romania

5. MG's journalist papers

6. MG with Princess Margaret

7. MG with Natalie Clifford Barney, in her garden

8. MG with Yehudi Menuhin and M. Celak, during the Enescu Festival

(Portrait of Miron Grindea when he came to Venice)

Publisher of the International Review (London — Rochester, N.Y)
'ADAM'

9. Portrait of MG by Daghani

10. MG with Olga Rudge, Pound's partner

11. MG visiting the dying Pound

ADAM

INTERNATIONAL REVIEW

Editor: Miron Grindea

"Sabra" Writing: Hebrew and Arab

To Old Books
a poem by
Paul Valéry

Half a sin   Yosl Bergner

51p. $1.50

'SABRA' WRITING: HEBREW AND ARAB

Nos. 352–354, Vol. XXXVI, 1971–

THE DEFIANT FLOWER ...

Hatred Breeds Poor Poetry

The greater part of this issue is devoted to Israeli literature. It is perhaps the first attempt in this country to bring together Jewish and Arab writers, poets in particular. The choice of the word 'sabra' was deliberate, for, apart from its purely botanical meaning – the fruit of the cactus – it refers metaphorically to a prickly exterior with a tender heart, which could be applied equally to the many tough, uninhibited yet well-disposed youngsters born in that turbulent area.[1]

We thought it a good omen that both Jews and Arabs attribute a special significance to this plant. Its very form – flesh surrounded by an unbearably thorny skin – may be seen in a symbolic light, accommodating as it does opposites found in nature. The etymology is as fascinating as it is controversial. *Sabr* or *sabbâr* are the Arabic for cactus (*tzabar* in Hebrew), which yields the form *subbair* (*opunctia ficus indica*, Indian fig). The latest (1966) edition of Hans Wehr's *Dictionary of Modern Written Arabic* gives *Sabr* as meaning 'patience, composure, firmness', because the cutting of the skin to avoid the thorns is a complicated process, requiring the help of a second person to lift out the sweet, juicy fruit after incision. (On the other hand, *sabra* also means unbearable ...) The 'sabra' defies all weathers – so do the constant endeavours towards a reconciliation between the Hebrew and Arab cousins. If for no other reason than the purely poetical, they have so much to exchange: the sophisticated quality of Arabic folk lyrics (some of them included in this number) could fuse with the deeper and more dramatic lyricism of the late Leah Goldberg and her younger followers. Also, those composers eager to establish a typical Israeli style should place more emphasis on using the immense fund of indigenous Arab themes – just as all architects of goodwill should relentlessly follow Marcel Janko's successful battle for the integral rescue of Ein Hod (now the Mecca of all Israeli artists), thus preventing any possible sacrilegious destruction of the traditional Arab architecture which has for centuries blended so harmoniously with the landscape.

Arab intellectuals are becoming more active artistically within Israel's boundaries – two in particular, Muhammad Wattad and Atallah

Mansour. The first wrote an unusual play dealing with the problems of an Arab youth trying to maintain his identity amid the predominantly Jewish culture. Significantly, Wattad translated his own play into Hebrew, and it was performed last year at the Haifa Municipal Theatre. Mansour's novel, *In a New Light* (1966), was written originally in Hebrew – 'something of a phenomenon', as David Pryce-Jones remarked in his foreword to the English edition published in 1969 by Vallentine Mitchell. A reviewer in *The Sunday Times* described the novel as a convincing portrayal of 'the social insularities of the Middle East'. Mansour himself wrote that 'Only in Israel could Arab writers freely express their opinions without fearing for their lives.' A dramatic contrast: while a number of prominent immigrant writers, bred in the best European traditions, found it insuperably difficult to express themselves in the modernised language of the Bible and were forced to hang on to their mother tongues, Palestinian Arabs showed that they could cope creatively and naturally with both Arabic and Hebrew. Think of the tragic predicament of several world-renowned German-language novelists and poets. Max Brod was not only the discoverer of Kafka but also the author of that sadly neglected novel, *Reubeni*; yet, although he lived in Israel for the greater part of his life, Brod died a 'linguistic refugee', isolated from the mainstream of Hebrew culture. Arnold Zweig, during the ten years of self-inflicted seclusion spent on Mount Carmel, showed total indifference to the overwhelming cultural environment, and as soon as the Nazi scourge came to an end he hastened to return to his old German milieu. Else Lasker-Schuler, rightly considered one of the outstanding women poets of this century, was also nothing but a guest in the Jerusalem which she celebrated in so many magnificent poems. As to Claude Vigée, in mid-career he still remains, we suspect, the French poet and essayist who has chosen the Holy City as his new creative home.

The problem of physical and spiritual co-existence is a gigantic one. While there is room for a divergent renaissance, Jew and Arab can survive only if they decide mutually to become part of the Mediterranean civilisation, as they have already been in history. Their respective languages have many common roots, enchanting inflections and *tournures de phrase*, parallel subtleties. A great many of each side's writers and artists who constantly try to overcome religious fanaticism, sectarian chauvinism and bureaucratic demagogy are eager now to bring about genuine cultural co-operation. For example, the novelist and playwright Aharon Megged proposed in recent years that all professional Arab authors become full members of the Israeli Writers' Association. Another Hebrew novelist, Benyamin Tammuz, played host to a number of joint gatherings of Jewish and Arab writers. Which brings us to a pertinent reflection: an opportunity for Jewish and Arab poets to meet was missed

by the organisers of the 1971 (fifth) Poetry International in London
(largely, as in the past, a festival of surrealistic planning and pitiless
tedium). Present were three gifted Israeli poets, two of whom have
already attended similar gatherings. One's natural reaction was 'ni cet
excès d'honneur, ni ...'. Surely, if a young, valiant literature ought to be
encouraged, someone should have thought of its masters – for instance,
the veteran Avraham Shlonsky, on a par with Ungaretti and Neruda in
terms of depth of vision and brilliant, vibrant rendering. How much
more imaginative would it have been to have heard two young Israelis,
one writing in Hebrew and the other in Arabic. It will come. *ADAM*'s
small anthology may be a step in that direction.

CONTRIBUTORS

Rashid HUSAIN and Nathan ZACK – *Five Arab folk songs* [translated]
Dalia RABIKOWITZ – *Death in the Family* [translated story]
T. CARMI – *Still Life* [translated poem]
Amalia KAHANA-CARMON – *The House with the Distempered Sky-Blue Stairs* [translated story]
Amir GILBOA – *In the Dark; Horses and Riders* [translated poems]
Chaim BE'ER – *The High Commissioner* [translated poem]
Jamar QUWAR – *Will* [poem in English]
Michel HADDAD – *Qayin* [poem in English]
Sameh AL-QASIM – *Cinerama* [translated poem]
Eyal MEDDEG – *From Pink Meadows* [translated poem]
Dalia RABIKOWITZ – *Around Jerusalem* [translated poem]
Mordechai GELDMAN – *Famous Poet* [translated poem]
Ariana HARAN – *All You'd Tried to Forget* [translated poem]
Yosef BAR-YOSEF – *The Sheep* [translated excerpt from play]
Muhammad WATTAD – *Co-Existence* [dialogues translated by the author]
Aubrey HODES – *The Test* [extract from *Intimate Portrait of Martin Buber*]
Zaki DARWISH – *City of Slumber* [translated story]
Abba KOVNER – *My Little Sister: Part Three* [translated poem]
Paul VALÉRY – *To Old Books* [poem + translation]
Michael EDWARDS – *Commonplace* [poem: note on this at end of *Views and Reviews*]
Jeremy ROBSON – *Between You and Me* [poem]

Views and Reviews: Sasson SOMECH, *Fadwâ Tuqnâ: Palestinian poetess* – Pierre ROUVE, *An innocent in Israel (Dorel Pascal)* – Amos OZ, *To be or not to be a Jew*

NOTE

1. According to Dr Elizabeth Boyko, a Vienna-born ecologist and world authority on cacti at
    the Arid Zone Agricultural Research Institute at Beersheba, none of the hundred and
    twenty species of the cactus plant that grow in Israel today (including the 'sabra') is
    indigenous. They are believed to have been introduced a few generations ago from Mexico.

INTERNATIONAL REVIEW

Editor: Miron Grindea

Francis Ponge

Octopus

Zygmunt Frankel

Summer Overtures

Clive Murphy

The two ADAM prize-winning novels

Christopher Fry

75p
$2.25

FRANCIS PONGE, ZYGMUNT FRANKEL, CLIVE MURPHY, CHRISTOPHER FRY

Nos. 361–363, Vol. XXXVII, 1972–

RE-MAPPING THE ROUTE

Must *ADAM* migrate yet again? A Kensingtonian for nearly thirty obstinate years, the journal is now being threatened with eviction from one of London's last surviving civilised areas. As if the pseudo-Kafkaesque masochistic 'design' of the Air Terminal were not enough, scores of streets and romantic gardens have in the last few months been mown down to make room for a bouquet of hideous redevelopments. Instead of putting up a fierce and possibly successful fight in defence of such innocent beauty, the young architects show the same grinning unconcern for urban debasement as their more established colleagues. Whereas many historical *arrondissements* in Paris can still count on their *communards*, London's landscapes are being rapidly and unscrupulously demolished by the bulldozers. After the destruction of St James's Theatre, after the outrage brought to the old façade of *The Times*, after what happened to the Ludgate Hill approach to St Paul's, now our SW7 is also being ruthlessly destroyed by cruel and perverse financial combines. Nearly half of Emperor's Gate, up to the very door of *ADAM*'s office, is at present a huge mound of rubble. Poems, essays and other original contributions continue to reach us from the outside, but they are being perused precariously on one limb, with contents for future issues discussed to the accompaniment of the pneumatic drill.

● ● ●

Driven back to our own old resources in England (after a happy three-year association with the University of Rochester), there was need for a halt for re-mapping the route. Woburn Press, a young but determined team of publishers operating from offices opposite the British Museum, have decided to harbour our in-and-out sailings for as long as readers and subscribers will show interest in *ADAM*'s cargoes. In addition, a few of the emerging literary historians at the University of Sussex have come forward with enticing offers of collaboration: for instance, no sooner had the theme of Francis Ponge been mentioned than there sprang an invigorating reaction from the still unpolluted surroundings of Falmer (the articles in this issue by George Craig and Christophe Campos). And there is hope for more in the future.

'*Enfin, Ponge vint.*' The deterioration of language as a vehicle for our understanding of one another is being exposed in contemporary writing at the same pace as the scientists' fear that the planet itself is approaching its final doom. Amidst these jollities it is perhaps not inappropriate to take a closer look at what is left of the poetical alphabet. We chose Ponge because, above and despite innumerable contradictions, 'Faut-il que l'époque soit bizarrement denuée pour qu'on attache à une littérature comme la mienne le moindre intérêt? Comment peut-on se tromper à ce point?' (*Le Grand Recueil*, II, 1961), in contrast with an equally baffling statement: 'Il me semble qu'il suffit que je m'ajoute à eux (Malherbe, Boileau ou Mallarmé) pour que la littérature soit complète' (*Le Parnasse*, 1928) – his 'rage de l'expression', spanning a full half-century, seemed to delineate most spectacularly the pangs of the present semantic dilemma. What a long way from Apollinaire or Max Jacob, for whom imagery was still the 'verbal angel'!

As early as 1919, long before he was granted entry into the *NRF* Parnasse, Ponge invoked the mysterious elements that might help him to express something new: 'O draperies des mots, assemblages de l'art littéraire, ô pluriels parterres de voyelles colorées [was this a *conscious* paraphrase of Rimbaud's *Voyelles*, A noir, E blanc, I rouge, O bleu, U vert? Ed], décors des lignes, bouches superbes des consonnes, à *mon secours! Concentrez, détendez vos puissances*' [our italics]. Any artist struggling so ferociously to break out of the limitations imposed upon him by the very tools on which his art depends arrests one's admiration. The poet may well attack his fellow-men: 'O hommes, informes mollusques, millions de fourmis que les pieds du temps écrasent … telles paroles, telles mœurs, ô société! tout n'est que paroles' (*Des raisons d'écrire*, 1939): or he may try to drive one away from his work by saying (tongue in cheek?), 'Les idées ne sont pas mon fort; je ne suis pas un grand écrivain,' in a non-essay with an intriguing English title, *My Creative Method*, or, 'pendant des années j'ai inventé toutes les raisons pour ne pas écrire' (*Préface aux papates*, 1935): then 'J'ai reconnu l'impossibilité de m'exprimer … je puis donc décider de me taire, mais cela ne me convient pas' (*Pages bis*, 1941). Which made Camus, one of his earliest admirers, wonder: 'C'est votre maîtrise même qui rend convaincant votre aveu d'échec' (*NRF*, 1956). At this point it is good to recall that, long before Camus, the late Betty Miller, an unjustly forgotten critic, questioned Ponge's utterance, 'Je ne me prétends pas poète' and thought this 'slightly contemptuous' self-denial came 'oddly from a man so patently infected by the malignant ardour of poetic curiosity' (*Horizon*, September 1947).

Greeted as a *chef de file* by the 'telquelistes' and held in high regard by a great many members of another group of restless and original experimenters (*l'Ephémère*, led by Yves Bonnefoy, for whom 'La parole c'est ce qui pose plus de problèmes qu'il n'y en a eu à résoudre,' and Jacques Dupin, whose latest cycle, *L'Embrasure*, contains 'une liasse noircie de frustrations et de torpeurs'), Ponge continues to add to the linguistic traps that bedevil the comprehension of so much of current poetical output. The elusiveness of language keeps him, as so many other poets, on tenterhooks; surely this constant uncertainty must be both exciting and pleasurable, since it can also be tormenting ...

The preparation of our tribute went through several stages of rearranging and postponement because 'le printannier et merveilleux Ponge', as his great contemporary René Char once called him, was late in sending us a few *inédits*. These reached us at the very last moment, yet in time to keep the two translations by Sacha Rabinovitch exciting company.[1]

•   •   •

Valéry

The English translation of Paul Valéry's *Collected Works* is now approaching completion. This most ambitious undertaking was bravely carried out through the joint efforts of the American Bollingean Foundation (subsequently taken over by the Princeton University Press) and Routledge and Kegan Paul in this country – an ideal tribute, coinciding with the centenary of the poet's birth. For *ADAM* the event is sadly associated, not only with a memorable compliment the ailing poet paid this journal when we visited him in May 1945, but also with the recent death of Cecil Day Lewis: for the Poet Laureate took part in our Valéry Memorial Evening, with T. S. Eliot in the Chair. CDL read his own version of *Le Cimetière marin* – an unforgettable experience, for Day Lewis's reading voice was (with the exception of that of Dylan Thomas) the most impressive of his time, enhanced by his virile and handsome appearance. Two lines only as a memorial to Lewis's rendering: 'Chienne splendide – Bright day star,' and 'Où marchent les colombes – Where dove-sails saunter by'; also, for the record, when Cyril Connolly met Valéry, in January 1945, he detailed to him CDL's 'magnificent translation', an opinion shared by the poet William McCausland Stewart but disputed by a Yale teacher, Kenneth Douglas (*MLQ*, December 1947).

Considerably less cosmopolitan than Eliot, Day Lewis cascaded with laughter when Desmond MacCarthy, another friend of the magazine present at the ceremony, told his own Valéry story. He happened to return from Paris the day after the poet's death (July 20, 1945), and he was more than perplexed to see the front pages of every French newspaper in thick mourning borders and entirely devoted to Valéry's life and work. No sooner had he reached Dover than he was equally struck by headlines lamenting a different national event: 'We've lost the Ashes!' MacCarthy was much comforted, though, when told of more than a dozen different versions of *Le Cimetière marin* (at the present moment there are more than twenty, not counting the latest annotated translation by Graham Dunstan Martin in the Edinburgh Bilingual Library, 1971).

Worth remembering is the brief creative period spent by the poet in England in the 1890s. In 1892 he met Meredith at Box Hill and was astonished to hear that, long before the brain, it is the stomach that brings a writer to ruin. Two years later he came over here on a *voyage mystérieux*, followed in 1896 by a three-month sojourn, during which he accepted tedious work as a translator for the British South Africa (Chartered) Company – a series of anti-German leaflets inspired by Cecil Rhodes. At this time he found himself 'au bord du suicide: un jour à Londres, j'avais envie de me pendre. Le jour était jaune et sulphureux. Les fumées descendaient des toits dans la rue. J'ai trouvé un volume d'Aurélien Scholl, j'ai ri et fus sauvé' (*Cahiers*, IX). The poet W. E. Henley, an old friend of Verlaine, offered him hospitality in his *New Review*, and Valéry's first important article, 'La conquête allemande', appeared in the May 1897 issue. He later recalled Henley's 'visage assez formidable'.

Just as Proust had the surprise of reading a first truly illuminating study on *Du côté de chez Swann* shortly after it came out in France (1913), Valéry was gratified to see *La jeune parque* reviewed in the *TLS* of April 23, 1917, only a few weeks after the poem was published by Gallimard. The reviewer was the same critic who wrote on Proust – young John Middleton Murry. 'Valéry had written to me to thank me in terms which were, to say the least, unsettling. Not only did I apparently understand the poem better than the French critics, but I had prolonged the music of the poem in a music of my own. But when, in 1921, we met in person for the first time, the mystery was partly solved. Valéry had called on Katherine Mansfield and myself in our room in a Montparnasse hotel, and he was explaining to her that the review, coming from England, gave him the assurance that the musical pattern of his poem had the universal validity at which he aimed. Anyhow, he surprised us both by quoting in an almost unrecognisable and unhesitating English – a whole paragraph which I had by then forgotten.' He then inscribed his books in 'curious English verse in which Valéry rhymed with Murry'.[2]

It took Valéry twenty-two years to revisit this country. On a bitterly cold Monday, October 30, 1922 (the poet's fifty-first birthday), he joined M. de Saint Aulaire, the French Ambassador, and made a speech at the unveiling of a plaque at 44 Howland Street, where Verlaine had spent the winter of 1872–3. The following day, a number of francophiles were invited to hear him talk in one of the most celebrated salons of the time. The layout for the invitation followed exactly the typography chosen by Arthur Symons for a lecture delivered on November 21, 1893, in London by Verlaine: 'Monsieur Paul Valéry, le grand poète français, fera une causerie sur *La Poésie et le Langage,* le mardi 31 octobre 1922, à Argyll House, 211 King's Road, Chelsea (avec l'aimable permission de Lady Colefax). Les places sont de 10s, et la présente feuille servira d'entrée.' The poet also read *L'ébauche d'un serpent,* much admired by the people afterwards invited to stay for dinner: George Moore (whom Valéry had met previously in Paris), Elisabeth Bibesco, Sir Edmund Gosse, Harold Nicolson, Vita Sackville-West. The greatest surprise of the soirée was the unexpected appearance, after dinner, of Conrad, who wanted to say how deeply impressed he was by the perusal of *Charmes.* Valéry returned to London the following year to talk about Victor Hugo at the Institut Français (October 16, 1923): this time he spent a whole day with Conrad at his country house at Bishopsbourne and wrote movingly of this visit in the special issue which the *NRF* produced on Conrad's death (August 1924).

In 1927 he came over, this time bearing the Academician's crown of thorns with a mixture of dyspeptic panache and irresistible charm. For here was now more than merely one of the forty immortals: he had suddenly become France's national poet, and for the last eighteen years of his life he slaved at a pace and in a variety of official chores that would have killed the toughest of our Poet Laureates. His photograph 'en grande tenue' was offered to Sybil Colefax 'de son ami très lauré'. John Galsworthy took the chair at an Anglo-French dinner given in Valéry's honour and greeted him in rather un-Galsworthian terms: 'Vous êtes essentiellement français, tellement français que, si vous veniez en Angleterre sous le nom de John Smith et si vous vous exprimiez en anglais, les gens vous suivraient très probablement en criant *Vive la France!*' At the same dinner Gosse proclaimed him 'au tout premier rang des poètes contemporains'.

Edmund Wilson, whose recent death has reminded everybody that we lost in him one of the most widely read and perceptive critics of the last two generations, was more restrained in his appreciation. While recognising Valéry's 'sculptural, marmoreal genius' in poetry, he seemed to detect a certain deviousness in the man's character. He had not been at all amused by Valéry's deliberate omission of the name of Anatole France, whose actual successor he was, in his official discourse under the Coupole. 'This address,' Wilson wrote, 'is perhaps his masterpiece of bad writing. Never has Valéry's viscous prose, his masses of clotted abstractions, been managed to worse advantage.' Another American author, who died this year, aged 97, the formidable Natalie Clifford Barney, also devoted to Valéry a chapter of subtle disappointments in her *aventures de l'esprit* (1929). It was she and Mme de Muhlfeld (a friend of Gide) who helped the poet both financially and socially in the early Twenties. The 'Amazon' was the first to translate *Monsieur Teste* into English (*The Dial*, February 1922) – 'Je fis ce travail avec le meilleur anglais qui me restait, et Valéry eut ses premiers dollars.' It was also at one of her famous 'vendredis' (January 3, 1923) that she introduced Valéry to Anatole France, the only occasion the two had met. 'S'occuper de Valéry était devenu le mot d'ordre de tout un déchaînement du mécanisme humain,' and Miss Barney, together with Princess Gaetani, devised a subscription system whereby the poet would get as much as 15,000 francs each year, but *NRF* opposed the initiative and took upon themselves the responsibility for the poet's welfare. The happy consequence of this well-meaning plot was that Ezra Pound, together with May Sinclair and Richard Aldington, set up a similar committee on behalf of T. S. Eliot, which resulted in Lady Rothermere's patronage for *The Criterion*.

Aldous Huxley's opinion of Valéry was ambivalent. When in August 1945 Victoria Ocampo asked him to join in a tribute to Valéry, he declined by saying: 'I was very fond of him personally and always derived much pleasure and profit from that almost incomprehensibly rapid and elliptic conversation, but I have never been unequivocally enthusiastic about his work … There was always a tendency in Valéry to pretend to a philosophico-mathematical profundity and precision of thought which in many cases he did not have. The result was a curious incongruity between form and substance.' Had Huxley by then forgotten what he had written to the poet from 3 rue du Bac, Suresnes, on 11 March 1929?: 'Je ne vous ennuierai pas avec l'expression de mon admiration'; or, on 4 January 1930: 'Je vous remercie infiniment de votre Léonard. Je l'ai trouvé plein de beautés – ou plutôt de beautés-vérités, car ce livre *est un bel exemple de la véritable œuvre philosophique, qui est une œuvre d'art*" [our italics].

Going back a few years, one is glad to see the esteem in which *The Criterion* held the author of the *Parque*. T. S. Eliot published a complete version of *Le serpent* in the January 1923 issue of his quarterly and subsequently, when Lytton Strachey turned the offer down, wrote an important 'Introduction to the Work of Paul Valéry' for a limited edition of the same translation, made by Captain Mark Wardle. An officer interested in early Valéry? This should not appear so intriguing if one remembers that Valéry himself, between 1897 and 1900, worked for the Ministry for War, and he once wrote that 'lire est une opération militaire'. T. S. Eliot, at any rate, must have liked Captain Wardle's writing, since he also published an original short story of Wardle's, *Periscope* (*The New Criterion*, January 1925). He was the author of *An Alphabet from the Trenches*, rhymes by Captain Mark Kingsley Wardle with sketches by Lt-Col. A Buchanan-Dunlop, published by Hodder & Stoughton, 1916, and of *Foundations of Soldiering*, Aldershot, 1916. Also in *The New Criterion*, F. Sturge Moore, the friend of Yeats, wrote an essay on Valéry's technique (June and October 1924); then, in *Hommage des écrivains étrangers à Valéry*, he published a two-hundred-line poem, *The Fount*, preceded by this dedication: 'Imitation is perhaps the only sincere flattery, hence the dedication of the poem which follows. As an iceberg throws back a dim and distorted image of the sun while drifting towards dissolution in the southern seas, even my stanzas seek to reflect the charm of yours whilst I am drawn irresistibly forward towards that Ideal Hellas, so near to readers of your Eupalinos, so fatally fascinating to myself.'[3]

> All that shone forth twixt and pure event,
> Tree, Serpent, Fountain – mirror of your essence.
> The drunkenness of acts, their iridescence:
> All move to make your shimmering monument!
>
> O diamond rigour, cryptic perseverance –
> Flouting the flash that tore the terrible schism!
> O crystal-gazer caught within your prism,
> Weaving clear arabesques on incoherence!
>
> Yet clear-leafed Plane, yet Patience of the Palm!
> O whirl, O Whorl, O flowering grace of feature,
> Loving – laughing at life, irked as a creature,
> Stirred to acclaim the God's eternal calm
>
> Echo of the Divine that seized your sight –
> You, dazzled by the mystery of light!

Among the English homages worth recalling is a Taylorian lecture for 1927, entitled *Paul Valéry*, which was delivered by The Right Hon H. A. L. Fisher. 'His verse,' the eminent historian wrote, 'is confessedly difficult, but perhaps for that very reason it has a curious power of transporting the reader into a magical world of its own.' Valéry himself delivered the Zaharoff lecture for 1939, when Oxford conferred upon him its Honorary DLit.

The preceding data, however amorphous, might possibly be of some use to a future scholar dealing with the Anglo-Saxon chapter in Valéry's secretive life. 'Que me fait ma biographie et que me font mes jours écoulés – ce n'est pas moi qui rechercherais le Temps Perdu,' he wrote in *Propos me concernant*, shortly before his death. We maintain, though, that the physical life of an artist can be of positive value in a future interpretation of his creative achievement, and among the many possible readings of a poet's work surely the biographical should find a place? Valéry himself wrote that each writer is by nature a comedian and that words are 'autant de mauvais instruments' (*Cahiers VIII*). Yet he had to put up with words, and for fifty uninterrupted years he never missed the passionate daily ritual of jotting down his thoughts. There are 40,000 pages of hitherto unpublished material awaiting a thorough and courageous sifter – a duty towards literary history.[4]

As for the state of emergency which so many poets are eager to trumpet, *ADAM* once again has the effrontery to say that poetry is with us still. Without disregarding the Byzantine complexity of the crisis of language, and while acknowledging the heated debates provoked by Noam Chomsky's ideas on linguistics, we find sense – and comfort – in André Chamson's confession of faith: 'Le langage n'est pas seulement la matière de la poésie, il est la poésie elle-même, puisqu'il est aussi la réalité ou, du moins, le plus expressif de tous ses symboles. Infirme ou triomphant, le langage n'est que l'écho de la poésie. Informe ou exprimée, la poésie est toujours au-delà des poètes' (*L'enfant qui veut être poète*). Also, three samples of immortal lines:

> Et les fruits passeront la promesse des fleurs *(Malherbe)*
> Le vent se lève ... Il faut tenter de vivre *(Valéry)*
> De toutes les maisons du monde
> Ne durera plus qu'un balcon:
> Et de l'humaine mappemonde
> Une tristesse sans plafond *(Supervielle)*

• • •

ADAM's Prizes – Like so many poets, Valéry hated the narrative art and dismissed the novel as being no part of literature. But literary history has taught us that poets have often attempted obsessively to be novelists as well, only to be forced to admit, with feigned deprecation, their inability to create characters in fiction.

The greater part of this issue consists of the full texts of the two prize-winning novels from *ADAM*'s competition held in London in 1968. While none of the entries for poetry and drama proved to be of sufficient artistic merit to be awarded the £100 prize offered in each category, there were twenty-two entries in the novel section, out of which six were important enough to be shortlisted. The members of the jury for the final decision were Mr L. P. Hartley, Mr W. J. Lambert (Literary Editor of *The Sunday Times*) and Mr Michael Ratcliffe (Literary Editor of *The Times*).

The verdict was not arrived at without a good deal of hovering, as should be the case in every such situation. Of the six, three names were kept for prolonged consideration. These were Richard Austin, Zygmunt Frankel and Clive Murphy. Ultimately, only the last two vied for the award, although one of the judges put on record that 'The virtues of Mr Austin's *The End of Summer* were calm, dignity and emotional honesty, with the supporting characters incisively done and the sense of dissolution ultimately real enough'. The dilemma increased when the jury concluded that, for different reasons, the remaining two works were of equal merit. Hence the decision to break the stalemate – to divide the prize between the two candidates.

Clive Murphy's *Summer Overtures* impressed the jury by 'its sulphurous sketches of life at several different levels of decay – personal, social, even in a sense political'. In spite of different techniques, the novel 'is reminiscent of Smollett, or perhaps Smollett re-written by Sterne' – in brief, a talent worth watching. As to Zygmunt Frankel's *Octopus*, the jury largely commented upon the subtle handling of the theme of guilt which, 'against the backcloth of the disaster of European Jewry in World War II (and harmonising in a way with the theme of Robert Shaw's *The Man in the Glass Booth*), is explored with a highly intelligent misgiving. Verbal or emotional fireworks are avoided, though description and reflection alike come up with a limpid warmth which is itself deeply involving.' If *Summer Overtures* is interesting 'for its sharp scene-setting and its proper contempt for life in the Metropolis', *Octopus* 'takes large historical themes, genocide, oblivion and the killer instinct and succeeds in battening them down under the structure of the story, so that they are always there but never erupt to destroy the narrative line of the tale itself'.

As the issues produced since 1968 have been of a constantly specialised nature, we have until now been unable to fit the full texts of these prize-winning novels. We do it now with a renewed belief that, like poetry, prose in the form of the novel can also be assured of its survival ...

CONTRIBUTORS

Francis PONGE – *The Match* [translated poem]
George CRAIG – *Matter and the Heart (Francis Ponge)*
Francis PONGE – *The Tortoise* [translated poem]
Christophe CAMPOS – *Wordpower (Francis Ponge)*
Francis PONGE – *La Simple; Le beurre (deux poèmes inédits)*

Zygmunt FRANKEL – *The Octopus* [full text of novel]
Hugo MANNING – *The Addendum of Phaedo* [poem]
Clive MURPHY – *Summer Overtures* [full text of novel]

Views and Reviews: Christopher FRY, *John Whiting, 13 pieces for London Magazine*

NOTES

1. There is an ample and interesting English bibliography on the poet. Jonathan Cape, in 1969, published a complete version of *Le savon* (*Soap*, 90p) by the American poet Lane Dunlop, who is also responsible for a number of meritorious translations which have appeared in the *Western Humanities Journal*. George Macbeth was even more successful with his translation of *La guêpe* (*The Wasp*, published in *The Strand* in 1965). Peter Hoy translated and published *The Mollusc* in one of his own many private presses, the Black Knight Press, 1968. He also wrote an essay for *The Luciad*. Heated debates have appeared in learned essays and searching reviews on both sides of the Atlantic. In an article entitled 'Omelette à la Ponge', a reviewer in the *Times Literary Supplement* (Sept. 30, 1965) wrote: 'What would we think of a cook who served up an omelette with the broken shells on the plate? The method seems now to have been applied, perhaps for the first time, to a work of criticism. It may have been the author's aim to compose a prose-poem on Malherbe in his typically fragmentary, tentative style. It is clear that in producing an unbook or an antibook of this kind Ponge is deliberately reacting against the fluency of academics – 'les incapables professionnels de la critique.' What he conveys most forcibly is the conviction that there ought to be a modern Malherbe, and he seems to be hoping that some future Boileau will be able to write 'Enfin, Ponge vint.' In a later review (Dec 12, 1968), *TLS* described him as a writer who 'takes great risks, tries lots of long shots, abandons commonsense in the hope of striking genius, and often comes a cropper'; yet, the reviewer admitted, 'Ponge harps on the fact that the contemplation of objects – any objects – can be a mysteriously poetical, and indeed religious, experience.' The American poet Richard Wilbur compared Ponge with William Carlos Williams and thought he will become 'more popular in the United States than the surrealists or Michaux'. After Professor David Plank, in an essay in *Modern Language Quarterly* (June 1965), placed Ponge as 'the discoverer of the man of the future', another American scholar, Professor J. Temmer, in the same periodical (*MLQ*, June 1968), attacked this characterisation as excessive and pointed out that 'Ponge is most successful when he follows Jules Renard's elliptic rhythm' – for instance: 'L'escargot n'a pas beaucoup d'amis, mais il n'en a pas besoin pour son bonheur, il colle si bien à la nature, il en jouit si parfaitement' (Ponge), as compared with Renard's *Escargot*: 'casanier dans la saison des rhumes, son cou de giraffe rentré, il se promène dès les beaux jours, mais il ne sait marcher que sur sa langue.' Two other critical essays worth mentioning for the benefit of future students of the 'chosisme pongien' are 'Ponge and the poetry of self-knowledge' (*Contemporary Literature*, Spring 1970), in which Professor Sarah Lawall insists on the artist's search 'for the image of man, creator and user of language', and 'Ponge, metapoet' by Professor Robert Greene in *Modern Language Notes* of May 1971. Finally, a thesis in French on Ponge as an art critic by Tullia Michelino, to be published soon by Exeter University, and a PhD on the 'textual linguistics', to which another young scholar, C. Butters, is now putting the final touches.

2. More than once Valéry told his young Irish friend, the poet William McCausland Stewart (they first met in Montpellier in 1922), of his concern over the hard life KM was enduring at the Gurdjieff 'clinic' at Fontainebleau, where she died in 1924. Two of Valéry's articles on 'La crise de l'esprit' appeared in Murry's *Athenaeum* (April 11 and May 2, 1919).

3. Another moving tribute, *Stèle for Paul Valéry*, appeared in William McCausland Stewart's *Tokens of Time* (Fortune Press, 1970), which Léopold Sédar Senghor described as 'admirable':

4. Valéry's *Cahiers* are full of English words. The one for 1895, for instance, is entitled *Self Book*. Monsieur Teste (alias the poet) kept a *Logbook*. He felt at self variance, or mixed French with English: 'En *some* ceci (cahiers et carnets) ce sont des tas d'études pour *some philosophy*, whose name I dislike or a miso-sophy.' Shortly before he died he wrote: 'Je connais assez mon esprit, *my heart* aussi.' But to our mind no other francanglais passage in Valéry's work equals this 'cipher': '*Story of the European one who gone in new land between savage people, live in a tribe of natives, and unveiled by ethics or other mistakes of the West, can*

learn something strong and noble – viz, natural – from the chief and the first men around him. He does evangelise or teach nobody, knowing himself be more ignorant than savages. His return to Europe. He applies the savage theory unformulated' (*Cahier I*. p. 500). Was this a 'note de travail' for an essay or a philosophical tale? As far as we know, these mysterious lines have never before been mentioned, so perhaps one is entitled to expect some revealing comment from a Valéry expert such as Professor L. J. Austin or Roger Shattuck. Oddly enough, Valéry considered himself enough of an expert to write about Conrad's 'bad' English: 'Il parlait l'anglais avec un accent horrible qui m'amusait [*sic*] beaucoup.'

ADAM

INTERNATIONAL REVIEW

Editor: Miron Grindea

Cyril at seventy – photographed by his old school-mate and life-long friend Sir Cecil Beaton.

"Mopping up more distant corners of the world that I must hurry to win from the jaws of decrepitude."

75p
$2.25

CYRIL CONNOLLY
Nos. 385–390, Vol. XXXIX, 1974–75

SANS TITRE

... to be talked about, to be remembered after death ...

The motto comes from one of Orwell's collected essays (*Why I write*, 1961). His Eton contemporary and friend, Cyril Connolly, wrote from entirely different motives: primarily, to anaesthetise himself against the insufferable obsession that he would never create the one and only masterpiece of which he had been dreaming from early youth. Result: for more than half a century and mostly under the pressure of having to earn a living, Connolly both enchanted and exasperated his readers with a capricious combination of classical background, inexhaustible imagery, gluttonous yet elegant *joie de vivre*, always singing the ecstasies and miseries of the heart. A man of countless complexities, he worshipped nature in its primeval splendour. He professed a connoisseur's allegiance to opulent food and, apart from the serene years he had found in his third and only happy marriage, he pursued a melancholy and often mortifying – baudelairian – quest for the *femme-chimère* (his own notion of 'das ewig weibliche'), constantly persuading himself that he had found the answer in morbid, pain-inflicting women. Above all, he never tired of professing his reverence for creativity ('I respect anybody who writes a book, that's a part built into me,' he confessed to Simon Blow in *The Guardian* on his 70th birthday), and to this creed he committed himself with selfless and total enthusiasm.

For a number of people, including myself, he symbolised the very notion of Literature to the extent of making life more tolerable (those unequalled editorials in *Horizon* for a full decade, 1940–1950, to be soon followed by what Richard Ellmann called 'one of the few solaces of Sunday morning in London', his reviews in the *Sunday Times*); hence the feeling of let-down, of unfillable vacuum which his death left. Yet it was *ADAM*'s cheerless privilege soon to find out that this shaman of Sunday-paper reviewing had almost as many detractors as admirers. While he was alive one was inclined to ignore the seriousness of Edmund Wilson's question put to John Wain in 1957: 'Why are so many people in England down on Connolly?' Alas, some of the replies received while assembling material for this memorial issue made the *cri de cœur* sound afresh, never perhaps to be clearly understood.

The first memorable spray of accumulated venom came from a cultured and still handsome old Etonian. 'Let me tell you something. If you really want to produce an interesting number, get someone who knew Cyril inside out; he might be willing [!] to write a demolition piece – X or Y, for instance. That would certainly balance some of the conventional[!] laudatory contributions you're bound to receive ...' Stunned, I nonetheless showed 'bonne mine à mauvais jeu'. The 'obliging' friend turned out among the first recusants – the 'No, certainly nots' – to the hundred or more letters that were sent out. The mere thought of having been invited to dwell on so 'unpleasant a theme' made him recoil in derision.

One of the finest poets in the English language thought he had nothing to say, not even about the glorious magazine to which he had often contributed, since, to use his own excuse, he had never 'belonged to Connolly's gang, so I don't feel qualified to write about him'. *Gang?* Unexpected word from a poet of universal amplitude. For days I was sunk in confusion until, unexpectedly, I met the poet's son, who recalled that some years back CC had upset his father over a contribution to *Horizon*; however, there followed a remarkable Canossa-like gesture – the repentant editor almost on his knees, having travelled a long distance to apologise and, in the hope of being forgiven, producing his wife from behind a porch as a talisman.

Another writer of distinction declined to contribute on equally flimsy grounds. 'I often admired his writing, especially about prints, animals and the pleasures of the senses – he had the Irish "edge" – but I do not feel I can write anything about him. One had to be one of his set and I was not.'

There followed a postcard with a reproduction of one of Henry Miller's gouaches [reproduced in this issue and now printed below]:

... Can't oblige. Have sight in only one eye. Do very little reading. Besides, I never liked Connolly! He is a snob, a dry intellectual, etc.
Good wishes!
Henry Miller

What a document to release, dismissing the one critic who did so much to establish the author of the *Tropics* as a respectable writer (see Durrell's piece in this issue). When, in 1970, I visited Miller at his luxurious villa on the hills of Los Angeles overlooking the Pacific, one of the questions the over-fatigued sage fired at me (while at the same time enjoying the luscious choreography of his latest Japanese naiad) was, 'And how is dear old Cyril?' He also once found it possible to write in his endearingly honeyed vein, 'Cyril, you are very wise, very understanding and really very kindly. I wonder that you remain the critic. You can go beyond.' (Part of a letter to Palinurus quoted in *The Unquiet Grave*.) Vive l'ironie!

These four first *accrocs* were sufficient to make me tumble deep, very deep into the pit of confraternals tearing each other to pieces. It gave me the feeling not so much of nausea as of sordid failure. *Qu'est-ce que j'ai cherché dans cette galère?* What had *ADAM* been doing all these years in the maledictory caverns of literary commerce? Whenever possible, we have tried to reveal some of the more offensive *canailleries*, whether hidden in forgotten books of criticism, memoirs and correspondence, or still prevalent in recent *bagarres*; but we never imagined that an artist who, for the last five decades, had been a passionate believer in creative truth would be denied the qualities which, for us, epitomise the fascination of the man of letters: munificence of outlook, all-embracing wit (even if marred sometimes by indifference to scholastic accuracy), constant renewal of style.

The list of 'No's' – and thus of disappointments – was much longer than it would seem necessary to reveal. Several of them, admittedly, had a plausible consistency, Sir Alec Douglas-Home's, for instance: 'As I declined to contribute to other publications on the same subject I could not possibly make an exception for *ADAM.'* Arthur Koestler: 'I do plan to write one day about Cyril, but the time is not yet.' (Incidentally, the author of *Darkness at Noon* will soon be seventy, and one can well imagine the piece CC would have written on the occasion – as inspired, surely, as the interview he took on AK's sixtieth birthday.) From Santa Monica, a heart-felt message from Christopher Isherwood: 'I work very slowly nowadays, and I am trying to finish a long book. I am all the more sorry to refuse because *I owe a great debt of gratitude to Cyril; he praised my work when I was beginning to write*' [our italics]. Finally, this note from Kingsley Amis, who, in an article now forgotten, has described *The Rock Pool* as one of the funniest novels written between the wars: 'Many thanks for asking Jane and me to contribute to your Connolly number. We have talked it over and, for various reasons, neither of us feels able to do what you so kindly suggest. We both had warm feelings towards Cyril, and both admired him as a writer, but neither of us seems able to lick anything publishable into shape.'

At the time Connolly died, I myself was experiencing the hazards of some major surgery in a London hospital, yet none of the ominous laboratory tests left me with as bitter a taste as Mr Geoffrey Grigson's explosion, under the guise of a letter to the Editor, exactly one week after his friend's death: 'As far as Connolly was concerned, some writers who are now taken to designate the Thirties were repelled by what they took to be Connolly's mixture of social and aesthetic attitude. In matters of value, they saw him as a late and provincial acolyte of much that they rejected' (*Sunday Times*, December 8th, 1974).

• • •

What was hidden behind this ferocious attack? After all, Mr Grigson had contributed to the very first issue of *Horizon* and along the years has been reviewing for the *Sunday Times*. From the portable telephone which breaks the dreariness of a hospital ward, I began bombarding various literary friends: What is he like? Tall, good-looking, soft-voiced, I was told. Happily married? Yes, very. Still capable of enthusiasm? Very much so. Then *why* this sudden dismissal of one of his most brilliant 'compagnons de route?' No real answer. Two weeks later, yet another welcome sedation at a time when everything in the ward is asleep: a whole hour of music in the 'Men of Action' series, with the names of Debussy and Satie pronounced with the correct French accentuation which, as a rule, the BBC seems to consider sacrilegious.[1] I missed the name of the broadcaster and this made the weekend unbearable, but what a joy on the following Monday to learn that the man of action was none other than Mr Grigson. By a strange coincidence I had then read his 'Noire Dame de la Beauce' – surely lines that must have captivated Cyril:

> I can hear la belle au bois dormant.
> I am hungrily going: I resume
> in the Beauceron wind,
> in the Beauceron dust.

This also helped me to remember that, on the largest placard displayed at the *ADAM* jubilee exhibition at the National Book League in 1965, there were two names proclaiming our ideal literary editors: Cyril Connolly and Geoffrey Grigson ... One never can tell: perhaps one day I will come face to face with the founder of *New Verse*. Will he give me the answer?

It is difficult for *ADAM* to accept, as some people would have us believe, that Cyril Connolly could be deliberately cruel or insidiously destructive. Maybe it was our special fortune to encounter only his generosity, although along the years the apprehension that we were barely more than an exotic footnote to his central literary pursuits never quite abandoned us. More than once *ADAM*'s relationship with him struck me as being sadly restrictive, our hero keeping us at a somewhat ill-defined, almost pharmaceutical distance.

I first met him in 1946, soon after the liberation of Europe, when one of our jubilations was the lifting of paper rationing that had kept *ADAM* prisoner for five agonising years. This requires a rather lengthy explanation.

Among the more naïve and self-defeating economy measures imposed by the British government after the fall of France in June 1940 was the stern – and in fact grossly wasteful – refusal of any paper quota to publications that crept up after that saddening date. Whereas *Horizon* and a host of less important periodicals were fortunately launched at the beginning of 1940 and had no paper worries, *ADAM* first appeared in September 1941 – thus infringing the law. The printer, the much-lamented Francis Matthew of *The Times* (he was also responsible for the production of *France*, the daily newspaper to which I was a frequent contributor) did not think it necessary to explain to me what was permissible and what was illegal. Perhaps he never thought that there was going to be a second issue! ... Besides – and here came the eccentric 'clause' of the restriction – one was allowed to consume as much paper as one could sniff out, provided one came out each time in a fresh disguise! A sympathetic official concerned with that rather surrealistic war-time paper anomaly, the late Sir Robert Fraser, gently summoned me to the Ministry of Information and with a twinkle in his eye suggested that each new number of the magazine should appear under a different title, thus posing as a completely independent and individual pamphlet. Why not call it in turn, he mischievously said, Eve, Cain, Noah, Moses, Jeremiah and other such evocative names provided by the Old Testament? Admittedly an amusing expedient, but for us a monstrous alienation from the symbolism of the original title – and so *ADAM* yielded to enforced retirement until the end of the war.[2]

Lansdowne Place (*Horizon*'s post-war office) had by then become the shrine for many a literary pilgrim. Connolly liked our anaemic-looking magazine (twenty-four pages) and right away offered it an unsolicited free advertisement. He had the eyes of a lynx. At the 25th anniversary of *The Listener* (January 1954), he spotted me in the crowd at Broadcasting House and dragged me over to Edmund Wilson with the unforgettable words: 'This is *ADAM*, one of the fighters on the London literary scene.' Yet when, some time later, I invited him to write a piece for our Entente Cordiale issue, the first question he asked was: 'How much do you pay?' I mumbled a moderate sum. The contribution never came, and finally we had to content ourselves by paying a reproduction fee for a fragment from *The Unquiet Grave*. It was worth it, though, as it justified the rather resounding, sardonical title on the front page, *From Julius Caesar to Cyril Connolly*. (Later on he said he nearly wanted to return the cheque; probably it was too late for him to do so.)

• • •

Another twenty years passed, with no real contact. Then a fairy-tale episode: J. W. Lambert, the literary editor of the *Sunday Times*, rang. 'We have a surprise for you. Connolly's next article will be devoted entirely to your journal. If you come round to our office next Wednesday afternoon, you can go through the galleys with Cyril.' Choking with emotion at our end of the line. The latest *ADAM* was entirely devoted to one of the most extraordinary figures of literary Paris, Natalie Clifford Barney, the self-proclaimed High Priestess of Lesbianism ('Elle a séduit les plus belles femmes de Paris,' Cocteau told me at the time); it had just come out, and I was performing the first administrative ritual – sorting out the subscribers' list – but Connolly had already bought his copy at Bertram Rota, and on his return journey home he avidly read the 200-page contents. Apparently he had refused to review a book on Aristotle, insisting that he should write about *ADAM* instead. A full review of a small, struggling magazine was an unprecedented event in English journalism.[3] For us, it meant reaching the moon. I never really understood how such a thing was possible, but it *did* happen. On the appointed day Cyril was waiting by the lift on the legendary and forbidding fifth floor in Gray's Inn Road; he handed me the proofs then for the next half hour stood still as if utterly bored. Not even the fact that I came accompanied by a graceful young lady drew a smile. Then, yet another typical eccentricity, but for us a beneficial unguent whenever in trouble: in a long essay on the high mortality rate of literary magazines during the last fifty years, written for *Art and Literature*, Connolly singled out *ADAM* as one of the three worthwhile survivors, next to *Partisan Review* and André Simon's *The Wine and Food Quarterly*.

How to thank him? Would he be our guest for a drink somewhere in the West End? He chose the Ritz, a place where I had been only once before – tea with Marthe Bibescu, though not *aux frais de la princesse*. Cyril was pretty punctual, but not alone: he came accompanied not only by his sunny Deirdre (whom I then met for the first time) but also by his *belle-mère*. Furtively I felt for my wallet, quaking as to the contents. A first polite question – how did I come to this country, and did I speak the language at all? Not the slightest interest when I said that, upon reaching these shores two days before the outbreak of war, September, 1939, I only knew two or three words of English. Nor when I confessed how bitterly I resented the strange closure of *Horizon* and the indignation I gave vent to in one of my editorials over what I regarded as a sacrilege.[4]

Almost an hour of indifferent talk – enlivened only by Deirdre's kind remarks about this and that. The heavy-going chatter was finally relieved by my dropping on the waiter's tray the one and only five-pound note which luckily I had on me, and so *ADAM*'s prestige was saved. A long-distance telephone call the next morning: 'It was nice of you to invite us all [*sic*] ... By the way, when are you going to collect your editorials in book form?'

He wrote to me only once – an incredible letter, asking whether I had absconded with the MS of an Auden poem (*Elegy for JFK*) which he had read in our 300th number 'when you last paid me a visit'. It looked as if he had written in all seriousness, with the usual copious disregard for punctuation for which Cyril was famed. Never a master of repartee, I surprised myself with an almost witty reply. 'How could I have had access to the MS,' I wrote back (in fact Auden, who was staying with the Spenders in St John's Wood, asked me to call on him and, during the conversation, scribbled a copy of the poem, which was then made into a block), 'since I have *never* been to your house?' Even this slightly indignant *mise au point* was ignored.

•   •   •

When I moved down to Sussex, I nurtured the vague expectation of establishing closer contact with Cyril. I knew that, on Auden's recommendation, he would sometimes travel from Eastbourne to look for a special pork pie only obtainable at a baker's just round the corner from where I lived, but in none of these expeditions did he make a move in my direction. He knew, though, that I, *too*, possessed a few rare French editions. He always telephoned to say: 'Yes, certainly, we must meet.'

ADAM's more painful regret is that Cyril never gave us the chance to introduce him to a number of fascinating local situations. After hibernating for more than a century in forgotten, crumbled chronicles, these 'crudities' sprang back to life in a steady procession. It soon became an invigorating exercise to spy them out from the vantage point of my Tante-Léonie window, overlooking the majestic public garden wedded to the seafront. Just as Connolly and his family came down to Eastbourne near 'one of the [Joycean] Martello towers erected as a defence against the threatened invasion of Napoleon', I soon discovered that I actually occupied the ground floor of the very first house which was built in the mid-Eighties by the great-grandfather of one of Cyril's oldest friends, the Proust-drenched Sir Henry D'Avigdor Goldsmid.

The place once witnessed some quite extraordinary happenings. A botanist with a spark of genius, Henry Phillips, chose the emptied site of a former piggery to erect thereon a gigantic glass and iron dome, wider in area than St Peter's. It was intended for the display of the largest tropical garden in Europe, with cedars and pine trees, exotic and decorative flowers, a pond for aquatic plants and rare fishes. How Cyril would have loved and sung this nearest equation to an English paradise! Alas, for reasons which were never clarified, the scaffolding was removed very shortly after the proud cupola (appropriately called The Antheum – *city of flowers*) was officially opened to the public on August 30, 1833. Tragedy followed: a local archivist recorded that 'The whole top of the Dome fell with awful rapidity, the huge iron girders collapsed one after another like a pack of cards, accompanied by a noise resembling the continued firing of cannons.' The shock was too much for the possessed designer: ten days later he became blind and died of despair, aged only fifty-three.

Sir Isaac Lyon Goldsmid (1778–1859), who had helped Phillips financially, returned to the scene twenty years later, had the rubble removed and, by special permission of William IV, began constructing what is now regarded as a fair architectural blend of Belgravia and Regent's Park – one of the architects was Nash's closest associate, Decimus Burton. He had by then also encouraged the expansion of an 'invigorating chalybeate Spa for the treatment of indigestion and crapulas of the system', as well as a 'Royal gymnasium by Sheik Dean Mahomet, who introduced the Indian vapour in the county'. In recognition of his services in settling an unwieldly clash between Portugal and Brazil, Queen Maria da Gloria conferred on him the sonorous title of Baron da Palmeira.

On the ruins of the ill-fated Antheum less than a dozen lonely sycamores and elm trees now keep vigil over the merciless fouling of the still-grandiose square. Uninhibited prostatic local dogs pull their owners in all directions from dawn till midnight. They have even succeeded in persuading them to join a syndicate – FIDO (Friends of Indigenous Dog Owners). But the story has only just begun. Thanks to the imaginative courage of a now-deceased mayor (surely a disciple of *Ubu Roi*, whom Connolly brought so close to our hearts by his exquisite translation of Jarry's masterpiece), the magnificent alleys and flower-beds were granted municipal protection by the erection of a number of receptacles (ten feet by six). 'In the absence of a more satisfactory description' – to quote the official annals – 'and especially as the American emblem, *Canine Relief Stations*, sounded somehow too flamboyant,' the compounds were signposted DOG TOILETS, each of them 'infilled with a layer of graded clinker'. Moreover, 'occupying pride of place a lamp-post and, for good measure, a bollard were to enable them to be easily seen and thus serve a badly-needed purpose', since 'dogs and lamp-posts are synonymous'. The dignified lamp columns were of 'sufficient height' and the 'proud owners expected to think individually'. Demonstrations took place, and representatives of the National Canine League were invited to make further suggestions. Unfortunately, none of the privileged strollers took the slightest notice of the offer and continued to perform their rituals *juste à côté* – until the municipality had to admit, repiningly, that 'The campaign initiated so hopefully had lost its impact [*sic*], and in practice the introduction of the dog toilets had made no material reduction in the fouling of the grass areas'. And so the proud clochemerles vanished as dadaistically as they first appeared.

• • •

Audio-visually, though, I had no grounds for grumbling, since right from the start I was plunged into a real Proustian sub-continent, its fauna clamouring for an all-dissecting story-teller. Perhaps, subconsciously, I was hoping to cajole Cyril into embarking on a sequel to 'The Rock Pool', based this time on the Sussex Riviera.

Within the breezy stretch of a few dozen square yards I gradually became acquainted with a new Promenade des Anglais, on which a well-intentioned, bizarre, fur-chested, lazy and yet formidable slice of humanity enjoys displaying itself as soon as the clouds lift. Each time the moody sun darts forth its brief javelins of light, this supposedly semi-retired populace emerges as if hit by some psychedelic tidal wave. Within seconds it has encircled the hideous line of dog-kennels duly hired for sunbathing. To the accompaniment of unremitting palaver, each of these sentry-boxes empties itself of its intricate equipment of chaise-longues, kettles, cups, saucers and jellies: unrepentant, jarring voices coalesce in a post-Schönbergian din.

Quite effortlessly, I recognised the unmistakable Madame Verdurin, pressing invitations to her cacophonous soirées at which repleted clerics unroll naughty rhymes and, by contrast, emaciated sopranos commit their vocal sins with homicidal irregularity. No sooner had I reached these gusty shores than I identified a few other familiar characters fit for a new *Recherche*: an endearing Dr Cottard, at least one strikingly beautiful Odette, arrogantly tall, with a slight edithsitwellian walk and tastes for dashing hats and trinkets, perversely oscillating between a shy, cultivated Swann and a minuscule, vulgar fisherman. You see what you have been missing, Cyril? Most probably, you did not all these years know that no lesser artist than George Painter has also moved down *dans ces parages*, although he continues to write as invisibly as in his BM days. But take note and rejoice!: someone heard him say that he never thought of you otherwise than as the 'Baudelaire of our generation'. Memorable description.

Alas, interspersed with this colourful shoal, echoes of bygone dramas are ghouling the air. *Pitié pour les femmes!*

How could one bypass Mary Heaviside's elopement 'in a preconceived manner' on March 9, 1840, with Dr Dyonisius Lardner, at one time professor of moral philosophy in a London college? The passionate couple spent nearly two agonising months on a post-chaise while making their way between Shoreham and Ostend, until they found a nest of lasting happiness at 21 rue Tronchet in Paris – though not before the injured husband, a captain left with three children to look after, crossed the Channel, tracked the amorous hideout and gave the satanic vicar an unforgettable thrashing and threw his wig in the fire.

Almost at the same time, an unexpected shade of Greek tragedy hovered over the young life of one of the Shirleys, a descendant of Teresia, Princess Ysha of Persia: she knifed and killed her adolescent lover on finding him in her daughter's arms. Finally, the aching saga of a mature and prolific novelist and critic, believed to live nearby. His gently written autobiography recently appeared under the intriguing *nom de plume*, Y, and was subtly prefaced by a local psychiatrist, Dr Solly Jacobson. He described this case history as a 'completely truthful human document' (Paul Elek, £3.50).

However remote, these people are still awaiting their author: an artist willing to identify himself with their unattended wounds. Who better than a Connolly, benignly confident in his autumnal creative powers, who would have loved to see them magically metamorphosed into *dramatis personae*? Where should they turn now? To a refreshed – Stendhalised – Anthony Powell, just recovering from his twelve-volume *roman-fleuve*? Or perhaps to a yet-unknown novelist, for whose recognition they would provide ample material?

But before turning from this possibly far-fetched dreaming of a solitary promenader, should one not risk a further journey, this time into the realm of ESP? How could one otherwise account for Cyril's continued presence in so many minds? The dialogue turns out to be not only indispensable but increasingly pleasurable ...

• • •

Looking recently again to one of Connolly's longer essays in *Horizon*, I began wondering how he knew that Gérard de Nerval wrote *Delfica* in 1843, when in fact it first appeared in 1845? Days of sterile research prying for reassuring evidence ended on a happier note than I had anticipated. Not only did I have the good fortune to discover a reliable *nervalien* in our midst, Dr Norma Rinsler, lecturer in French at King's College, London, but I also traced Connolly's review of her *Les chimères* (*ST*, October 21st, 1973). Cyril had actually *seen* the manuscript of 'Delfica' when it belonged to Paul Eluard and, *indeed*, Nerval wrote this hauntingly obscure sonnet during his voyage to the Orient in 1843. Since Connolly wished one day to see an English rendering of the poem, let me inform him (should he not know) that no less than four different translations have appeared over the last thirty years. To toast the prolonged life of *Delfica*, here goes the inter-spatial emission of the first stanza from Brian Hill's version in *Fortune's Fool* (Rupert Hart Davis, 1959):

Under the myrtles, Daphne, do you know this old refrain,
Under the silver by the sycamore's foot,
Under the trembling willows, or where the olives shoot –
This age-old song of love, always renewed again?

The only time he asked me to visit him was in May 1973. I do not think that the compulsive collector wanted to watch my envy as he paraded his first editions of Gide, Pound and Proust – he had, for instance, paid £450 for *Sodome et Gomorrhe* inscribed to 'Monsieur J Middletone Murry – hommage admiratif et reconnaissant d'un écrivain que vous avez toujours protégé et soutenu et qui voudrait avoir une heure de santé pour vous remercier moins brièvement'. He insisted on showing me at least half a dozen copies of *ADAM*, kept in his working room upstairs among his *livres de chevet*. Refusing as he did all his life to learn to type, he spent his nights writing his reviews in longhand. The bedroom resembled nothing I was used to expecting, even from a bibliomaniac. The gilded four-poster bed was outrageously rumpled – which made me think of our own editorial elephantiasis (whether the daily or the monthly 'paper-work'), spread over all floors, as looking relatively neat ...

What impressed me in particular was that, instead of contradicting Deirdre when she gave away no less than several thousands of hotel and restaurant bills from the early Twenties onwards, together with similar mementoes that were carefully stored in cupboards throughout the mansion, Cyril seemed to regard this as something quite normal. From his student days he had belonged to that lucky tribe 'who never throw anything away'. The less fortunate paper-addicts – working in fear of fulminating wives intent on subjecting all printed matter to the furnace, in the unshakeable belief that *rien ne se perd, tout se met en cendres* – had every reason to covet Connolly's solidly tamed household! What might become of such paperasses, once the *pater familias* has gone, is a different matter altogether ...

During our only face-to-face conversation, I struggled hard to provoke the raconteur, but failed. However, as he enquired what would our future issues contain, I mentioned that for years I had been thinking of a special issue on the history of *Horizon*. He beamed in response: 'What an exciting idea! I could let you have a great deal of material.' Too late now, alas, since, like his Library, most of the archives are bound to be dispersed *à tout vent*. A biography, on the other hand, remains a fascinating possibility.

Surely, if a *cabotin* of Frank Harris's dimensions has, during a single generation, been the subject of half a dozen biographies, Cyril's life will be infinitely more rewarding to explore.[5] Despite all his ambiguities of heart and mind, his was a continuous and passionate odyssey, for it sketched the artistic as well as the moral background of two-thirds of the century. What he modestly – and morbidly – regarded as his negligible work ('Journalism has destroyed me to a large extent,' he told Simon Blow sadly: 'What survives of me are a few tufts on a fruit tree when I should have been a forest giant') is in reality brimming with invaluable information and comment on a wide variety of themes: *belles lettres*, visual arts and, as I was thrilled to discover during my visit to Eastbourne, music.[6]

Connolly was too often rashly judged to be somewhat of a 'sterile' writer; but anyone prepared to look into his work will above all be impressed by the marvellous abundance of ideas bursting forth from almost every article and essay. One hopes that, in time, the pieces available in the four volumes of criticism, as well as those still hidden in the over-abundant corpus not yet anthologised, may come to be considered a major contribution to English prose.

Since even an editorial must come to an end, here is a final (although inconclusive) thought: was it worth dying, Mr Connolly? June 1974: do you remember our telephone conversation shortly after your final Icarus flight to the Riviera in pursuit of yet another obsessive dream! I wanted you to hear Simenon's noble farewell to a life of creative writing: *chacun essaie si fort d'exister* – a perfect *pendant*, I thought, to your own affirmation, *to stay alive is the greatest contribution a man can make to posterity*.

Now, in case you may wonder – why this issue in your memory? Frankly, no straight answer comes easily to mind. Was it necessary as an act of self-exorcism? A doubtful exercise, since one cannot free oneself from your presence. Or maybe a gesture, an attempt to campaign against Time itself? Readers will decide.

It is so much pleasanter to imagine that you are still watching what is foaming on the Literary scene since you left us. Did you feel the reverberations of that recent bombshell in the columns of the *New York Review of Books*? Noel (Lord) Annan wrote an ocean-wide article which sank us in confusion. Four months later he apologised – implausibly. Over here, the publication of all your letters to Noel Blakiston (*A Romantic Friendship*, Constable, £5.50). By getting them out so soon, NB wanted to 'provide unquestionable evidence of [your] tenderness.' Christopher Sykes, in his compact and dignified biography of Evelyn Waugh (Collins, £4.50), had to admit that, although 'Evelyn's relations with you were among the most ambivalent of his life', there was an undeniable streak of 'affection, almost of amorous infatuation, towards you'. So far, so good!

•   •   •

Perhaps the best way of acknowledging our debt to the many Connolly enthusiasts who helped in compiling this memorial issue is to have brought the project to completion. A single name, though, should be mentioned, that of Mr F. E. Brazier, the late Reference Librarian of the *Sunday Times*, who produced the precious files needed during the research. Kind Mr Brazier! Now he, too, is gone. It is fitting to link his memory with that of Cyril, whom he admired so much but never met.

It is also good to recall here that, as soon as I returned from Eastbourne, Cyril telephoned to say that he had forgotten to tell me something which should be a source of pride for *ADAM*: he believed that our issue on Proust and Virginia Woolf had been the very last thing that Elizabeth Bowen had read. He took it to her in hospital, and she thanked him only a few hours before her death. Need one add that it would not have been Cyril had he not, in the same breath, admonished me for considering an issue on John Cowper Powys: 'How *could* you? That self-serviced bore!'

D'accord, Mr Connolly, we'll go on arguing.

CONTRIBUTORS

Raymond MORTIMER – *Jottings for a Memorial*
Cyril CONNOLLY – *Sonnet (Balliol, circa 1924)*
Cyril CONNOLLY – *Small quote from* Previous Convictions
Robert LOWELL – *Four Poems: Not Cleared of Killing; 1938–1975; An Ear of Corn; The Day*
Alan PRYCE-JONES – *A Socratic Elder*
Stephen SPENDER – *Cyril Connolly, November 1974* [MS repro of poem]
Lord KINROSS – *The Young Cyril*
Henry d'AVIGDOR GOLDSMID – *Du côté de chez Connolly*
Enid BAGNOLD – *Cyril*
William SANSOM – *CC – From a Pupil*
Connollyana (from Previous Convictions)
Peter LEVI – *For Cyril* [poem]
Lawrence DURRELL – *Style and Generosity*
A. E. ELLIS – *Te Palinure Petens*
Denys SUTTON – *The discerning Judge of the Arts*
T. C. WORSLEY – *Lament for Cyril*
Georges BERNIER – *Voyages d'agrément avec un anglais*
Michael WISHART – *He Died of Living (for Deirdre)*
Matthew HODGART – *Connolly's Rock Pool*
Michael KELLY – *Ovid's Amores, 1, 5* [translation]
G. S. FRASER – *On not Knowing Cyril Connolly*
Martin SEYMOUR-SMITH – *The Generous Reviewer*
T. S. MATTHEWS – *A Note on Cyril and Edmund*
G. S. FRASER – *Winter Drawing Near* [poem in memory of CC]
Robin MAUGHAM – *The Legend*
David BATHURST – *Christie's Book Consultant*
Fred UHLMAN – *Mistaken Identity*
Andrew ROSSABI – *A Carp for Epicurus*
Frank LISSAUER – *The Gnat* [poem]
John BYRNE – *Gentleman among Players*
Norma RINSLER – Delfica *(Gérard de Nerval)*
Alan PRYCE-JONES – *The Kind Sad Benefactor ('stele' for Peter Watson)*
Roland PENROSE – *Cyril and Peter [Watson] – Complementary Opposites*
Priaulx RAINIER – *Personal Recollections [of Peter Watson]*
Michael WISHART – *Peter and Others*

David MELLOR – *A Taste for Tragic Excellence [Peter Watson]*
Isabella FEY – *The Fox* [poem]
Paul ROGERS – *The Auction* [poem]
Mary SANDBACH – *Letter to the Editor [re the young Auden]*

NOTES

1. The only comforting exception to this phonetic misconduct during the last twenty years of broadcasting continues to be Patricia Hughes, but what will happen to the Third Programme when she retires?
2. A second issue, celebrating H. G. Wells' seventy-fifth birthday, had already gone to press and was allowed to come out *without* any volume number ...
3. Lord Kemsley made a great fuss when Desmond MacCarthy reviewed the first number of Connolly's *Horizon*. (See *The Pearl of Days*, The History of the *Sunday Times*, p. 194)
4. At the time (November 1949), very few people knew what Connolly's real intentions were, so I wrote: '*ADAM*'s 200th issue coincides with the sad news that *Horizon* – that literary phenomenon we have come to marvel at and often to enjoy – has suffered a temporary eclipse. In the last issue, Mr Connolly has tried to persuade us that by taking a twelve-month respite, he would have a better chance of perfecting himself as a writer. The argument sounds painfully unconvincing. There is no real dilemma for the editor who is also a creative writer in keeping a balance between these activities . The very *raison d'être* depends upon his never giving up – unless he dies, of course. There is no true editorship when everything is safe and prosperous.' Alas, the decision to take the 'year's break' proved to have been a signal for final departure. An inadmissible retreat, we thought, from the small company of fellow-strugglers.
5. In the early Sixties, Connolly, at the expense of overcoming 'a deep horror of himself', seemed willing soon to embark on writing his memoirs – the main reason he asked a number of old friends to return all the letters he had written to them. Noel Blakiston was the first to comply with this request, and in his letter of acknowledgement Cyril even hit upon a title, 'Over the Hump', for 'the erotic biography of a cryptopath, one million copies sold before publication, over 1,500 pages, only 63/-'. As was to be expected, it was one more of his irrepressible fantasies, although his concern over what 'more material from other friends' might reveal sounded genuine: 'It will become a poor man's Nuremberg.'
6. When he drove me back to the station, he made a considerable detour, especially to show me the front of the Grand Hotel, where, in 1903, shortly after he had completed the scoring of 'La Mer,' Debussy eloped with Madame Bardac. It was then that Cyril spoke about the composers he cared for – Vittoria, Palestrina, Scarlatti, but above all Mozart and Debussy. What impressed me most deeply was his passionate reaction to the agonies of wounded love, which Mozart's music illumines so poignantly. Stendhal helped him towards this. I shall always remember the emotion with which he quoted this burning sequence: 'J'avais une curiosité singulière à connaître toutes ses infidélités. Je m'en faisais reconter tous les détails.' Which particular love made him memorise and seek desperate solace in this typical stendhalism? Yet another tantalising query for his biographer. While still at Balliol he wrote to Noel Blakiston about 'this Debussy weather, very disturbing like the *Unquiet Grave*' (Jan 1927). Also, when commenting on Ivy Compton-Burnett's *Brothers and Sisters*, he singled out the 'Scarlatti-like dialogue'. And this exquisite description of *Pelléas*: 'The music is of a consistent fragile beauty, a luminous green world of which one can never have too much.'

ADAM

INTERNATIONAL REVIEW

Editor : Miron Grindea

Les Liaisons Dangereuses
Blandine McLaughlin

Choderlos de Laclos "l'homme honnête
par excellence, le meilleur des maris."
(Proust)

Onion Soup - Latin Quarter Poems
Francis Scarfe

Two Short Stories and Poems

Dennis Holmes,
Desmond Hogan,
Craig Raine

Proust - once again
William Carter, Frances Stern

£1
$2.25

LES LIAISONS DANGEREUSES AND OTHER PIECES

Nos. 413–415, Vol. XLI, 1979–

'LE PLUS EFFROYABLEMENT PERVERS DES LIVRES'

La volupté unique et suprême de l'amour
gît dans la certitude de faire le mal.

Baudelaire, *Fusées*, 1851

Ce n'est pas la bonté de son cœur, laquelle était fort grande,
qui avait fait écrire à Choderlos de Laclos les Liaisons dangereuses.

Proust, *Le temps retrouvé*

Pour être méchant il faut de l'expérience,
une connaissance exquise du cœur.

Sartre, *Saint Genet*

Anyone who reads *Les Liaisons dangereuses* for a second or third time is faced with an increasingly aggravating riddle. How is it, one wonders, that this masterpiece is still so imperfectly known? Less known still is the author, Pierre Ambroise François Choderlos de Laclos (1741–1803), a frustrated artillery officer in the pre-Revolution army, although reputedly a resourceful manipulator of political intrigues under different regimes – particularly the Reign of Terror – and possibly at times a clumsy demagogue who nevertheless escaped being beheaded when his own 'patron', the Duc d'Orléans, was guillotined. The problem which a number of critics are still trying to solve is whether a provincial *rousseauiste* (with *La Nouvelle Héloïse* as his 'bible de sensibilité'), author of a few mediocre poems, could have written one of the most gruesome and at the same time subtlest psychological novels in all Western literature.

Born in Amiens of a family recently accepted into the *petite noblesse*, he studied mathematics (' … science fort utile', he wrote, 'pour régulariser la tête et calmer l'imagination trop vive'), became lieutenant at the age of twenty and started a dull garrison life in a succession of provincial towns, among which Grenoble, whose 'vie mondaine' fascinated him, with nothing that he observed there being later reproduced by halves. A native of the city and an ardent disciple of Laclos, Lieutenant Henry Beyle, spoke of the sexual debaucheries which he thought must have supplied the raw material for the *Liaisons*. It came out as an epistolary novel in 1782, the same year as Rousseau's *Confessions* and one year before Mirabeau's *Erotika Biblion*. It was literary dynamite, with all the decaying aristocracy denouncing the author as an arch villain and instantly ostracising him from their midst. If one can understand the wrath of Mme de Genlis, author of 'educational' books and mistress of Laclos' protector (' ... livre exécrable par ses principes et fort mauvais sous les rapports littéraires', she wrote in *Mémoires inédits*),[1] the indignation of a close friend such as Marie-Jeanne Riccoboni (1713–1792) – translator of Fielding's *Amelia*, who took upon herself the formidable task of completing Marivaux's *Marianne* – was simply silly. Indeed, she attacked Laclos in rather Aunt Edna-ish terms: 'C'est en qualité de femme, Monsieur, de Française, de patriote zélée pour l'honneur de ma nation, que j'ai senti mon cœur blessé ...' Putting on a mask of excuses two centuries before Proust (a much more gifted mystifier), poor Laclos had to write here, there and everywhere, hoping to assuage the fears and suspicions of the decaying aristocratic set, who saw themselves ruthlessly depicted in the novel. Remembering the Duchess of Gramont's epigram, 'Les mœurs ne sont faites que pour le peuple,' he made elegant use of his rapier by reassuring prudish Mme Riccoboni that all these 'femmes méchantes et dépravées' *did* in fact exist and that he could not possibly eradicate 'aucun des traits qu'il a rassemblés dans la personne de Mme de Merteuil sans mentir à sa conscience, sans taire au moins une partie de ce qu'il a vu'.

Two years later this uniquely incendiary bestseller appeared in a four-volume English edition under the title 'Dangerous Connections, or, Letters collected in a society and published for the instruction of other societies.' The editor of the *Monthly Review* (LXXI, 1784) promptly obliged: 'A villain of quality, ambitious of being distinguished by a pre-eminence in vice, disdaining the easy conquest of a young and unsuspecting virgin, singles out a married lady, of the first character for virtue, religion and good sense, by way of experiment, to shew how far the power of seduction may operate, and what effects may produce. In a series of letters addressed to a female confidante of more decent fame than himself, but of principles equally corrupt, this abandoned libertine, who seems to wish rather to ruin than to possess the object of his pursuit, delineates every step of his progress in this infamous intrigue, and lays open its secret springs, with all their immediate and remote influences and effects ... He who could trace the currents of human action through all their intricate channels to their hidden source in the heart, and unfold its most secret springs, could not be ignorant of the tendency of the present publication.'

During the Restoration, and most probably under the waspish influence which Mme de Genlis still exercised over her former pupil, Louis Philippe, a Paris tribunal ordered in 1824 'la destruction de cet écrit dangereux, pour outrage aux bonnes mœurs.'

Misgivings and conflicting appreciations of the *Liaisons* continued to appear throughout the nineteenth century. The first creative artist to acknowledge the novel's greatness was Baudelaire, although even he made a few typically paradoxical assertions – for instance, after hailing 'ce livre de moraliste aussi élevé que les plus élevés', he abruptly defined 'tous les livres' as being 'immoraux'. His admiration was amply vindicated when the same tribunal which, in August 1857, banned *Les Fleurs du Mal* once again condemned the *Liaisons* (May 1865) for 'outrage à la morale publique'. Remarkably, amidst this outcry, the respectable Larousse showed more than courage and good taste when praising, in its 1873 edition, 'ce roman de moraliste, *le seul qui pût effrayer cette société en décomposition et lui faire peur d'elle-même*' [our italics]. It mattered little if Taine, too busy to read the book, dismissed the author as 'un Machiavel subalterne'.

Surprisingly, no literary historian has yet shown, to my knowledge, Laclos' deep admiration for English literature, which he regarded as 'plus moderne' than the French. Long before he accompanied the Duc d'Orléans to London (14 October 1789 to 10 July 1790), he was an insatiable reader of Richardson, Fielding (*Tom Jones*, 'ce roman le mieux fait') and Fanny Burney, the future Mme d'Arblay. He frequently spoke of *Clarissa Harlowe* as 'Ce chef d'oeuvre du roman', and in *De l'éducation des femmes* (1783) he admitted that 'On ne peut assurément se défendre d'estimer beaucoup et même de respecter l'héroïne de ce roman'. In a moment of excessive *rousseauisme* – perhaps also tongue in cheek? – he further pointed out that 'Cependant Clarisse a fait à peu près la plus grande faute qu'une jeune fille puisse faire, puisqu'elle a fui de la maison paternelle avec son séducteur.' He qualified this, however: should one explain to young (French) readers that the heroine 'a été nécessairement entraînée dans tous les malheurs dont elle finit par être la victime, alors il y aura peu de lectures plus utiles' ...?

Two years after the publication of his novel, Laclos wrote a very long and rather stodgy essay for *Mercure de France* on Fanny Burney's *Cecilia (ou les mémoires d'une héritière, par l'auteur d'Evelina)*. What was interesting was the distinction he drew between the two nations by suggesting that – while the English 'exigent peut-être que l'auteur d'un Roman commence par leur faire connaître les personnes avec qui il va, pour ainsi dire, les forcer de vivre pendant quelque temps' – in France, 'au contraire, ou d'ordinaire le sentiment précède la reflection ou, presque toujours, c'est par les évènements qu'on s'intéresse aux personnes; on veut, avant tout, être intéressé et, même en lisant Richardson, presque tout lecteur français est tenté de laisser là les personnages ou aller s'informer de leurs aventures.'

Upon returning from England, Laclos rejoined the army, though for only a short time, as he was arrested in 1792; after a mere breath of freedom he was re-arrested (sharing the same prison as de Sade, although, alas, hardly having an opportunity to ... exchange notes with his *confrère*, one must assume) and was finally freed, thanks to the intervention of Vicomte Paul de Barras, a member of the Directoire. One last volte-face in 1800 – a sycophantic praise of Bonaparte which brought prompt reward: he was promoted general with the French army in Italy. Three years later he died at Tarento.

To return to the nagging question of the gulf between the creator ('homme vertueux, bon fils, bon père, excellent époux') and his characters – how one would wish to find an answer! What a long journey, from Henri de Régnier, who queried the fame of the *Liaisons* as having 'je ne sais quoi de suspect' (*Revue Bleue*, 1912), to the militant communist Roger Vailland ('un Laclos marxiste', as Pierre de Boisdeffre defined him), who thought that the author subconsciously saw himself as Valmont – 'l'insolent qu'il aurait tant envié être'. A great many contemporary writers, mostly French, have volunteered highly contrasting opinions. Benedetto Croce saw him as a mere pornographer; Léon Daudet, as 'capable des pires cruautés'; Maurois thought that 'Laclos admire ses monstres mais les condamne', while, on second thoughts, the author of *L'Immoraliste* decreed that 'Il n'y a point de doute que Laclos n'ait été la main dans la main avec Satan' (preface to a new English edition of the *Liaisons* in 1940). This did not prevent him on a previous occasion from acclaiming the *Liaisons* as one of the 'two greatest French novels, the other being *La Chartreuse de Parme*'.

There is ample room for a sober study of the controversies surrounding Laclos' only novel. Students interested in the subject will find *A la recherche des Liaisons dangereuses* by A. and Y. Delmas (Mercure de France, 1964) most profitable, with its many suggestions as to Laclos' influence on modern writers – Svevo, Virginia Woolf, Faulkner, Huxley. One should also recommend Philip Thody's study (Edward, 1970), which has a number of original observations, such as the fact that the *Liaisons* make the first mention ever of contraception in a literary work; the imaginative chapter 'Libertinism and the Novel' by Richard Veasey in *French Literature and its Background* (OUP, 1968); *Das Böse in den Laclos' Liaisons dangereuses*, by Helmut Knufmann, (München, 1965).

Laclos, the trained mathematician and military strategist, organised Valmont's 'seducting campaign' according to the rules of warfare, just as he built up the personage of Mme de Merteuil as a totally liberated woman *avant la lettre*; but even this does not sum him up and cannot account for the vast range of his detached psychological mastery. *ADAM* ought to return to this fascinating subject ...

•   •   •

'Dear Robert,' the first short story in this issue, marks the literary debut of a City gentleman in his late sixties, now in rural retirement. Dennis Holmes began writing only surprisingly recently. Craig Raine, author of a first volume of poems, *The Onion, Memory* (OUP, 1978), won first prizes in the Cheltenham Festival of Literature in 1977 and 1978. Another book of his, *A Martian Sends a Postcard Home*, is due shortly from the OUP. Francis Scarfe, formerly Director of the Institut Britannique in Paris, is author of three novels (*Promises*, 1940, *Single Blessedness*, 1941, and *Unfinished Woman*, 1954), poetry (*Inscapes*, 1940, *Underworlds*, 1959) and criticism (*Auden and After*, 1949, *The Art of Paul Valéry*, 1954). Desmond Hogan was born in 1951, at Bullinasloe, Western Ireland. His first novel, *The Ikonmaker*, appeared in 1976. A second novel, *The Leaves on Grey,* is due to come out in February 1980. Both Blandine McLaughlin and William Carter are teaching French at the University of Alabama. Frances Stern, also American, is the author of an exhaustive *Concordance* of Proust and Dante (500 pp of text), due for publication next year.

CONTRIBUTORS

George D. PAINTER – *Chateaubriand and the Brothers de Laclos*
Blandine McLAUGHLIN – Les Liaisons dangereuses – *A Quest for Freedom*
Francis SCARFE – *Onion Soup – Latin Quarter Poems (15 poems); Le peintre de dimanche* [in English]
Dennis HOLMES – *Dear Robert* (story)
Craig RAINE – *Two Poems: The Great Wall of China; Rhinoceros*
Desmond HOGAN – *Memories of Swinging London* [story]

Views and Reviews: William CARTER, *Proust's views on sexuality* – Frances STERN, *The 'Septet' – A key to the* Recherche

NOTE

1. The antipathy was mutual. Indeed, in a six-line poem Laclos entreated Mme de Genlis to give up writing: 'Change donc, ma fille, / Ta plume en aiguille, / Brûle ton papier; / Il faut te résoudre / A filer, à coudre: / C'est là ton métier.' She was also one of Proust's *bêtes noires:* 'Si je vais avec vous à Versailles je vous montrerai le portrait de l'honnête homme par excellence, du meilleur des maris, Choderlos de Laclos, qui a écrit le plus effroyablement pervers des livres, et juste en face de lui, celui de Mme de Genlis qui écrivait des contes moraux et ne se contenta pas de tromper la duchesse d'Orléans mais la supplicia en détournant d'elle ses enfants' (*La Prisonnière*). Comte de Genlis, together with his wife's lover, Philippe-Egalité, were among the first Girondins to be guillotined in 1793.

INTERNATIONAL REVIEW
Editor: Miron Grindea

George Enescu: 1881-1955

A tribute by Marcel Mihalovici, Yehudi, Hepzibah and
Yaltah Menuhin, Joseph Szigeti, Niculae Caravia,
Robert Simpson, Doda Conrad, Gigi Tomaziu, Jean Mouton,
Sergiu Comissiona, Viorel Cosma, Lory Wallfisch, John Amis,
Norbert Braiain, Manoug Parikian

Care român n'are talent?

A selection of post-war Roumanian poetry and prose:
Arghezi, Banus, Blaga, Bogza, Cassian, Fulga, Jebeleanu,
Macovescu, Neagu, Radu Tudor Popescu, Preda,
Sorescu, Stanescu

A glimpse of the Danube Delta

Iris Murdoch

£1.25
$2.50

NOTES ON A GENIUS

Nineteen eighty-one is not only the centenary year of Bela Bartok's birth but also that of the protean Roumanian George Enescu. His was a bewildering and in many ways a frustrated life: it contained so many equally brilliant *careers*, as he was one of the outstanding violinists, pianists, conductors and teachers of this century – but at the same time it sadly overcast the only aspect Enescu really cared for, that of creative artist. He was never able to solve the constantly agonising conflict between the multiple performer and composer – too much for a single human life to bear, yet Enescu had to go through with it. Uniquely great in so many ways but not spectacular enough to catch the 'masses'.

However hard I may try, I cannot be rigorously objective – an inability stemming from the fact that Enescu has been the hero of my whole life, and now it would be rather late to change course. As he always represented for me the *total* artist, I was considerably relieved when no less a musician than Pablo Casals, in a conversation we had in Bucharest in 1937, reassured me that Enescu (whom he had known intimately since 1895) was the greatest musical phenomenon since Mozart. So there ... the ritual of worship could go on uninhibited. A year later, also in Bucharest, I heard Maurice Ravel saying, 'Georges fut le génie de notre génération.'

As good fortune would have it, shortly after the end of the Second World War I was privileged to spend long periods of time in Enescu's company. These were the last nine years of his life – most of which he spent under unimaginable physical discomfort; years also of financial hardship and of emotional malaise. The artist who, for nearly half a century, has been unquestionably one of the most handsome and impressive performers on any concert platform, arrived from Roumania crippled beyond any medical repair.[1] It was heartbreaking to watch him walk bent double. Every movement was agony for him; and yet, as soon as he was helped onto the rostrum, he became a transformed person. 'I can hardly carry my carcass,' he would say to his newly-acquired friends among orchestral players, who followed his discreet but pain-laden baton in a state of reverence and awe. All English musicians who had met him for the first time between 1947 and 1953 still speak of him as of someone un-replaceable and unforgettable.

The main purpose of the present tribute is not so much that of expressing a personal debt – this might one day materialise, I hope, in a more substantial form – as the ardent desire to awaken and widen musical awareness of Enescu's creativity.

George Enescu is an ocean of a subject, and even if, for personal reasons, his life cannot yet be revealed in all its complexity, there is already a distinct move in the right direction; that of paving the way towards a biography – not a protective or a mock-pious one, but a true account of memorable triumphs, often followed by the humiliations and defeats which he bore with great dignity.

Long before his richly imaginative, although sometimes a trifle too polite, conversations with Bernard Gavoty went on the air and subsequently appeared in book form, Enescu spoke of his ups and downs with great frankness and with a racy brand of wisdom.

The story of so many torments should be told one day. It is true that many witnesses of vital importance, such as the composer Mihai Jora, Thibaud, Yvonne Astruc, Theodore Fuchs and A. H. Cohen are no longer alive; but one can still draw upon Enescu's half-brother, the painter Caragea, his cousin Gigi Tomaziu and, above all, the two sprightly nonagenarians, the pianist Niculae Caravia and Romeo Draghici, the valiant founder and curator of the George Enescu Museum in Bucharest. The fifty years of uninterrupted collaboration with the same agent – the slavishly faithful Cohen, with whom Enescu travelled from one corner of Roumania to another, stopping in the most obscure towns and hamlets to make people acquainted with Sarasate, Vivaldi or Debussy – are an epic in itself. No effort should be spared in finding material relating to this extraordinary association. The magnificent text in this issue by Marcel Mihalovici, the distinguished composer who succeeded Enescu at the Institut de France, indicates also how much one can still expect from this noble artist.

From my own store of recollections I will rather root out first a few samples of the great wit who used to invest the most distressing situations – and they were not a few – with droll dignity and panache. I last visited him at Hôtel Atala, off the Champs Elysées, two months before he died, on May 4th, 1955. As I came accompanied by a young lady – inevitably one of the admirers firmly determined to have a glance at the legend – he threw an impish look at me, and his hardly intelligible words, in Roumanian, were: 'How naughty of you.' Another and perhaps even more memorable illustration of his *Galgenhumor* came after his very last recital in Switzerland at the beginning of 1953. His accompanist was a young, talented pianist afflicted by a slight hunchback. Asked how the concert went, Enescu answered mischievously: 'C'était une harmonie parfaite, moi avec ma bosse à gauche, lui avec sa bosse à droite ...'

He is generally remembered as the perfect courtier, impeccable in manners, often excessively so. Except for the players in the symphony orchestras he conducted in Roumania, he addressed most of his friends in French – a tradition irritatingly adhered to by the upper class and by a great many snobbish apes. His wife he addressed not only as 'Domnitza' (*Princesse*), but always in the third person. This was the style: 'Is the *princesse* ready to go?' or 'May I disturb my Ram?' (*bélier* in French, an endearing nickname, no doubt part of a secret mythology, which probably none of the Master's close contemporaries ever dared to query). To me he spoke only in Roumanian, a lively Moldavian brand, with occasional *osés* expressions just to please me and not infrequent bawdy verses, such as 'Incetinel si leganat, iaca, mireasa s'aaa ...' (Gently and lilting, the bride ...). Yet whenever he answered my letters, he wrote in French. His urge for pun-making was irresistible and of the highest order, as in the following *billet* [hand-written, here reproduced and transcribed as follows]:

De la part de   *26-4-54*
GEORGES ENESCO

vœux et amicaux remerciments à ADAM,
respectueux souvenirs à mADAMe, et
bons baisers à mADAMina

Alas, there are not only happy recollections that keep me attached to the memory of this many-sided genius. I also knew a tragic Enescu, and the conflicts underlying his daily life no doubt hold the key to a better understanding of his creative aspirations and achievement. 'I have been an insatiable lover,' he once told me, 'and this also made me horribly jealous.' He did not only throw a three-stringed toy fiddle into the fire as a lonely and oppressively pampered child; in a moment of sentimental drama, he broke one of his real violins, a Guarnerius, to smithereens, just at the time the Paris Opera was starting rehearsals for his masterpiece, *Oedipe*. This episode alone would make the subject of an entire book, but let us rather recall the date which marked the greatest joy in his whole tormented career. March 13th, 1936: the world première of his only opera, which took him a quarter of a century to write (in between ruthlessly crowded concert tours) and which fellow-composers and prominent critics greeted as the most significant music drama since *Pelléas*. Honegger wrote: 'Nous nous trouvons sans aucun doute devant l'un des plus grands maîtres, sa composition atteint les plus hautes cîmes de l'art lyrique: elle possède une originalité absolue.' The only personal detail I may add is what Enescu proudly told me, that both

Furtwängler and Karajan expressed keen interest in *Oedipe* and hoped
to conduct it at a festival in Germany.

The staging of this great work still implies enormous problems, as
the recent performance given by the Bucharest Opera at the Lausanne
Festival amply proved; but the difficulties surely cannot be more unsur-
mountable than were those attending Schönberg's *Moses und Aaron*. A
great many musicians, among them Menuhin, believe that the work is
destined to be one of the revelations of the twenty-first century. My
humble view is that, if a truly courageous producer were to fire the
imagination of Covent Garden, La Scala, the Metropolitan or the
Edinburgh Festival for a new production, any of the unprepared audiences in the West would suddenly discover a new idiom as important as
that of *Wozzeck*. Should this remain a mere idle speculation?

• • •

Enescu rarely took a violent dislike to anyone – I found him a mild,
rather reluctant hater – although he enjoyed frightening me sometimes
by raising his huge, sculptural hands with the words 'These are a mur-
derer's hands' – *astea-s maini de ucigator* (in Roumanian).

I saw him flare up on three occasions. While being enraptured by
Kathleen Ferrier's seraphic voice, he couldn't come to terms with the
style of another soloist in one of the Bach works he conducted in the
main BBC Studio. The lady felt the Maestro's refrained displeasure and
seemed to enjoy exasperating him even further, both at rehearsals and
during the actual performance. 'C'est une impertinente,' were his grave
words.

The second time I saw him angry was when he recalled one of the
preliminary sessions he so graciously undertook to initiate a French
orchestra into the pastoral subtleties of Elgar's music, prior to Sir
Edward's recording of his own *Violin Concerto* with 15-year-old Yehudi
as a soloist. The legendary Freddy Gaisberg was then still the undisput-
ed tyrant of the recording world. He exploded while Enescu, with his
unflinchingly civilised tempi, was obtaining the results he wanted: 'Will
you tell these chaps to hurry?' Gaisberg expostulated. Enescu's reaction
matched the engineer's rudeness: 'How dare you call my colleagues
chaps?' and whenever he remembered Gaisberg's behaviour he saw red.
Finally, an incident at Central Hall during a rehearsal of Mozart's *A
major Concerto* (*K488*) with Walter Gieseking. Everything went well
until the last movement, which, surprisingly, the soloist wanted to play
faster than anyone else. The Boyd Neel Orchestra found it impossible to
keep pace. Enescu, with his usual modesty, intervened: 'But Meister, my
friends in the orchestra simply cannot cope with your tempo.' To which
Gieseking retorted arrogantly: 'This is the tempo *I* want.' Turning

towards the players, Enescu said: 'Gentlemen, this is Herr Gieseking's command. I am only the conductor, so let us practise.' The performance took place, but the Maestro never addressed another word to his defiant 'colleague'.

The late Ernst Wallfisch, who, through his strict musicianship, belonged to both worlds – that of Casals and that of Enescu – told me how he sensed an air of repressed sadness when he described the Prades Festival to the latter. Casals may well have proclaimed George as the supreme musician, yet he never thought of inviting him to conduct the *Brandenburgs* or some Cantatas. One of Enescu's very rare philosophical murmurs was that conductors are usually too glued to their batons to lend them to anyone else, even for a day (*dirijorii nu lasa batul din mana*). This did not prevent Casals from sending an emotional cable when he heard of Enescu's fatal stroke: 'How could you do this to me, mon cher Georges? Have you forgotten that we are the last two survivors of the 1890s?'

One's memory can spill out innumerable other episodes of equal poignancy, but they can be told at a later date. One scene only, however, ought to be disclosed now, I think. After his very last concert in London in 1954, when we had to wheel him through the tortuous corridors of the V and A, Enescu had an indescribable moment of despair. He seemed to have forgotten all his countless triumphs – now obsessed only with his physical decline. It was sheer anguish to hear one of the greatest artists of our time belittling his genius. Bewildered, I felt incapable of uttering even the slightest word of conventional objection.

By way of contrast, a final, beautiful sight shortly after this *cri de cœur*: the bed-ridden Master, once again his own struggling self. With a finely sharpened knife – his trustworthy companion from which he never separated during endless nights of composing – he was scraping all the notes he considered superfluous. 'J'ai été toute ma vie un raseur,' he said self-mockingly; 'You see, mon cher, a true artist must always have the courage to clear the jungle of notes he has written and leave only those which are essential for the meaning of the work.'

Long after the composer's death, I came across the extraordinary evidence that no lesser colleague than Bruno Walter intervened with the Soviet authorities in 1924 to release Enescu's manuscripts, which, for safety reasons, had been evacuated to Russia during the First World War. Walter sent the following letter to his friend, the diplomat Leonid Krassin:

My dear Herr Krassin,   *München,*
                                                         29.VI.1924

Many thanks for your kind letter of 14th June. I would dearly love to come back to Russia and conduct in Moscow and Leningrad, but this year I am fully engaged from September until May. I should, however, most certainly be glad to visit you in the forthcoming season.

May I take this opportunity and raise another matter which is very close to my heart? I recently met in America George Enescu, who has scored a great success equally as a violinist, composer and conductor. He is an unusually gifted musician and, moreover, an extremely endearing and dignified person. This dear friend of mine, who has devoted the whole of his life mainly to creative achievement, and was fully justified in doing so, has for some time been in great anguish of mind. In the throes of the war, either July or August 1917, a large amount of his completed works were evacuated to Moscow together with the Roumanian National Treasury. (Enescu is a Roumanian, by the way, but with no political allegiances – a pure artist.) Among those valuables there was a large white wooden box marked 'Lot No 91' and labelled 'Musique Manuscrite Georges Enesco.' I should be most obliged if you would kindly enquire whether this precious box is still somewhere in Moscow, and then let me know as soon as possible in München, Mauerkirchestr 43. What should eventually be done with the music could be decided at a later stage. Since Enescu has been deprived of his manuscripts for seven years, he may just as well wait a little longer, perhaps until I can come to Moscow and bring the music back to him. Obviously, I would like to be able to give him some reassuring news in the meantime – after all he is anxiously awaiting such news. At the moment he is like a father who assumes his sons are missing in action.

By the way, if you'd like to hear a quite amazing young violinist in Moscow, do invite Erika Morini over. She has also been in America and had a sensational success there. She's a really phenomenal player.

Warmest greetings and best wishes for your good health. I recall with so much pleasure our days in Moscow together.

Your ever devoted,

Bruno Walter

As a postscript to the above document, here is a letter I recently received from Marchesa de Casa Fuerte:

Paris, août 1981
15 rue de Remusat

Cher Monsieur

J'ai été l'élève de Georges Enescu après avoir quitté le Conservatoire de Paris où j'avais reçu un Premier Prix de violon en 1913; pendant toute une année j'ai travaillé avec lui le *Concerto* de Brahms et j'ai gardé de ces leçons un souvenir merveilleux et inoubliable.

C'était 26 rue de Clichy dans un appartement qu'il a gardé très longtemps. Avant d'entrer au Conservatoire j'ai été l'élève de Marsick qui, vous le savez, a été le maître de Jacques Thibaud, Enescu et autres. Mais, s'il est vrai que j'ai aimé et travaillé mon violon toute ma vie, je n'ai pas fait une véritable carrière de violoniste. Je me suis mariée et suis allée habiter l'Italie avec ma famille.

J'ai revu Enesco pour la dernière fois à un dîner donné à New York pour les 75 ans de Fritz Kreisler, en 1950. Il était le même, toujours aussi génial et plein d'esprit et de bonté. J'étais à table entre lui et mon ami Samuel Dushkin et je me souviens de cette soirée très gaie et mouvementée comme si c'était hier. (Bruno Walter était parmi les convives.) Je ne savais pas que je ne devais plus les revoir.

Yvonne de Casa Fuerte

As I hinted at the beginning of this informal introduction, it would have been improper for me to just gloss over the judgments of his fellow composers or the recollections of Enescu's few friends still alive. My personal reminiscences and marginal comments have a single aim, that of shedding new light upon one of the most amazing artists of this century. There should be room for Enescu's complex genius.

• • •

During my lengthy and adventurous search leading to the current Table of Contents, I was encouraged by a great many people. Unreserved acknowledgements are due to Romeo Draghici, a true apostle of the Enescian gospel but above all editor of a hitherto unknown and vast *Correspondance* by Enescu, the child and the adolescent. The second volume of this important work has been awaited since 1970, but meanwhile the author has had his ninetieth birthday! Another researcher, Dr Viorel Cosma, lays greater emphasis on the musicological aspect of the many works by Enescu which have been discovered in recent years. I must also express my deepest gratitude to a perfect English eccentric, Mr Cheniston Roland, who has spent over thirty years of his life hunting through many thousands of old 78s hidden in cellars and markets all over Europe and America. Needless to say, he owns every record, public and private, that Enescu made between 1924 in New York and the early Fifties with the Bach *Partitas*. I got to know this extraordinary *violin historian* through yet another original, Yorkshire-born Miss Wendy Rhodes, who, out of love for Enescu, has taught herself Roumanian and is now enthusiastically engaged in translating several works by Roumania's post-war writers. I am also indebted to David Cumming for his constant editorial vigilance and zeal.

•   •   •

To mark this year's centenary celebration, *ADAM* is founding a George Enescu biennial prize of £100, to be given for a work of chamber music by a composer under 25 years of age. The prize will be awarded at the Menuhin School at Stoke d'Abernon if the winner is of English nationality or at the Menuhin Summer Festival at Gstaad if the award will go to a musician from any other country. Further details will be announced in our next issue.

CONTRIBUTORS

Joseph SZIGETI – *One of the Least 'Promoted'*
Marcel MIHALOVICI – *Hommage à Georges Enesco* [in French]
Yehudi MENUHIN – *My Great Master*
Hepzibah MENUHIN – *Facsimiled letter to Enescu on his 65th birthday*
Yaltah Menuhin RYCE – *Childhood Memories*
Niculae CARAVIA – *Fifty Years of Friendship* [translated]
Gigi TOMAZIU – *'Mosh' Georges* [in French]
Sergiu COMISSIONA – *The God-Given*
Jean MOUTON – *Enesco dans l'intimité*
Robert SIMPSON – *He was Made of Music*
Doda CONRAD – *'Maître'*
John AMIS – *Master Classes at Bryanston*
Norbert BRAININ – *What the Amadeus Quartet owes Enescu*
Manoug PARIKIAN – *The Phenomenon*
Jacques FESCHOTTE – *Albert Schweitzer chez Enesco* [in French]
Lory WALLFISCH – *Magic music-making*
Viorel COSMA – *Roumania's two geniuses* [translated]
George ENESCU – *Master to Disciple [12 letters to Yehudi Menuhin]*
George and Marie ENESCU – *9 letters to ADAM (with 2 PPS from Mme Enesco)*
Marie CANTACUZENE-ENESCU – *Pynx: le créateur*
Adolphe BOSCHOT – *Letter sent with medal to Enesco one year before his death*
Iris MURDOCH – *A Glimpse of the Danube Delta*
Which Roumanian is no Poet? – A selection of poetry and prose [translated]

NOTE

1. The late Dr Cârstea, with whom I discussed Enescu's medical history in 1974, thought that from early youth he showed symptoms of scoliosis (lateral curvature of the spine), which, with the years, degenerated into a decalcification of the vertebrae. An inflated aorta also caused him irregular breathing.

INTERNATIONAL REVIEW

Editor: Miron Grindea

Arguments about Dostoevsky

A two-act play
by Friedrich Gorenshtein

Ce Russe sublime

Proust, Claudel, Gide

A story of incompatibility

Leonard Schapiro

£1.25
$2.50

DOSTOEVSKY
Nos. 437–439, Vol. XLIII, 1981–

THE CRITICS' SEE-SAW

Am I really so great? I sometimes asked myself in
timid exaltation. Do not laugh! I never afterwards
thought I was great, but at the time ...
                                    A Writer's Diary, 1877

Arguments about Dostoevsky (*Spory o Dostoevskom*), the play in this issue
published for the first time in the West, may not be a theatrical event –
though in the hands of an imaginative director it could be shaped into
lively entertainment. Written in the shape of Gobineau's *Scènes his-*
toriques, it mirrors with much vivacity and humour some of the tragi-
comic ideological clashes between officialdom and isolated intellectuals
who, at their own peril, beg from time to time to differ. It also illustrates
the zigzagged course of Dostoevsky criticism in Russia.

Although bibliographical material on his work appears to be among
the largest ever compiled on any of the major Russian authors, the history of his appreciation in his own land has recurrently see-sawed
between extremes of adulation and disparaging invective. With the
publication of his first novel, *Poor Folk* (1846), he was acknowledged as
'an extraordinary and original talent' by the most influential critic of
the time, Vissarion Belinski (1811–1848). The assessment was
prophetic, as it focused upon the element of the pervasive tragic,
'unlikely to be immediately understood and recognised'. Another early
critic, Valéryan Maikow (1823–1847), went even further when presenting Dostoevsky as an unusually perceptive psychological writer who
'gazed so fearlessly and feelingly into the workings of human emotions'. It did not take the critics long to denounce this 'reactionary pro-
pounder of much hodgepodge' (the progressive *narodniki* in particular
were incensed by the publication of *The Devils*, a satire of some of the
exponents of radical ideas). As Vladimir Seduro points out in his well-
informed study, *Dostoevsky in Russian Literary Criticism* (Columbia
University Press, 1957), Nikolai Mikhailovski (1842–1904) 'set the
tone of much of what was to become the Soviet critical literature'. Ever
since the 1860s, political criteria prevailed over the philosophical, aesthetic and mystic interpretations of those who glorified him as 'the
prophet and spiritual leader of the Russian people' (Vasili Romnov,

Yevgeni Solov'yov and Dmitri Merezhkovski were among the more prominent eulogists).

By the start of this century, Marxism became the predominant approach of most Russian critics, with predictable results. Lenin, for instance, in 1914, angrily dismissed a Ukrainian writer, V. Vinichenko, whose novel *Testament of Fathers* he regarded as 'an ultra-bad imitation of an ultra-repulsive Dostoevsky' ... an opinion which he obviously must have changed profoundly, since, four years later, he authorised the unveiling of a monument to the 'forerunner of the Revolution' on the Tsvetnoi Boulevard in Moscow. After the collapse of the 1905 uprising, Dostoevsky was 'readopted' for a while, only to be rejected once more on the eve of the 1917 events. While recognising the genius – the equal of Dante, Shakespeare, Cervantes and Goethe – Maxim Gorky relentlessly attacked the reactionary views of the 'medieval inquisitor, his torment-ing and barren writing, the complete autonomy of the personal element, the decadent apologia for passion, thus generalising the negative traits of the Russian national character'. Remarkably, even the great Tolstoy, in a letter to Gorky, found it 'curious that Dostoevsky should be so much read – I cannot understand why, for he is so painful and useless, all those idiots, adolescents, Raskolnikovs, are so unreal'. Moreover, Tolstoy even believed that 'there was something Jewish about him!' In defiance of Gorky's conformist and unsparing opinion, Anatoli Lunacharski (1875–1933), the westernised intellectual and the first ever to write in Russia on Proust, had the temerity to hail Dostoevsky's love of 'the heav-enly reaches above the stars'. Alas, in the end he, too, had to yield to pressure, and he expediently warned his fellow-Russians that 'To be car-ried away by Dostoevsky would mean to put a millstone around your neck and, once you have dived into the slough, you remain there for ever'. 'Although,' he added, 'it would be improper for the new man born of the Revolution not to be acquainted with such a giant, it would nonetheless be *socially unhealthy* [our italics] to fall under his influence.'

If, during the Second World War, for purely patriotic reasons (the struggle against everything that was German), Dostoevsky's work was being made use of as a suitable temporary therapy – 'Despite his faults', the official slogan ordained, 'he was and remains a deeply Russian writer who loved his people' – with the advent of Zbdanovism in 1946 the medicine was abruptly decreed as being much too risky for further consumption. The war-time attempts to promote him as an inspiring socialist were followed by abusive attacks in both literary publications and academic discourses. An uncompromising *volte-face*: once again he became 'one of the fiercest opponents of socialism and democracy'. V. V. Yermilov, the influential editor of *Literaturnaya Gazeta*, denounced him in a pamphlet, 'Against the reactionary ideas in Dostoevsky's writings', as a precursor of the decadent Céline, Henry Miller and Sartre. With the curtains henceforth closed, only occasional chinks here and there were allowed to shine through. One such occurred in 1952, in the *Soviet Encyclopaedia* entry under 'Dostoevsky', a wisely anonymous piece, markedly moderate and reasonably objective for the period. Yet at the same time, *Classics of Russian Literature*, a collection for young people, did not even mention the name ... None of his works were included in any school curriculum.[1]

For a detailed analysis of further criticism during the last three decades, one must once again turn to Vladimir Seduro, this time to his *Dostoevsky's Image in Russia Today* (Belmont, Massachussets, 1975). The works were rehabilitated as part of the general relaxation during the post-Stalin era, though the referees had great difficulty in finding the requisite 'quotes' to substantiate the new policy. Providentially, one of the pundits remembered what Lenin had once said of *The House of the Dead* – 'a work unsurpassed in Russia and world literature which gives a wonderfully clear picture of how the people lived under the Tsars' ... , and this provided, in 1956, the perfect *raison d'être* for the 75th anniversary of the master's death. Exhibitions in museums and libraries all over the Union presented vast miscellanies of memorabilia such as the translation of *Eugénie Grandet* in 1844, Dostoevsky's first published work. A Moscow street was renamed in his honour, novels were once again dramatised, and the cinema also took him up, culminating in Kulidhzanov's epic production of *Crime and Punishment* (1970); hundreds of foreign dignitaries and writers attended the State celebrations. A ten-volume edition of *Collected Works* (1956–1958) was followed by the Academy thirty-volume edition (1966–1973), which included the correspondence and a considerable amount of hitherto unpublished texts, among which were the long-awaited *Notebooks* (1860–1881), (English edition, Ann Arbor, USA, 1973). However, even this encouraging relaxation in the scholarly publication of so much source material did not much alter the Marxist-Leninist approach ('the disintegration of old social norms, the baseness and animal egotism of bourgeois society' etc), and, for obvious reasons, critics were still careful not to dwell on Dostoevsky's philosophy of art and aesthetics. The ambivalence persisted, with the only difference that scholars were able, surreptitiously, to stress the vast heritage: in Seduro's words, 'in the light of the historical and literary facts, sweeping away all artificially erected barriers and distortions and gradually gaining the upper hand in this prolonged argument over Dostoevsky'.

Naturally, there is also a considerable field of research, pursued in totally uninhibited freedom, by emigré literary historians both in Europe and in the United States. One of them, Pavel Berlin, in a long study, *Russkaia literatura i evrei* (Russian literature and the Jews, *Novyi Zhurnal*, New York, 1963) tackled the rarely explored aspect of Dostoevsky's attitude towards Judaism. 'Jewish motifs of the struggle with God resounded in his soul,' Berlin wrote, and the 'persistent questions to which Christianity gave no answers' impelled Dostoevsky, however unintentionally, to come into contact with Judaism. Vladimir Jabotinsky, in one of his *Feuilletons*, and Nikolai Volski on the other hand, traced in the novels and especially in articles for various periodicals a great many passages which make Dostoevsky appear as a consistent anti-Semite. The subject was re-examined at exhaustive length in *Dostoevsky et les juifs* by David Goldstein (Gallimard, 1976), recently translated into English by the author (University of Texas, 230 pp, 1981).

One is surprised to learn that the only play Dostoevsky ever completed (at the beginning of his career, before banishment to Siberia) was *The Jew Yankel*, a stereotype used also by Gogol when in need of a caricature. The pitiable figure in *Taras Bulba* is 'praying, enveloped in his rather soiled shawl, according to the rites of his faith'. The Yid Isai Fomish in *The House of the Dead* ('Even now', Dostoevsky wrote later, 'I can't think of him without laughing') started his morning prayer by 'wailing, sputtering, pirouetting wildly and absurdly; on his arms he fastened maniples and on his forehead a little wooden box of sorts, secured by a band, so that it looked like some ridiculous horn sprouting out; what was so absurd was the way in which Isai seemed to make a display of his ritual'. *Crime and Punishment* contains other conventional descriptions, such as the moneylender Alyona Ivanovna, 'rich like a Jew', or Louzhin, 'stingy like a Yid'; but more important, in the same great novel, is an intriguing episode which has received much critical comment. Svidrigailov, after a nightmarish dream in which he nearly rapes a five-year-old child, rushes into the street determined to kill himself but is stopped by a grotesque figure whose face expressed the 'fretful sadness which is the centuries-old mark of the Jewish race'. Goldstein finds the choice of a pitiful-looking Jew as a ... fireman in Tsarist Russia not only 'insolite, mais inconcevable.[2] L'écrivain a beau ironiser en coiffant le petit Juif craintif du casque d'Achille – incarnation resplendissante de la beauté virile, de la force et du courage – tout se passe comme si Dostoevsky découvrait dans sa créature autre chose que le reflet dérisoire d'une grande vie passée. Par sa seule présence, ce Juif fantomatique conteste au peuple russe le rôle messianique que Dostoevsky entend lui réserver; (car) il a refusé à admettre qu'il n'est de messianisme qu'hébraïque, ou encore, comme le dira Berdiaev, que la conscience messianique à l'intérieur du christianisme est toujours une rejudaïsation du christianisme. Dostoevsky ne peut légitimer le rôle qu'il réserve à la Russie qu'en anéantissant – en quelque sorte figurativement – cet autre peuple dont l'existence même est la négation de ce privilège.' Dwelling on Goldstein's laborious interpretation, the American critic Robert Adler argued that 'By stages, Dostoyevsky's own perception of the messianic vocation of the Russian nation became more extreme and with that shift, his xenophobia grew more important. Inflamed with a vision of the degeneracy of the West and Russia's redemptive role in history, he also became obsessed with the Jews as the arch-enemy of the great Christian consummation that could be achieved only through the Russian people'.

The *Correspondence* and *Notebooks* testify indeed to his constant state of turmoil and neurosis, exacerbated by the savage pressure under which he had to write. One simply has to accept the blatant contradictions between the creative artist and the hurried, often naïve, political journalist. In one of his *notes de travail* one finds, for instance, this amazing *cri de cœur*: 'It would be better if I myself believed in anything I had just written'. One must take many other extreme statements in one's stride.[3] In his own periodical, *Vremya* (Time), Dostoevsky impetuously took issue with those who used in print the word *zhid* instead of *yevrei*, just as he protested against the increasing attacks on the Jews: 'Are we to suppose,' he asked, 'that the Jews are not human beings, but wild beasts dangerous to the moral order?' – only to make the same people appear in his novels as 'speculators, thieves, lickspittles, even ritual murderers'. In *A Raw Youth* (*The Adolescent*), he forecast that the doom of society will be brought about by the reign of the Yids (*zhidovskoye tzarstvo*), 'until the paupers will destroy the shareholders, confiscate their shares and take their places'. Having given this warning – 'If the people don't come to their senses, in no time they'll fall into the clutches of Yids of every stripe' – he slyly asked himself, in *The Diary of a Writer* (1877): 'Am I really an enemy of the Jews?' ... Only to accuse, one year later, 'the Yids and the *kabal*, spreading like wildfire', of having largely forced him to stop publishing the *Diary*. It was also relevant that at the monstrous Beilis Murder Trial, Chief Prosecutor O. Y. Vipper based his indictment on the 'prophetic words of our renowned Dostoevsky, who had warned the Russians that the Yids will be drinking the people's blood'. More significant still was the fact (noted by Goldstein) that all offensive references to Jews in Dostoevsky's letters to his wife have been removed from the 1956 edition of the *Collected Works*.

Returning, briefly, to the bewildering changes in the critical treatment in the USSR: one must salute the first modern *Biography* of Dostoevsky, written by a prominent scholar, Leonid Grossman (1888–1965) and published in Moscow in 1962, in both Russian and French. Another daring work, *Dostoevsky's Personality, a novel research study* by B. I. Bursov, while inevitably Marxist, was described by Seduro as 'having penetrated beyond the pre-ordained boundaries of the materialist doctrine – a distinct achievement in Soviet Dostoevsky studies'. Throughout the last four decades, the duality persisted: 'The struggle to accept Dostoevsky as against the tendency to reject him continues to this day.' And yet one should perhaps not grumble too much when, so far away from his mother country, an artist so passionately Russian as Vladimir Nabokov was capable of writing this silly and arrogant comment: 'No doubt Dostoevsky is waiting at the door of my [campus] office to discuss his low marks'; furthermore, while Tolstoy and Chekhov would have found *Lolita* objectionable, 'Dostoevsky would have hugely envied and perversely loved it'.

So much, then, for Dostoevsky in Russia. While in Germany and France most novels were translated not long after their publication in Russia, *The Insulted and the Injured* (1861) and *Crime and Punishment* (1866) appeared in English only in 1886. Henry Vizetely, the publisher, defied the National Vigilance Association, whose campaign against 'immoral' literature chose Russian fiction among its main targets. George Saintsbury ordained that 'the healthiness and beefiness in the English temperament was a guarantee against our people ever falling prey to the sterile pessimism which seems to dominate Russian fiction'. The *Athenaeum* spoke of such realism as Monsieur Zola and his followers 'did not dream of', while the *Academy*, unaware of the fact that the author had died five years previously, advised Mr Dostoevsky to 'learn the art of condensation and above all to study Zola who, despite his faults, is never wearisome'.

The year 1886 also saw the publication of *Dr Jekyll and Mr Hyde*, and when J. A. Symonds suggested that, instead of killing himself, Dr Hyde should have given himself up to the police 'as Raskolnikov did', Robert Louis Stevenson reacted in a memorable manner: 'Raskolnikov is easily the greatest book I have read in ten years. … Many find it dull; Henry James could not finish it because the character of Raskolnikov was not objective, and at that I divined a great gulf between us and the existence of a certain impotence in many minds of today, which prevents them from living *in* a book or a character. All I can say is, it nearly finished me, it was like having an illness.' While acknowledging at one stage a 'strong quality of genius' in Dostoevsky, James nonetheless described the novels as 'fluid puddings'.

Among the salient *bêtises* of the period, there was George Moore's description of the author (in a preface he wrote for the first translation of *Poor Folk* in 1894) as a 'Gaboriau with psychological sauce, and that of the inferior kind'. Gissing, on the other hand, in his study of Dickens (1898), spoke with remarkable insight of the Russian's superiority in his bold treatment of extreme psychological situations, which 'Dickens was obliged to ignore or to hint, with sighing timidity'; such powerful scenes were 'beyond Dickens as we know him; it would not have been so but for the defects of education and the social prejudices which forbade the gifts to develop.'

As to 'the continued vitality of Dostoevsky's influence on French literature ever since the apotheosis conferred on him by Gide, Suarès and Fauré', this has been expertly explored by Professor F. W. J. Hemmings in *The Russian Novel in France* (OUP, 1948). According to him, 'So long as the workings of the sub-conscious forces of man remain something of a mystery, readers in France will continue to come to him, as the men of the ancient world to the oracle of Delphi, to receive answers, some satisfying, some dissatisfying, but nearly all of them enigmatic'.

While Bergotte detested Dostoevsky, the narrator in *La prisonnière* dwelt at some length on 'la beauté neuve que Dostoevsky apporte au monde, création d'une certaine âme'. A bewildered Albertine takes him to task, asking for the meaning of 'le côté Dostoevsky de Madame de Sévigné', and the answer is, 'J'avoue, lui dis-je en riant, que c'est très tiré par les cheveux' … Still dissatisfied, Albertine wants to know if 'Dostoevsky a jamais assassiné quelqu'un, (car) les romans que je connais de lui pourraient tous s'appeler l'Histoire d'un Crime'. The narrator is evasive, but he shows that Proust had read *Les frères Karamazov*. He admits that 'Il devait être un peu criminel, comme ses héros, qui ne le sont pas d'ailleurs tout à fait' [*sic*]. On the other hand, 'C'est un grand créateur; d'abord, le monde qu'il peint a vraiment l'air d'avoir été créé pour lui, une humanité plus fantastique que celle qui peuple *La Ronde de Nuit* de Rembrandt'. Follows the protestation of an impassioned fellow-writer (although, only a few sentences before, he had declared … 'Je ne suis pas romancier'). As to Lafcadio, Gide's hero in *Les caves du Vatican*, he is 'very evidently, Dostoevsky's Raskolnikov', just as 'The conspiracy owes much to the nihilist gang in *The Possessed*,' and Gide himself, like Raskolnikov, 'told to the market-place of his contemporaries the crime that had made him great'.[4] Similarly, Dostoevsky had a marked influence on Duhamel (*Salavin* in particular) and Camus; a source of inspiration for Nietzsche;[5] the fascination of his work on Hauptmann, Hamsun, Thomas Mann and Faulkner was equally fecund, but the subject overflows …

Among the many tributes recently published in the West, the one by Professor Richard Freeborn sums up best Dostoevsky's lasting impact on modern literature – 'His death centenary is to be remembered in the same terms as are those of Dante or Shakespeare or Goethe: it can be said of him that he not only anticipated Freud or existentialism, but in his influence he was the first major Russian writer to bear witness to a Russian ideal of spirituality'.[6] As far as *ADAM* is concerned, I should like to acknowledge the information I found in the early studies of Dostoevsky by Janko Lavrin (1922) and Gerald Abraham (1936), in David Magarshak's biography published in 1961 and in Robert Lord's essays on *Russian Literature* (Kahn and Averill, 1980). I also received much valued advice and assistance from the Russian Department of the University of Nottingham, Dr Francis Williams and Judith Bumpus (BBC), Vanessa Wolley and Anthony Woodrow.

• • •

The Enescu Prize. We were hoping to be able to announce full details of the George Enescu Biennial Prize in this issue. The task of assembling a truly representative international jury requires, however, more time than we had anticipated; this, and conditions for participation in the competition, will be announced at a later date.

CONTRIBUTORS

Friedrich GORENSHTEIN – *Arguments about Dostoevsky* [translated two-act play]
Marcel PROUST, Paul CLAUDEL, André GIDE – *Ce Russe Sublime* [3 French views]
Leonard SCHAPIRO – *A Story of Incompatibility: Dostoevsky and Turgenev*
Jean MAMBRINO – *Adam* [translated poem]
David MAGARSHAK – *Translating from the Russian*
Roger CARDINAL – *Winter to Me* [poem]

Views and Reviews: Sergei HACKEL, *Dostoevski, prophète manqué* – Alexander PIATIGORSKIY, *Roszanov and Dostoevsky* – Zinovy ZINIK, *Has* The Raw Youth *grown up?* [translated] – Virgil CÂNDEA, *A Roumanian Connection* [translated]

NOTES

1. Twenty years ago, I attended the International Symposium on Tolstoy, organised by the *Fondazione Cini* in Venice (see *ADAM*, Nos. 284-6, 1960). It was noticeable that all the Russian delegates had ambivalent feelings towards Dostoevsky; clearly, the Tolstoyan gospel was officially regarded as less harmful.
2. The critic John Bayley made an interesting comment on this episode: 'Not fireman, surely, but one of the imperial guardsmen on ceremonial duty in St Petersburg, who wore an Achilles helmet. One should never underestimate the range and potency of the novelist's humour, a solvent of every sort of crackpot or disagreeable belief which the doctrinaire Dostoevsky may have held. Svidrigailov, the ideal Orthodox Slav, is the accursed and wandering Jew, while the real Jew in his imperial Russian uniform makes the proper pronouncement of nationalistic orthodoxy – "You can't do that here!"' (*TLS*, 17 VII 1981)
3. In the introduction to his lively new translation of *The Devils* (Penguin edition), the late David Magarshak warned readers that 'It would be absurd to take Dostoevsky's political views seriously; his spite and hatred not only of his opponents, but also of all imaginary "enemies" of Russia, was perhaps entirely in harmony with his religious obsessions'.
4. *André Gide, a critical biography*, by George Painter (Weidenfeld, 1968).
5. 'Dostoevsky was the only psychologist from whom I had anything to learn: he belongs to the happiest windfalls of my life, happier even than the discovery of Stendhal. This profound man, who was right ten times over in esteeming the superficial Germans low, found the Siberian convicts carved from about the best, hardest and most valuable material that grows on Russian soil' (Nietzsche, in *Twilight of the Gods*).
6. The *Times Higher Education Supplement*, 30.1.81.

Our 45th Year

ADAM

INTERNATIONAL REVIEW

Editor: Miron Grindea

I am drinking a large glass of whisky to
you in Antibes on the 45th anniversary of
Adam. You have certainly made a fine art
of survival (even Cyril Connolly failed
with Horizon.) My best wishes in advance
for your 50th anniversary in case I am
not able to toast it in the same fashion.

Graham Greene

DODECATRIBUTE to M.G. at 75   *DAVID GASCOYNE*

M any years, many memories, my dear Miron . . .
I met you early, ignescent incomer,
R aw yet ready to recognise your rare repute
O f openess to all original output.
N ow none can ignore your initiative nous.

G reat is our gratitude for your genial gift:
R ampart of rance amidst Ragnarok's rioting,
I ndispensable international index,
N one such never needless of normative notions,
D oyen of discerningly diglot dossiers,
E xemplarily edited for an era—
A dam, acme of annals of authentic art.

£5.00
$10.00

DEBUSSY ETC – AND *ADAM*'S 45TH AND MIRON'S 75TH BIRTHDAY TRIBUTES

Nos. 443–445, Vol. XXXXV, 1983–

I am drinking a large glass of whisky to you in Antibes on the 45th anniversary of Adam. You have certainly made a fine art of survival (even Cyril Connolly failed with Horizon). My best wishes in advance for your 50th anniversary in case I am not able to toast it in the same fashion.

[signed] Graham Greene

DODECATRIBUTE to MG at 75

David Gascoyne

M any years, many memories, my dear Miron …
I met you early, ignescent incomer,
R aw yet ready to recognise your rare repute
O f openness to all original output.
N ow none can ignore your initiative nous.

G reat is our gratitude for your genial gift:
R ampart of rance amidst Ragnarok's rioting,
I ndispensable international index,
N one such never needless of normative notions,
D oyen of discerning diglot dossiers,
E xemplarily edited for an era –
A dam, acme of annals of authentic art.

HONORIS CAUSA

And the Lord God caused a deep sleep
to fall upon Adam, and he slept.

(Genesis 2.21)

An accumulation of factors, each one more frustrating than the last, has delayed various editorial projects during the last two years. As can be imagined, this was far from making me happy, but, as so often in the past, I clung once again to trust in our readers' forbearance. Perhaps,

perhaps the present anniversary issue might prove worth having waited for. At any rate, it should at least justify a few stray reflections.

Far from deriving unqualified pride from the mere fact that we have lasted for so long, I often think with sadness of the many literary casualties in this country – publications which started with an enormous amount of skill and enthusiasm and yet succumbed after two or three issues. Even *ADAM*, despite its longevity, still feels like a newcomer making its debut – clumsy, unwanted, unrecorded. One aspect of neglect in particular causes pain, which is when a special issue, consisting either of surveys of foreign literatures or a number devoted to an individual writer, is not considered worth mentioning in any of the bibliographies devoted to these specific subjects. Such issues require intensive, often frenzied research and are motivated solely by the anticipation that the material would one day be of use to new researchers.

An infinitely greater source of frustration continues to be the discouraging attitude of wholesalers and bookshops. Nor have public libraries at any time shown a friendly inclination to support us. Could this be our fault? Has *ADAM*, in some indefinable way, been wrong in belonging to no school and in propounding no ideology? Readers might find an answer ... Anyway, sooner or later (a few more years, or, with luck, after reaching the half century) the journal is bound to come to an end. New ideas, fresh sensibilities, a different vision of what one would expect from a literary magazine in the late 1980s – these are some of the thoughts that keep weighing on our mind. On the other hand, so many commitments undertaken in recent years! Two in particular have remarkable stories attached to them.

The first one. Many years back, a well-known musicologist contacted me with a perplexing proposition: would *ADAM*, he asked, be prepared to publish a 150-page issue with hitherto unknown material on Debussy, classified by a French collector totally lacking in practical sense? 'What is the idea?' I asked in some bewilderment. The amazing answer was: 'It will help me at a later date in a work on the same subject.'

So thunderstruck was I at the suggestion that, out of an incorrigibly perverse curiosity, I agreed to see the MS. The musicologist entrusted it to me. Two days later, he panicked and changed his mind: 'I've decided that it might be unwise to part with the text, so may I come to collect it?'

• • •

From time immemorial the literary world has been blighted by similar acts of piracy. *ADAM* alone, in its modest trajectory, has witnessed some equally offensive episodes ... Hence the decision to perform an urgent act of editorial justice (another one in our next issue). Rollo Myers, 92 next year, found among his dormant MSS a rich and interesting compilation of criticisms illustrating how Debussy's work has fared in Europe and in the States. It would be a pity, I thought, if this work on Debussy (overlooked, surprisingly, by a number of London publishers) were to fall into the hands of yet another 'enterprising', unscrupulous researcher, who would be only too glad to offer this valuable material to the world. I was determined to secure in time the copyright.

Concerning Debussy: I was the author of one of the most monumental gaffes imaginable. In 1945 *ADAM* arranged a performance of a duet from *Pelléas et Mélisande*, sung by the legendary Maggie Teyte and Pierre Bernac, with Francis Poulenc at the piano. I unpardonably failed to make a recording of this unique musical event, and for years I tried to forget my blunder, until recently I was reminded of it by a footnote in Garry O'Connor's absorbing biography.[1] Isn't it extraordinary that the first Mélisande, in 1902, was a Scottish singer, Mary Garden, and the second, in 1908, a girl from Wolverhampton?

As Rollo Myers' meticulous compilation appears here as a precautionary measure to protect various data from being forgotten or badly exploited, I take the liberty of including a personal recollection from my conversations with George Enescu. He said: 'I attended the world premiere of *Pelléas*, accompanied by Richard Strauss, who was totally *décomposé* by the effect of the orchestration.' Enescu added: 'In fairness to the creator of *Salome*, one should also reveal that my own great master, Gabriel Fauré, surrounded by a few disciples, was not more favourably impressed by the score. I myself recognised the genius, although as a colleague Debussy could sometimes behave abominably' (a mild equivalent of the Roumanian word *scârba*).

● ● ●

1983 brought us an unexpected joy. The year began auspiciously, with an official announcement that 'the Council of the University of Kent at Canterbury have unanimously accepted a recommendation that we should offer you an Honorary Degree of Doctor of Letters'. Naked *ADAM* in the Garden of Akademos! After having been so frequently accused in official quarters of lack of discipline, eccentricity, lawlessness! The highest official status at a time when we were becoming conditioned to isolation ... Once the excitement was over, I realized that, by an uncanny coincidence, the University of Kent is surrounded by some of the most opulent orchards, yielding, year after year, the divinely delicious Cox's orange pippins. I found it simply impossible to ignore the scriptural connection between the magazine and the forbidden fruit. The drollery went even further: Dr David Ingram, the Vice-Chancellor, invited me to make the speech on behalf of the graduands – the other two being no lesser figures than Cardinal Hume and Mr Robin Leigh-

Pemberton, the newly-elected Governor of the Bank of England –
supreme polarities of the spiritual and high finances. I could think of
nothing better than publicly to confess *ADAM*'s sinful career in this
country, starting from complete blackout during the blitz and indulging
in interminable bibliographical convolutions. I still cannot fathom my
audacity – indeed, I addressed the learned congregation in impudent
verse. This is what followed:

ADAM's Somersaults

Let him try in doubtful meters
To narrate just how he stumbled
From the passionate blue Danube
To the lazy shores of Thames.
Banks unknown, full of phantoms,
Tides of phosphorescent voices,
Shreds of meaning in the darkness.
Greedy, groping for a syntax,
All he nets is rage and blackout –
Harder words to catch than trout.
Feeble angler, frightened exile.
Give the game up altogether.
Conquer English? How's that done?
Clutching syllables still tempt him,
All emerge from Eve, no doubt –
And they drive him fast along.
Notions blossom all around him,
Hard to grasp, their subtle charms.
Golgotha, but fifteen stations.
Metaphors pile up in traffic,
He is choking, gasps for air,
Then the genesis of scanning,
Nightmare, pain and fascination.

Poems clutter with no mercy,
Claiming all his prompt attention.
Manuscripts from Erewhon,
Epic dramas and new lyrics,
Business easier said than done.
How to stop this wild invasion?

Perhaps one day he will be lying,
Toothless beggar, hard of hearing,

Nothing left for him but apples
(Eve has dropped them, just to tempt him).
'Penny for an Editor!'
Do not trust him. 'He would promise,
Well-intentioned, no more issues,
Final end to printing errors.'
While Dame Fortune lets him rummage
Through the pastures of Belles Lettres,
You will find his vow is broken,
He will scout beyond permission,
Bills of fare or à la carte.

Snouts have gone too far and how!
Drastic steps ought to be taken:
Why not sound the Chancellor?
It's high July, exams are done for,
Stop him, Dr Ingram, burn him
In the furnace of the shadows.
Doctor Adam? You are joking –
Brand him Dishonoris Causa.

• • •

I am greatly indebted to Henry Raynor, Sybil Perceval, Dick Perceval, Colleen Gardener and Simon Jenner for their enthusiastic and valuable assistance. Thanks are also due to Mr Arthur Heath for producing this issue in an exceedingly short time.

CONTRIBUTORS

Rebecca WEST – *A Message (letter to Carola Grindea)*
Ondra LYSOHORSKY – *In Difficult Years* [poem translated by Christopher Fry for the 75th]
Francis SCARFE – *ADAM* [poem]
Fernand AUBERJONOIS – *'Nul ne parle quand j'interromps'*
John SMITH – *A Sussex Eden (for MG)* [poem]
Prof. Brian SIMPSON – *Oration for ADAM* [delivered to the Convocation of the University of
    Kent at the presentation of Miron's honorary doctorate]
Christopher FRY – *Greeting*
Yehudi MENUHIN – *Letter*
Marie-Jacqueline LANCASTER – *Brief Encounters*
Anthony RUDOLF – *Old Adam: An affectionate memoir*
Anthony FARRELL – *A See-Saw Association*
Michael MOTT – *Courageous Taste*
Rollo MYERS – *Debussy – An outline of his life and work; pro and anti critical assessments of his
    music*
Erik SATIE – *Debussy (Les Commandements du Catéchisme du Conservatoire)* [poem in French,
    with 3 translations]
Simon JENNER – *Debussy's Chart (a Leo)*
Rachel LASSERSON (aged 10) – *A Portrait of my Grandfather (Miron G)* [facsimile]
Francesco MALIPIERO and Darius MILHAUD – *Musical MSS on ADAM theme*

Views and Reviews: Norma RINSLER, *Aragon, Apollinaire and War (including an unpublished letter from Aragon)* – Vanessa DAVIES, *No Helpmeet for Adam?*

NOTE

1.   *The Pursuit of Perfection: A Life of Maggie Teyte*, London, 1979.

ADAM

INTERNATIONAL REVIEW

Editor : Miron Grindea

61
96F 00

André Gide — pianist

C'est tout ce que je puis vous dire.
J'espère que vous allez bien et que Adam
vivra autant que l'espèce des artistes."

£6
$12

GIDE AND MUSIC

Nos. 468–480, Vol. XLVIII, 1986–

IN MUSIC'S COMPANY

The larger part of the present issue is taken up by a detailed study of the crucial role music played in André Gide's life and creativity. Its author, Dr Patrick Pollard, recently co-ordinated a symposium on 'André Gide et l'Angleterre', obtainable from Birkbeck College, London, and is now preparing an important study for publication, *André Gide: the homosexual moralist*. Meanwhile, in the pages to follow, readers will find hitherto invaluable, unexplored material, based on Gide's correspondence with Debussy, Stravinsky, Dukas, Milhaud and Schmitt, as well as a far-sighted analysis of the presence of music in works such as *La porte étroite*, *Les faux-monnayeurs*, *La symphonie pastorale*, and above all the *Journal*.

ADAM's own research on this fascinating subject was interrupted by the accidental discovery of a set of posthumous diaries in which Gide was branded as one of the most pernicious figures in French literary life. Only a short while ago, belatedly, I came across *Le livre de l'amertume* (470 pages, Mercure de France, 1983) by Georges Duhamel, whose work and friendship had greatly influenced my youth. His 'book of bitterness' unleashed memories going as far back as adolescence, some of them relevant to music – hence the ensuing lengthy digressions.

The personal side first. I fell upon a totally unexpected entry: 'Jeudi 31 octobre 1929. Visite d'un très jeune écrivain roumain, Miron Grindéa, qui m'affirme que je suis en train de supplanter Gide dans l'estime de la jeunesse roumaine, car il y a un retour vers un art plus sain [*sic*].' The surprise was just as great when, on the page opposite, I read: '22 octobre. Visite de Ernst Robert Curtius, 43 ans. Il représente ce genre d'hommes, lettrés étrangers qui ont été tout de suite fort adroitement accaparés par le clan Gide. Bah! Ils finiront peut-être par nous découvrir un jour.'

I may have spoken the words quoted by the well-known author (then aged 43), and if the episode had become hazy over the years, to see it recorded in print, more than half a century later, gave the memory a jolt – a cascade of flashbacks!

The year is 1927. At a time when a large part of the Roumanian intelligentsia was engulfed by the sinister Iron Guard ideology, about half a dozen sixth-formers used to gather several times a month at the feet of an eighteen-year-old guru called Mircea Eliade, indisputably the most prodigious polymath of our generation. A twentieth-century Pico della Mirandola! Two years my senior, it was his intellectual exuberance that first gave me the impetus to write. Moreover, it was in his garret in Melody Street, overflowing with books in practically every European language, that I first heard of Roger Martin du Gard and his roman-fleuve, *Les Thibault*, of Giovanni Papini's *Un Uomo Finito* and, above all, of André Gide's *Les nourritures terrestres*. The effect of the last was entrancing ('enflammer les lèvres d'une soif nouvelle'), but this state of 'ferveur livresque' and inebriation did not last long. By the time of matriculation, two other French masters were offering a spiritual out-look totally different from the permissiveness of the *acte gratuit* exalted by Gide. They were Romain Rolland with *Vie de Beethoven* and *Jean Christophe* (up to *La Révolte*, the fourth of the ten-volume cycle) and Georges Duhamel with *Vie des martyrs* and *Civilisation* (Prix Goncourt, 1918). Heading a surgical unit in the 1914 war, within earshot of enemy guns and unable even to see the faces of the mutilated soldiers, he per-formed during fifty appalling months more than two thousand opera-tions. Little wonder that metaphors such as 'Il existe une véritable langue universelle – c'est la voix de la souffrance' had a magnetic effect on the youth of the Twenties. 'Au fond des plaies,' the message reverber-ated, 's'agite et s'exalte une âme furtive qui ne se manifeste pas aisé-ment, mais que je souhaiterais tant vous faire entendre.' *Confession de minuit* (the first of the five-volume saga *Vie et aventures de Salavin*) intro-duced me further to an unforgettable character; impossible not to love 'à raison même de ses tourments et de son noble désespoir.' Duhamel became a witness and his gospel of loneliness a source of strength to me between leaving the capital city (at that time still considered the 'Paris of the Orient') and my first encounter with the real thing – Lutetia.

My introduction to the fifth arrondissement, during an early period of student gloom, culminated, naturally, in the discovery of the 'ruelles odorantes de la Montagne Sainte Geneviève' – Salavin's country. Twenty years later, in the wake of the liberation of Paris in 1944, the first pilgrim steps took me to the same site, Place du Panthéon. The five-storey, pompously-named Hôtel des Grands Hommes, where I had stayed in the late Twenties, looked dismally abandoned with its blinds lowered. Otherwise the place showed no scars: Contrescarpe, Lycée Henri IV, rue Descartes, the wooded courtyard at 17 rue du Cardinal Lemoine (where I once caught sight of Valéry Larbaud, the aphasic wizard of *Barnabooth*) had not been touched by the enemy. Rue Vauquelin, round the corner, seemed to be glad to let passers-by rediscover its old spell. It was there, in 1929, that at least once a month I would climb to the fourth floor at number 28, where a group of happy amateurs (twenty at most) used to meet every week to play through the *Brandenburg Concertos* or a Haydn or Schubert symphony. Sometimes the conductor was a middle-aged, shy-looking musician by the name of Hector Laisné, while the flautist was none other than the host, creator of Salavin.[1] (The Dostoevskian character of the novel was also a flautist trying to come to terms with the oppressive routine of daily life, and 'perceiving the true dimension of man' through the sound of the instrument.)

Music soon became a lasting bond between us, and whenever I met the Maître I had the privilege of joining him in the never-ending game of tossing musical quotations back and forth: Mozart and Wagner operas, symphonies, string quartets, all sources of happiness. So much so that, when the implacable globetrotter ('J'ai toute ma vie voyagé sans regretter jamais un seul voyage') decided to visit Roumania in 1938, and I went to greet him at the frontier (Jimbolia), he enacted an extraordinary scene in front of two bewildered customs officials. Leaving behind his wife, the actress Blanche Albane, and his other companion, Jean-Louis Vaudoyer,[2] he started humming in his husky voice the theme from the slow movement of Beethoven's *Second Symphony* which, over the years, had become our signature tune.

While he was our guest in Bucharest, I took him to the Opera to a performance of *Zauberflöte*. Watching the tears of joy streaming down Duhamel's rubicund, beaming cheeks during Papageno's 'chat' with the magic flute was a touching sight. The solo flautist in the orchestra pit was Vasili Jianu, one of the best-known virtuosi in Europe. I had no difficulty in persuading him to join in a harmless musical cabal. The following day, while the Duhamels were having lunch in our flat, Jianu appeared surreptitiously and without much ado took his instrument out of the case. Duhamel hardly had time to grasp what was happening before the young artist settled into Mozart's *Concerto in D major* ...

A similar manoeuvre took place after the war, this time with the connivance of Blanche Albane. As her husband had been unable to attend the debut recital in Paris of an English Duo, the musicians were amused at the suggestion to stop off for one hour on their way back to the Gare du Nord and call at 31 rue de Liège, Duhamel's home. The Maître listened enraptured to a Sonata originally written for flute and harpsichord by John Stanley, the seventeenth-century blind composer. This made a welcome change, Blanche Albane remarked radiantly, at a time when the rage among young French musicians, including their composer son Antoine, was dodecaphonic music, with René Leibowitz as the new oracle – anathema to parents brought up on classical and romantic music. (Born in 1925, Antoine Duhamel has in the last three decades written a large amount of vocal and instrumental music, including three Operas: *Lundi, Monsieur, vous serez riche*; *Les Oiseaux*; and *Les Gambarins*.)

So many more recollections come to mind. Suffice it to mention that during the London Blitz I once again, clandestinely, reached Duhamel in occupied France at the time when his books were banned by the Nazi authorities. I invited him to become Honorary President of the International Arts Guild which I had set up in 1943 with the inspiring help of Henry Moore, Benjamin Britten and Stephen Spender – the other patron was Pablo Casals, at that time still a voluntary exile from Franco's Spain in Prades, on the Spanish-French border.

• • •

Back to 1939: my final migration to the West on the very day World War Two broke out (September 1st). When, two years later, I re-established contact with the beleaguered Duhamel and asked him to help me resurrect the exiled *ADAM*, he at once sent this vibrant message: 'A l'heure où j'écris ces lignes la France est dépécée. Quel est le moins mortel de nos trésors terrestres? C'est assurément notre langue et notre littérature.' Words bound to instil courage and purpose in the journal's first steps in a new, intimidating cultural environment. Hence the journal's determination to allot as much space as possible to everything that illustrated French civilisation. Doubting Duhamel's advice that no-one ought to venture into literary editorship before the age of fifty, I had little hesitation in cajoling him through the years; and his contributions on Balzac, Rimbaud, Verhaeren, Proust and Strindberg were memorable. (To this day, I suspect they have not been recorded by any French bibliographer.) In more than one way he sustained the magazine throughout its most critical period, and this is something *ADAM* will never forget.

> L'homme, ce misérable tas de secrets.
> André Malraux: *Anti-mémoires*

Two choices often face addicts of literary history: that of practising *ce vice impuni, la lecture*, which Valéry Larbaud, even during his many years of agonising physical suffering, worshipped with undiminished glee, or that of resisting the *punishable* vice of rummaging through posthumous diaries. Oh! the imprudent probing of internecine wars between fellow-writers; the ghoulish disclosures of new facts and never-ending cross-references. And yet, however heavy the penalty, how oft had *ADAM* really shirked temptation?

Treading over Georges Duhamel's stabs of bitterness, I stumbled over far too many judgements and moods in sharp contrast with the image of the man and artist I had built up during my formative years. In 1925 (February 2nd) he confided to his *Diary*, 'Je ne me trompe pas: si je regarde attentivement dans le fonds de mon cœur, je n'y vois rien qui ressemble à de la rancune.' What could have then caused, I wondered with increasing sadness, so much acrimony and irritability in a public figure so widely acclaimed as a 'maître de conscience' and whose long career has been showered with more honours than any of his French contemporaries would normally have been able to cope with? Neither his considerable output – scores of books – nor the extent of official recognition (member of the Académie Française, 1935, of the Académie de Médecine, 1937, of the Académie de Chirurgie, 1940, of the Académie des Sciences Morales et Politiques, 1937, member of dozens of literary juries) seem to have brought him peace. 'L'on me demande tout,' he sighed; 'l'on pourrait m'emmener en brancard pour mourir très vite à la tâche.' Yet he never tired of arguing, charting, vindicating. 'Je ne sais plus me reposer,' he went on fretting, 'mon seul repos est de changer de travail, le seul remède à la souffrance.' His friend Roger Martin du Gard scolded him, trying to dissuade him from ever joining the French Academy: 'Fais attention, mon vieux. Ouvre l'œil. Ecarte les flatteurs et ressaisis-toi. Si tu veux t'asseoir chez la vieille dame tu es définitivement foutu, et ton œuvre sera derrière toi' (12 January 1928). 'Tu es un véritable ami,' Duhamel replied despairingly, 'mais ton conseil est administré comme un coup de bâton. Je ne crâne pas, je gronde, je vais hurler.' The friendship lasted, although, as will be revealed, at a heavy cost.

> *Les amitiés littéraires reposent toutes*
> *plus ou moins sur le mensonge, du*
> *moins sur les précautions et les*
> *prudences, et c'est pourquoi elles*
> *sont illusoires: elles n'existent pas.*
> François Mauriac: *Bloc-Notes*

During *ADAM*'s final research for the present number, an eminent literary historian, Arlette Lafay, produced a meticulously annotated edition of the entire correspondence between Georges Duhamel and Roger Martin du Gard, *Témoins d'un temps troublé, 1919–1958* (500 pages, Editions Minard, 1987). This outstanding work of scholarship is, alas, one more illustration of Mauriac's cynical comment quoted above. Indeed, beyond the illuminating exchange of views concerning the creative endeavours and achievements of two great artists, one glimpses only too frequently the painful side of a needling relationship.

The fact that – probably lacking the courage to call on Gide for practical advice – Martin du Gard, as early as 1913, appealed to his *perpétuel ami* to read his major work while it was still in manuscript form, flattered

Duhamel. In 1948, Martin du Gard recalled 'le soir où je t'ai infligé l'analyse détaillée des 36 volumes que je projetais d'écrire pour *Les Thibault.*' Here is Duhamel's version of the same episode. 'Il me pria d'être son premier lecteur. Je me rendis avec élan à cette invitation. Un cahier sur les genoux, je prenais des notes, aiguisais mes critiques, vivais parmi les rêves et les fantômes familiers de mon ami.' (*Revue de Paris*, December 1952). In March 1928, Duhamel spent one more 'laborious time' reading new drafts but found that the work 'added nothing new to the great naturalistic novel'. Roger, for his part, knowing how little Gide cared for the author of *Salavin* and obviously inclined to amuse the Master, told him slightly mockingly that he was eagerly awaiting the visit of the *automobiliste Duhamel*, 'lequel vient corriger les *fautes d'ortographe'* [my italics]; 'Il est irremplaçable,' he added, 'pour cet office. Il me revoit mes textes avec une conscience de correcteur d'imprimerie et une science de puriste *incomparable* [my italics]. C'est un Littré à lunettes.' The same night, Duhamel consigned to his *Diary*: '*Les Thibault* – aussi bien que possible, et pourtant je crois que c'est un immense effort sur une forme d'art épuisée. C'est quand même une grande œuvre [*sic*]'. Roger's criticisms of his friend's works were no less severe ('Vous écrivez trop et vous vous habituez à n'être plus assez difficile; trop de complaisance et de générosité, une tendance à prêcher'); they were all administered with a scalpel-like directness! He couldn't help, he admitted, using stern words, but nonetheless he was quite happy to anticipate that 'Nous vieillirons comme une vieille paire d'amis'. One year later (September 16, 1929), another *cri de cœur*: 'Sache que je traverse un dur défilé en ce moment. Un mot de toi me ferait du bien.' The answer came the following day: 'Je suis désolé de savoir que tu es en panne. Conserve-toi pour les amis qui t'aiment de tout leur cœur même quand tu les comprends mal.' Suddenly an unexpected remark: 'Ce qu'il y a de secret dans ma vie n'est pas dans ma correspondance.' Then back to the diary: '17 septembre. Roger s'est donné pour mission de peindre les passions. L'idée qu'il pourrait n'en pas avoir l'inquiète beaucoup. Ce brave homme casanier, méticuleux, déjà obèse, se plaît volontiers à croire qu'il est le vase de tous les vices. Il fait des pieds et des mains pour se donner quelques aventures, et se donner ainsi l'illusion d'une vie tourmentée, tragique. Telle que doit l'avoir l'auteur des *Thibault*'.

However, despite so many mutual strictures, the two friends took their 'belles et vivantes querelles' in their stride. Georges wrote: 'Tu es parmi les plus généreux des amis, un des derniers avec qui j'éprouve quelque plaisir à parler de mon art, auquel j'ai donné ma vie.' A moving message followed, addressed to his *vieux frère Roger* (September 1931): 'Il y a tant de sécurité dans l'amitié qu'on se retrouve toujours.' There were moments when they even came close to admiration for each other's writing. Martin du Gard was ready to admit that, in Salavin, 'Duhamel a créé peut-être [*sic*] un type immortel' (*Les Nouvelles Littéraires*, 1935), whereas Duhamel, more generously disposed, wrote: 'Roger Martin du Gard par son œuvre honore les lettres françaises' (*Mercure de France*, 1936). Unfortunately the bomb exploded by the perennially unpredictable Swedish Academy threw a number of French authors, including Valéry, Romains and Duhamel, into utter disarray: the Nobel Prize for literature landed in Roger Martin du Gard's courtyard. Only a few hours before the name of the new laureate was announced, the newspaper *L'Intransigeant* informed its readers that 'Au cours de ces derniers mois il a été beaucoup question chez les 18 [the eighteen members of the Nobel Committee] de Georges Duhamel.' And when, several weeks later (December 8), Duhamel visited Bergson (winner of the much-coveted prize in 1927), the ailing philosopher told him: 'J'ai eu une déception. Je pensais que vous auriez le Prix Nobel. J'apprécie les ouvrages de Martin du Gard, mais je pensais que c'était vous qui l'auriez.' At least there was some consolation for Duhamel in his disappointment to know that Bergson considered him 'le romancier de l'époque'. According to Lafay, the letter or telegram of congratulations which Duhamel undoubtedly must have sent to the winner 'n'a pas été retrouvée'.

The relationship between the two lived on. Georges in 1953 expressed his anxiety: 'Te verrai-je encore en ce monde? Je me le demande parfois.' A painful reply from Roger: 'Cher vieil ami, je ne t'oublie pas. Simplement je *vieillis*. Tu verras comme elle va vite quand elle commence, la dégringolade.' Mercilessly, the signs of bodily decay crept up on both, making life a misery – Martin du Gard, bedridden for long periods, with fits of suffocation, '*méchamment éprouvé, abattu la proie d'une grande somnolence:* je m'attends au pire … je n'ai même plus l'espoir d'avoir le temps de mourir avant le sinistre' – Duhamel, who suffered practically all his life from an injured vocal chord (so much so that his wife often felt that he would have given up most of his honours if only he could have recovered his voice), also becoming an invalid. Distressing as their physical condition was, more disturbing still is Arlette Lafay's conclusion that both Duhamel and Martin du Gard, undoubted masters of the French novel for more than a generation of readers, are now amongst the Great Forgotten.

● ● ●

Admittedly, the creative process can never be a smooth one, and what most readers look for in a writer's *notes de travail* are intimations of his unnerving struggle with the demons of doubt. ('If a writer loses his doubts,' Arthur Koestler believed, 'then he is finished.' *Writers at Work*, Penguin). But this is rarely to be found in Duhamel's *Livre de bord*. 'Je m'applique,' he wrote, 'à ne glisser ici ni méditations, ni découvertes fatiques. Nulles pensées; des faits, ce que l'on peut raconter après une journée de fatigue, quand il reste encore une goutte de courage au bout de la langue.' His *Logbook* is largely a record of incidents related to fellow-writers constantly asking for favours concerning their careers and social ambitions.

Here are a few morsels illustrating the intrigues and gossip that only too often afflict literary life in France: '*27 oct 1927*. Gallimard me prie de pousser la candidature de Durtain au Prix Goncourt. *16.2.28*. Réunion du Prix de la Renaissance. Je pose la candidature de Durtain avec énergie. D'abord en pleine séance, puis auprès de chacun des types. Chaude bataille préparatoire. *12 juin 1929*. Prévost me demande mon appui pour le Prix de la Renaissance. Pourquoi pas? *12 janvier 1929*. Chamson qui, après une longue conversation assez cordiale bien que très businessman, finit par me demander s'il a des chances au Prix de la Renaissance. Hélas, comme il est difficile d'être aimé pour soi-même. *29 mars*. Réunion préparatoire du jury de la Renaissance. Le fait que Martin du Gard soit candidat oblige un peu tout le monde à voter pour lui. Je joue sans pudeur de cette corde après m'être bien assuré que Prévost n'a aucune chance de passer. *7 mai*. Je vais à Paris pour le Prix de la Renaissance. J'avais promis à Jean Prévost de faire tout ce que je pourrais pour lui. Je l'ai fait longuement. J'ai vu tout de suite que cette candidature n'avait aucune chance et, en effet, Prévost n'a obtenu que deux voix. Comme parmi les autres candidats il y avait au moins Jolinon qui est bon copain et semblait avoir des chances, j'ai décidé d'abandonner Prévost et de m'unir à Dorgelès pour faire passer Jolinon. Ça n'a pas été sans les plus grandes difficultés. Il a encore fallu quatre ou cinq tours de scrutin pour arriver à éliminer le nommé Rival avec sa *Reine Margot*. A part ça le déjeuner a été très gai, très amical. *8 octobre 1930*. Visite de Prévost. Il a grossi. On voit déjà la longue figure de l'homme. Je lui dis: "Vous êtes intelligent, vous écrivez bien, mais vous n'êtes pas sympathique et l'on dirait que vous prenez à tâche de décourager ceux qui pourraient s'intéresser à vous. Le nombre de ceux que vous avez maltraités ou déçus va croissant ..." Il sourit le pauvre et, tout aussitôt, il me parle du Prix Goncourt et me demande expressément de le recommander à Descaves; "Quant à Ajalbert," dit-il, "Gallimard s'en charge, l'ayant acheté." Il parle sans cesse de ses trois petits-enfants comme d'un fait social qui crée des obligations à tout le monde.' An endless saga.

Many other people infuriated Duhamel, as he thought that they behaved below his expectations and principles. Here is an angry comment on one of his oldest friends, the composer and conductor Albert Doyen, who had exerted a great influence on Duhamel by widening his musical knowledge and music appreciation. '*17 nov. 1929*. Pendant plus de vingt ans j'ai sans lâcher pied soutenu Doyen contre tous et contre lui-même. Il n'a jamais passé ma porte que pour me demander des services. Il m'est devenu indifférent du jour au lendemain. J'en ai assez de ces gens à lubies, à caprices dont j'ai souffert toute ma vie.' At times Duhamel saw himself 'assez dépourvu [*sic*] d'un certain esprit d'aggression' and free of sarcasm, 'dont l'empire est grand chez nous et l'usage toujours facile.' Nonetheless, when dining with Paul Reynaud he couldn't help pointing out that he had 'l'air d'un petit chacal – hélas, ce n'est pas ce bonhomme-là qui sauvera la France.' The same evening (May 5th 1938) he was vexed by another presence at a table close by: 'Nous voyons s'installer le duc de Windsor, ex-roi d'Angleterre et empereur avec sa pernicieuse petite femme. L'ancien monarque a l'air d'un garçon de café. On ne peut pas regarder sans mépris ce déserteur du trône.' Anthony Eden disappointed him for a different reason (May 1939): 'Il y a quelque chose de féminin dans sa manière de faire la séduction. Malgré de si grands dons physiques il n'est pas sûr que ce beau jeune homme (40 à 43 ans) serait un bon conducteur de peuples.'

There were moments when he noticed a lack of understanding in himself 'que je reproche si volontiers aux autres'. Commenting on Paul Valéry (May 1938), he spoke of his 'douce lâcheté'; then he wrote: 'J'honore sa merveilleuse intelligence et pourtant il me choque par je ne sais quelle avidité.' Fortunately, not all entries were strictly consistent – the sullenness expressed one day gave way shortly after to a more serene mood, as in this hilarious picture of the author of *Le cimetière marin*, gazing at the not-so-blue Danube in Budapest: 'Valéry est à l'âge où les gens nerveux ne peuvent pas ne point penser à leur vessie (de manière générale à leurs réservoirs et à leurs sphinctères). Il y pense et il parle bien: les longues cérémonies académiques sont un supplice pour les vieux académiciens et ils en crèvent. A l'enterrement de Foch j'en étais moi-même torturé. Mais les autres! Leur vessie était peinte sur leur visage. Poincaré en est mort.'

He was also critical of de Gaulle, who, as first President of the Fifth Republic, particularly as constitutional 'Patron' of the French Academy, had often sought his advice. 'Il n'est pas beau, même le front est étrangement étroit, mais il a de l'air,' he wrote in 1949. On one occasion, after diagnosing the general's need of a bilateral cataract extraction, he commented: 'Il ne sourit presque jamais. Je l'ai vu un certain nombre de fois, je ne l'ai jamais entendu rire. Ce n'est pas de la froideur, c'est plutôt quelque chose d'inhumain.'

The fiercest entries are those on Jules Romains and André Gide, the author's *bêtes noires*. 'De bon cœur j'aide quelques amis. Je l'ai fait quand Romains a souhaité d'entrer à l'Académie. C'était justice sans doute, mais il y avait aussi chez moi un vif désir d'avoir la paix, de faire le nécessaire pour que Romains n'eût rien à envier. Même au repos, de toute sa courte personne, il exprime l'ambition effrénée, maladive.' The sad erosion of this *amitié douloureuse*, as described by Professor Bernard Duhamel, who edited the *Livre de l'amertume*, originated in the sceptical attitude taken in 1921 by Duhamel and other people in the medical profession when Romains announced that he possessed extra-sensory powers – a *vision extra-rétinienne*. It is also worth recalling the fact that the author of *Les hommes de bonne volonté*, the longest stream-novel in any literature – twenty-seven volumes poured out between 1932 and 1946 'as though a tap had been turned on and the author was a duct' – made his debut with *La vie unanime*, a book of poems set and printed in 1908 by his 'vieux frère', twenty-year-old Duhamel at the Abbaye, the short-lived community of dreamers at Créteil. Forty years later, he had become 'un voyou intelligent, une bête sauvage'. Need one add that Romains lost little time when, during an intimate supper in honour of Gide, he informed his guest that 'Duhamel ne perd jamais de vue sa carrière, jamais d'imprudence surtout.' 'Ah! l'imprudence,' Gide remarked mischievously. 'Comme je prise l'imprudence, si peu d'êtres en sont vraiment capables.' Romains, whose poetry was warmly greeted by Gide in the very first issue of the *Nouvelle Revue Française* (January 1909) – 'Je tiens ce livre de débutant pour un des plus significatifs que nous ait donnés la génération qui s'élève' – did not hesitate, though, to spill in his autobiographical book *Amitiés et rencontres* (1970), one of his last drops of venom over the founder of the *NRF*.[3]

Furthermore, in 1946, freshly elected to the Academy, he couldn't resist making yet another nasty remark about Gide: 'Jules R, qui sait tout, nous a dit qu'il avait *interrogé* [my italics] les gens de la police et qu'il n'existait pas un dossier Gide dans les cartons de ces messieurs' (Duhamel's *Diary*).

Here we are. Two major figures, who made their literary debuts at the same time and, occasionally, had a good word to say about each other, in their years of achievement behaved like two 'écorchés vifs'. (Georges writing to Jules: 'Tu as fait une carrière magnifique à laquelle j'applaudis. Je ne me plains pas de la mienne. Le monde est assez grand pour nous deux.' But was it?...) Commenting in *Le Monde* on literary backbiting, a much respected critic and academician, Bertrand Poirot-Delpech, asked this painful question: 'D'où vient que les écrivains français, car c'est un sport national, s'abaissent à tant de mesquineries? C'est le métier qui le veut. Les catholiques brillent à ces joutes de préaux, sans doute par goût des repentirs compliqués. Mauriac était le champion de la rosserie aussitôt regrettée, la main sur la bouche, mais décrochée quand même.' He then singled out a rarity amidst the fauna: 'Le protestant André Chamson réussit dans *Il faut vivre vieux* à ne pas dire l'aube d'une méchanceté sur qui que ce soit.' At the other end of the spectrum – one could find the enriching metaphors of an artist famous for the elegance with which he tamed his most ferocious enemies: 'Si je pouvais haïr je ne saurais haïr que la haine. Brouille, brouille, brouille. Elle naît presque toujours d'un malentendu qui s'allonge par le fait que les protagonistes s'éloignent l'un de l'autre. Les griefs se fabriquent d'eux-mêmes et la réconciliation, si facile au début, devient difficile à la longue.' The poet concluded with legitimate pride: 'Il m'est arrivé de débrouiller les brouilles' (Jean Cocteau, *De la brouille*, Liège, 1960).

While conceding that contemporary life in this country has often been punctuated by the thrusts and parries of such skilled duellists as Wyndham Lewis, D. H. Lawrence,[4] Roy Campbell, F. R. Leavis ('If nothing had been known but Pope's works,' the embittered Cambridge don remarked in *Scrutiny*, 'would envy, venom, malice, spite and the rest have played so large a part in the commentary?'), Edith Sitwell, Geoffrey Grigson, to name only a few, one must admit that the art of mayhem appears to be less obnoxious on this side of the Channel.[5] Talking of Pope, in a masterly analysis of eighteenth-century literary feuding and of *The Dunciad* in particular, Cyril Connolly used a memorable epigram: *nothing dates like hate.*

Long before Cocteau, in *Conseils aux jeunes littérateurs*, Baudelaire tried to appease his contemporaries in a more dramatic manner: 'La haine,' he wrote, 'est une liqueur précieuse, un poison plus cher que celui des Borgia – car il est fait avec notre sang, notre santé, notre sommeil et les deux tiers de notre amour! Il faut en être avare!'

• • •

Back to one of the most deep-rooted and mildly enraging rituals performed by any chosen French author who knows that, sooner or later, he too will have to knock at a number of doors. At last, it was Georges Duhamel's turn:

'*15 nov.* Visite à Bourget, à Hermant, à Bergson, trois d'un seul coup, à une heure d'intervalle. Ça va très vite, et c'est très amusant, parce que je ne suis pas du tout décidé à me présenter. Hermant adore l'intrigue, rien qu'à parler des jeux académiques, il jubile. Je comprends qu'il sait où, sans rancune, se présenter sept ou huit fois. Si Benoit passe c'est parce qu'il a consenti à ne pas se présenter avant Chaumeix. Alors on lui doit quelque chose. Tous les gens que j'ai vus prononcent la même phrase étonnante: Benoit a si bien fait sa petite cuisine que c'est à peu près sûr de passer. Personne pour avoir une autre opinion, qui serait par exemple littéraire. C'est à mourir de rire. *18 nov.* Marcel Prévost m'a bien entendu parlé de l'Académie. –Nous espérons faire enfin passer un homme jeune, Pierre Benoit. Il est prudent, si vous le voulez bien, de ne pas

troubler notre jeu car sûrement vous lui enlèveriez des voix. Attendez
un peu et quand je jugerai le moment convenable ...' The race continues: 'Ce même matin j'ai vu Barthou. Il a l'air antipathique mais rusé et
somme toute intelligent ... Venez-vous me faire une visite académique?
–Sûrement non, mais ça pourrait arriver. –Eh bien, la chose est claire.
La fois prochaine, je ne prendrai d'engagement avant de vous avoir vu.
19 nov. Rendez-vous avec Poincaré. Il paraît que je suis de ceux que l'on
ne pourra pas faire attendre. Il m'est tout acquis, bien entendu. Si j'avais
pris rang avant Benoit mes chances auraient été plus considérables. *21
nov.* J'ai vu Nolhac. Il me dit: ma règle est la suivante, je vote d'abord
pour mes vieux amis et puis, ce devoir accompli, je vote le tour suivant,
pour le bien de l'Académie. Benoit passera dans un sourire général,
mais il passera.' A brighter interlude: Jules Cambon (1845–1935) was
elected in 1918, and towards the end of his colourful *vie mondaine* had
reasons to feel sorry for himself – 'J'ai vécu parmi les duchesses et maintenant j'obéis aux infirmières.' He startled the young, ambitious Benoit
by asking him: 'Pourquoi vous dépêchez-vous d'entrer à l'Académie? La
vie est si longue.'

Four years later the game started in earnest, with Duhamel both
player and dupe. '*17 oct, 1934.* On a tué Barthou il y a huit jours et
Poincaré est mort avant-hier. Il paraît que je perds sûrement une voix,
peut-être deux. Régnier m'a confié sous le sceau du plus grand secret
que Bourget est dans une clinique et qu'il va peut-être mourir. Ce n'est
pas la foire aux fauteuils, c'est plutôt la foire aux cercueils.' Duhamel
began to have doubts, was almost ready to give up. 'Ce traffic d'influences est horrible,' he decided: 'Je sens grandir un fort et salubre désir
de me retirer de tout ça.' And yet 'Quelque chose me dit que je combat-
trai peut-être' [*sic*]. His friend Mauriac thought that it was too late to
withdraw. 'Il écarte avec horreur l'idée d'une retraite. Est-ce par humil-
ité chrétienne qu'il me dit à tout instant en me touchant l'épaule, "Vous
êtes plus grand que moi par le talent"? Je lui dis, "J'étais il y a deux mois
un grand seigneur des lettres, et maintenant je suis un solliciteur." Il
répond comme tous: "Barrès a échoué une première fois et ce n'était pas
un petit bonhomme".' Mauriac is further quoted, this time with regard
to Paul Claudel's candidature. After a typical first volley – 'Ce grand
bonhomme est une brute' – the author of *Le baiser au lépreux* told a number of fellow-academicians that it would be safer to prevent the great
poet from exposing himself to the traditional round of visits; and with
his irresistible mischievousness Mauriac explained: 'Si nous décidons
Claudel à se présenter à l'Académie, il ne faut plus qu'il fasse des visites: chaque fois qu'il fait une visite il perd une voix.'

• • •

On November 21, 1935 (having failed the year before to obtain a sufficient number of votes), Duhamel joined the immortals.[6] In his accept-
ance speech, he denounced 'le XXe siècle (qui) est brutal et hagard, pas
favorable à la lecture'. Judging from the many entries in the *Diary*, his
long academic span was marked by sharp changes of mood. In October
1937 he was complaining already: 'L'Académie me désespère et parfois
me dégoûte. Toute la bande des anciens pédérastes ... On sent bien que
tous ces gens sont incapables d'être d'accord sur quoi que ce soit; vraiment incapables d'élan, de raisonnements, d'actes volontaires – les trois
fonctions de l'âme!' There follows an irresistibly funny description of a
séance: 'En hiver, au crépuscule, l'Académie est lugubre. Il y a une table
dont la vue est presque macabre. Le maréchal Franchet dort debout
comme un soldat, évidemment. Le cardinal Baudrillart pique du nez
par secousses et finit par s'abattre, la face sur le tapis vert. Entre les
deux, le duc de la Force, immobile, a l'air d'un fantôme. Il dort les yeux
ouverts. On se demande avec horreur si l'on vit encore ou si l'on est déjà
parmi les ombres. Le cardinal Baudrillart est tout petit, enormément
ventré et le devant de son habit est fort sale, débris alimentaires. Son œil
brille d'une flamme que je connais bien, celle de la jalousie littéraire.'
Yet this and many other sorry sights did not in the least deter Duhamel
from canvassing on behalf of several prominent figures. Ignoring du
Gard's entreaty, twenty years earlier, he urged the author of *Les Thibault*
to present himself: 'Je te dis encore et avec insistance, songe à venir nous
rejoindre' (12, XI, 1944). Writing to Gide, a few days later, du Gard commented mockingly: 'Duhamel m'a convié à devenir académicien;
comme on est mal connu, hein?'

Unrepentant, having convinced himself that it would be a pity to let
the old house collapse – after all, it was 'une des plus vieilles institutions
de notre malheureuse France' – Duhamel went as far as to try and 'convert' the man he detested most, the 'maître de la pedérastie française'.

Another sample of the tragic-comic literary strategy in France.
'Quelque temps après l'élection de Claudel j'ai rendu visite à Gide pour
lui parler de l'Académie. L'idée de voir Gide une fois par semaine ne me
transportait pas d'enthousiasme, mais nous étions plusieurs à penser
que l'Académie doit présenter une sorte d'inventaire de la littérature et
que Gide est, de toute manière, une des figures marquantes de ce temps.
Bien que j'eusse déjà quitté le fauteuil de Secrétaire perpétuel, je venais
de remporter plusieurs succès quasiment "personnels", les élections de
Claudel, de Romains, de Mondor. J'étais encore sur ma lancée. Ce devait
être, si je ne me trompe pas, à l'automne de 1946 ou au printemps de
1947. J'engageai la conversation sans la moindre précaution oratoire,
disant en substance: "Nous avons un fauteuil pour vous. Si la chose vous
agrée, vous serez sûrement élu. Nul ne s'avisera d'exiger de vous une

visite. Parmi les gens de votre génération, si je mets à part ceux qui sont morts tôt, les autres sont venus à l'Académie. Claudel vient d'y entrer. Je ne me fais d'illusion sur l'Académie, la proposition que je vous fais, elle est surtout pour moi une affaire de discipline, j'entends de discipline pour la vie des lettres françaises." A ce petit discours Gide répondit d'abord par un silence, puis par des mots non sans hésitation: "Eh bien! ... non ... non, Duhamel ... Je suis trop vieux ... Il n'est plus temps ... Ah! je ne dis pas que si l'on m'avait offert le siège de Valéry ... Mais puisque le siège de Valéry a été donné, alors, je renonce ...'" It took Duhamel some time to realise that he had been taken for a ride. Indeed, at that time Gide, 'l'illustre vieux singe, le prix Nobel (et) une élection à l'Académie, aurait sûrement compromis la machination Nobel.' He consoled himself by reflecting that there was not a single homosexual among his close friends. 'A l'Académie peut-être, mais l'Académie est un omnibus, ce n'est pas une famille d'amis choisis.'

A year later, ... Duhamel preferred to think that 'le Prix Nobel a somme toute sauvé cette malheureuse Académie de la honte et du ridicule'. What he was unaware of was the fact that, as early as 1919, friends of Gide had insisted that he put his candidature forward. 'Mais c'est un impératif,' voiced Mme Jeanne Muhfled, the excitable hostess of a highly manipulatory literary *salon* (competing fiercely with the one presided over by Natalie Clifford Barney); 'Il faut que vous y entriez, quelqu'un qui écrit comme vous!' – followed by Gide's disingenuous excuse, 'Non, ce n'est pas dans ma ligne, je m'y déformerais, et puis, je ne veux entrer nulle part d'où l'on pourrait me chasser, ce qui pourrait bien arriver!' Indeed, had he joined the Company, who knows how the more conservative fellow-academicians might have reacted to the gospel of *Corydon* ...? What 'ce bon Duhamel', as he was mockingly described in the *Journal*, also seems to have forgotten – or misunderstood? – was the sarcastic letter in which Gide asked him to ... congratulate the Academy for having chosen him among the immortals!

What a distressing pleasure to stand on the edge of a literary battle-field and compare what a writer has confided to his *Diary* about a particular 'cher confrère' with what that other person has written down, perhaps at the same time, in his own notebook or diary. Gide could not guess how he would appear in the *Book of Bitterness*, thirty years after his death, whereas Duhamel had been smouldering for many years, each time he remembered how little he counted for with the High Priest of the *NRF*. 'J'ai parlé de la perfidie de Gide,' he lamented, 'je ne rêve pas. Chaque fois qu'il a senti ou compris que j'allais marquer des points, il a, très discrètement d'ailleurs, posé des mines flottantes. Quand j'ai publié *Cécile parmi nous*, j'ai pu constater, en France comme à l'étranger, que Gide avait tout de suite, et par provision, prononcé un jugement défavorable.' It is worth mentioning that, as early as 1912, the *Journal* recorded that Duhamel (who had already been published by Gallimard) actually attended an editorial session of the *NRF*, together with Alain- Fournier and Fargue, while Gide himself was busy checking the subscribers' lists … Shortly afterwards, in a letter to a friend, the poet François-Paul Alibert, Gide dismissed 'ce grand niais qui a nom Duhamel', only to report (November 23, 1920) a stimulating encounter in the Luxembourg Gardens: 'Excellente conversation sur le roman; Duhamel comme moi se débat contre les critiques de Martin du Gard. Il proteste que ces petits récits épurés que Martin du Gard critique ont plus d'espoir de durer que le complexe roman que je souhaite d'écrire aujourd'hui.' In several recently discovered letters addressed by Gide to Duhamel, one is not surprised to come across the usual conventional words, such as 'Croyez à mon affection bien fidèle', or 'Très heureux de vous revoir – surtout si je pouvais vous être utile en quoi que ce soit'. However, there is one letter from Cuverville (June 26, 1926) in which Gide praised *Lettres au Patagon* – 'Les pages sur le nationalisme sont parfaites (et) j'aurai plaisir à les citer, car je ne sache qu'on ait écrit rien de plus sensé sur ce sujet.'

• • •

Shortly after the *Livre de l'amertume* came out in 1984 – the year celebrating the author's birth centenary – Professor Lafay published a provocative survey entitled *La sagesse de Georges Duhamel* (Editions Minard, 500 pages), an analysis in depth of the totality of the oeuvre. This compelling study also highlighted many instances of the vituperation and abuse to which Duhamel had for so long been subjected. Between the two world wars, and particularly in the 1950s, he received harsh treatment at the hands of some of his French contemporaries. In the gossip beehives of the Saint Germain literary cafés, Jean-Paul Sartre, seldom reluctant to savage a fellow writer if the opportunity arose (one cannot forget, for instance, his attack on Albert Camus), was at one stage alleged to have anointed Duhamel one of the *sept péchés capitaux de la France*, next to de Gaulle. Many more vicious labels accumulated in the catalogue of *vacheries*. A ferocious one – *romancier des familles nombreuses* – came from Paul Léautaud, renowned hater of fellow-writers, unsurpassed *canaille* of the Parisian literary scene. But the most inexplicable was the violent and inept onslaught by Denis Saurat, a friend of long standing, when he wrote: 'Salavin? abominable bonhomme, un fou qui n'est pas encore enfermé' (*Marsyas*, 1934).

The discerning reader will no doubt find for himself countless samples of duhamelian wisdom in Arlette Lafay's well-documented study; however, more significant than these is the disclosure of a lesser-known aspect of the author's emotional life: his mortifying spiritual torment, his *poignante tristesse* confronting our mad and criminal world.[7] 'Il a perdu le cœur de toute sa vie, sa foi en l'homme,' commented the critic Dominique Bona. The *Diary* ended with these despairing words: 'Les civilisations croulent comme des pyramides de sable et le sable s'envole au vent.'

• • •

Fortunately, a last glimpse in this tortuous, sad story offers a truly serene note. The heroine of *Cécile parmi nous* (the seventh volume in the Pasquier cycle, which Gide so intensely disliked) has been living in this country for the last fifty years – on the banks of the Thames! What a moment – to come face to face with the reality of an enchanting fictional character. In the novel she appears only as a diaphanous Mozart player who teaches the piano. An unforgettable instance occurs in Chapter viii, when she beseeches one of her pupils, 'Mais non, Gertrude, faites le silence autour de vous, faites le silence en vous, purifiez le monde entier par un grand et calme silence.' Cécile actually studied both the piano and the violin at the Paris Conservatoire under an extraordinary teacher, Simone Plé-Caussade. (A prolific composer herself, counting Pierre Boulez among her pupils, she finally joined a Carmelite Order and died as recently as 1986, aged ninety, under the name of Sœur Marie-de-l'-Incarnation.

> *Gide jusqu'à sa mort et même par-delà*
> *la mort n'a pas fini de nous surprendre*
> *et nous scandaliser.*
> François Mauriac: *Mémoires intérieures*

Taking leave of Duhamel's *Catalogue* of frustrations, one readily crosses the threshold and returns to that other artist for whom music also had a life-long fascination. 'Dans le doute,' Gide wrote, 'je retourne à l'étude du piano comme vers un opium où se calme la turbulence de mes pensées et j'apaise mon inquiet vouloir. J'y ai passé, chacun de ces jours derniers, quatre ou cinq heures – Concertos de Mozart, Orgelchoralvorspiele de Bach-Busoni et Goyescas de Granados' (*Journal*, 22 January 1931).

Nearly twenty years ago, in an issue covering the centenary of André Gide's birth (*ADAM*, Nos. 337–339), I propounded that, although he was a lesser creative artist, a study of his life would prove a much more daunting undertaking than Proust's. Such a work so far refuses to emerge, but one lives in hope ... Roger Martin du Gard warned us that 'La complexe personne de Gide sera difficile à cerner'. In the words of Jean Lambert (Gide's son-in-law), 'Peut-être un jour, quelque biographe idéal et patient ... quand tout ce qu'on pouvait dire sur Gide sera dit ...

(mais) nous sommes encore assez loin de ce jour' (*Gide familier*, 1958). A similarly cautious view was expressed by the late Arnold Naville (Gide's bibliographer): 'Il faudra beaucoup de temps pour que, dans le futur, quelqu'un qui ne l'aura pas connu puisse comprendre ce qu'il fut réellement, s'en imprégner, l'aimer et rendre alors vraiment vivante l'image qu'il laissera à l'histoire' (privately printed *Mémoire*, Geneva, 1952).

For the last thirty years, the supply of Gidean knowledge has been replenished in France by the omniscient Claude Martin, indefatigable secretary of the Association des Amis d'André Gide (Sainte Foy-les-Lyon, France), by the no less erudite Professor Daniel Moutote (Université Paul Valéry, Montpellier), in Canada by Professor Jacques Cotnam (York University, Toronto) and in this country by three younger scholars, Dr Peter Hoy (Merton College, Oxford), Dr Patrick Pollard (Birkbeck College, London) and Dr David Steel (Lancaster University). Since Gide's death in 1951, the bibliography has grown steadily. Long before his monumental work on Proust, George Painter wrote *André Gide, a critical biography* (1951 and 1958). It was followed by Justin O'Brien's 400-page study (1953); there was also the well-documented two-volume *Jeunesse d'André Gide* by the well-known psychiatrist Jean Delay, member of the French Academy (1958). As to Pierre de Boisdeffre's *Vie d'André Gide, vol 1: Avant la fondation de la NRF* (1970), one refuses to imagine that, even after a delay of twenty years, there will be no sequel to this laborious enterprise. On the other hand, between 1945 and 1977 four invaluable volumes of recollections appeared: *Les Cahiers de la Petite Dame, Notes pour l'histoire authentique d'André Gide, 1919–1951*. Although some Gidean experts seem inclined to treat a number of the disclosures as romantic exaggerations, one is grateful nonetheless to be able to juxtapose this 3000-page panorama by a twentieth-century 'Boswell-Eckermann' with Gide's own *Diaries*. The author was the formidable Maria van Rysselberghe (1866–1959), referred to in Gide's *Journal* as Mme Théo. For nearly forty years she was the closest witness and confidante of Gide's private and intellectual life. He, the chain-smoker of cigarettes, she addicted to the pipe, they occupied adjacent apartments interconnected in the same house at 1 bis rue Vaneau in the seventh arrondissement. Every day they met for long hours, playing patience or exchanging comments on innumerable literary figures of the time. 'Nous sommes pareils,' Gide once told her, 'en ceci que nous mettons toute notre sagesse au service de nos folies.' If one sometimes wonders whether indeed the Petite Dame's remarks cover only what Gide may have been too inhibited to find space for in his *Journal* – according to André Malraux, 'Le *Journal* de Gide est fait de ce que Gide ne pourrait pas noter, car nul ne se voit sans miroir' – one must nevertheless accept the references as being as close to the 'truth' as one might desire ...

• • •

Among the most relevant observations are naturally those relating to music. As is well known, all his life he was an inveterate amateur pianist. His *Diaries* abound in original remarks on piano practice and interpretation, with his interests insatiably spanning from Bach to Paul Dukas. Unlike the egregious Duhamel, who acquired the rudiments of music during the first world war in the trenches, Gide was bullied by his domineering mother to sit at the piano from an early age and do his 'gammes, arpèges et un peu de solfège'. After a tedious initial period under Mademoiselle de Goecklin – 'Elle était toute fluette, pâle et comme sur le point de se trouver mal, je crois qu'elle ne devait pas manger à sa faim' – the child was fortunately taken over by an inspiring teacher, Monsieur de Lanux, a former pupil of Liszt, through whom he may well have met Chopin, so movingly evoked in *Si le grain ne meurt* and also portrayed as Monsieur La Pérouse in *Les faux-monnayeurs*. Gide played mostly for himself, although occasionally he felt the need to 'perform' for a few friends. For instance, in January 1907: 'Jean Schlumberger, je m'efforce à lui jouer les *Variations* de Paul Dukas et parviens à ne m'énerver pas trop sur les premières.' He tells Mme Théo: 'Ah! que je voudrais arriver à jouer avec assurance devant autrui, comme quand je suis seul!' La Petite Dame relates on May 9th, 1922: 'Roger Fry et sa fille Pamela à dîner. C'est cordial et sans beaucoup d'intérêt; pour leur faire plaisir, Gide essaye de jouer de l'Albeniz et du Granados, mais il est si nerveux qu'il ne peut continuer.' According to her, 'Il passe environ deux heures par jour au piano; quelle infinie patience dans sa manière d'étudier avec des mains sans souplesse.' Gide himself found, however, that 'Il est inutile, fâcheux même, de s'obstiner trop longtemps de suite sur un même passage; mieux vaut y revenir et souvent, c'est à cela que se reconnaît la patience'. One soon gets an intimation of Gide's jealousy and fear of professionals. *14 mai 1921*: 'Je suis resté découragé, sans plus oser rouvrir le piano de douze jours. Qu'on s'étonne après cela si je n'aime pas les pianistes! Toute la joie qu'ils me donnent c'est rien auprès de celle que je me donne en jouant moi-même; mais en les entendant je prends honte de mon jeu. Mais il va de même quand je lis Proust; je hais la virtuosité, mais toujours elle m'en impose et je voudrais pour la bien mépriser en être d'abord capable. Je *sais* et *sens* par exemple que la *Bacarolle* de Chopin doit être jouée beaucoup plus lentement que ne fait Mlle X, qu'ils en font tous; mais pour oser la jouer devant d'autres aussi *loisiblement* qu'il me plaît, il me faudrait savoir que je pourrais aussi bien la jouer plus vite, et surtout sentir que l'auditeur en est convaincu. Jouée de ce train la musique de Chopin devient brillante, perd sa valeur propre, sa vertu ...' Whereas musicians like Milhaud and

Nadia Boulanger agreed with much of Gide's approach to Chopin, there were others who didn't take his views too seriously. If one can more or less understand the impatient reaction of a universally acclaimed interpreter of Chopin's music like Arthur Rubinstein, when he described Gide as 'a frustrated and embittered amateur pianist who has tried in vain to dominate the difficult keyboard for the last sixty years' (*New York Times*, October 16, 1949), one finds it more difficult to accept and forgive the vicious comment of someone who collaborated with Gide on an opera, *Perséphone*: 'That Gide understood nothing whatever about music in general is apparent to anyone who has read his *Notes on Chopin*' (Stravinsky, in *Memories and Commentaries*). Two years before his death, Gide read with keen interest a lengthy analysis of his ideas on Chopin written by the well-known pianist and pedagogue Yvonne Lefebure (*Contrepoint*, No. 6, 1949).

• • •

Of particular interest are Mme Théo's notes on Youra Guller, the legendary Roumanian-born pianist, the equal of Clara Haskil and Dinu Lipatti. Schnabel, Rubinstein, Solomon and many other contemporaries spoke with awe of her magical tone. She entered the Paris Conservatoire at the age of ten and, two years later, won the Premier Prix – 'Cette enfant n'a plus rien à apprendre,' decided Gabriel Fauré. She gave her first concert in this country on October 13, 1923, in the series of Wigmore Hall Recitals by Great Pianists, which included in the same month Busoni, Paderewsky, Rosenthal, Sauer, Bauer and Donhanyi. One of her devoted disciples, the Argentinian pianist and conductor Albert Portugeis, had the inspired idea of organising a Golden Jubilee Recital fifty years later in the same Hall, on the same day of the month; with the same programme. One of those rare musical experiences that enable one to come to terms with mankind.

Meeting Youra after that memorable evening in 1972 (she was then in her late seventies), I tried to make her reminisce about Gide, as I knew that she had often played at the Pontigny *Rencontres*, and on several occasions she had even partnered him in piano duets. 'Il aimait la musique,' was all that she was at first prepared to say, but in the end she became quite garrulous. She didn't have too many kind words for the Petite Dame, unaware at the time that her name would appear so frequently in the *Cahiers*. Here are some of the entries. August 1926: 'Je le trouve au salon étudiant avec Mme S[chiffrin] le final de la *Sonate en si bémol mineur* de Chopin. Il est fort frémissant, tout tremblant d'excitation, rempli de regrets d'être nerveux au point de ne pouvoir jouer devant plus de quelques personnes. Un autre soir Youra Guller joue deux sonates de Scarlatti et les deux premières parties de

Petroushka. Ici Gide est sans restrictions, tout à fait transporté ... *20 août*: Mme Schiffrin se met au piano. Elle joue un *Concerto* de Philip Emmanuel Bach, puis des mazurkas de Chopin. Je sens Gide content, approbateur ... *29 août*: Je lis sur le visage de Gide qu'il n'est plus content. Il dit, "Beaucoup de choses sont perdues, les mouvements sont trop rapides en vue de l'effet."' Inevitably, gossip was in the air – a welcome diversion for the Petite Dame. 'J'apprends que Gide s'est lié d'amitié avec les Schiffrin,'[8] she records on January 11, 1927, and points out that 'Son jugement sur eux semble pourtant suspendu; malgré leur réelle attirance, il trouve leur façons avec lui, il ne sait comment dire, à la fois Dostoevsky et aussi un peu sémite. Schiffrin, généreux, très grand seigneur dans ses procédés d'éditeur. Elle semble partie pour la grande passion, ce qui me donne, dit Gide, un trac abominable.' Things began to ... develop, at least in Mme Théo's imagination. She was thrilled to be able to record Gide's panic: 'Youra a dû jouer un peu gros pour me faire comprendre sa passion pour moi [September 11th 1927]; c'est certes une curieuse créature et je la tiens pour une grande comédienne. Vous allez voir que d'ici très peu de temps elle va avoir une grande aventure, c'est tout à fait le genre; ce ne sera pas avec moi et ce ne sera pas de ma faute. Je suis loin d'aimer toujours la manière dont elle joue.' The scenario changes in March 1928, when Gide informs his confidante: 'Youra et Sacha Schiffrin sont séparés; ils continuent pourtant à vivre ensemble. C'est Youra qui me l'a raconté d'un air assez frémissant, un jour que je déjeunais chez eux.' Two more episodes delectably told by Mme Théo: 'Youra l'a beaucoup engagé à aller la voir, mais très lâchement Gide s'est abstenu, redoutant les confidences et de devoir prendre parti. Il ne dit pas ce que je sens [*sic*].' Furthermore, at a meeting organised by the *Union pour la vérité*, Gide was seated 'à côté d'une jeune femme élégante, à laquelle il a fini par tourner le dos, un peu de son côté. Il se retourne, salue, sourit gauchement, ne reconnaissant pas la personne et bredouille de vagues paroles. Après la conférence, la voyant d'un peu plus loin, une lueur lui traverse l'esprit, il se rend compte que c'est Youra! Consterné, confus, il se confond en protestations, très exagérées naturellement. Un dialogue horriblement pénible.' Gide's own comment: 'Je ne savais quelle tête faire, genre Phèdre et Hippolyte. Je ne supporte pas du tout ça! Voila ce que c'est que de ne pas reconnaître les gens, ça me joue toujours de mauvais tours.'

• • •

The quotations concerning Gide's piano playing, as well as his rather histrionic relationship with Youra Guller, are only a small part of the source material in Mme Théo's *Cahiers* (described by Claude Martin as being 'sans équivalent dans l'histoire des lettres'). Students still looking for plausible clues to the innumerable hallucinatory episodes in Gide's life could do no better than resort – with caution sometimes – to the Petite Dame's revelations. She was an unusual character, worthy of a great novelist (Proust in particular would have adored spying on her insatiably, before introducing her in the *Recherche*). Think of it: from being the legitimate mother of Elisabeth van Rysselberghe, she became the common-law mother-in-law of Gide himself and common-law grandmother of his daughter, Catherine, to end as *legal* mother-in-law of Pierre Herbart, one of Gide's acolytes, who left his own uncompromising account of the great man, warts and all. Clearly no promiscuity there – just an amazing set-up. Admittedly, going through the *Cahiers* as available now, one often gets lost in the chronology, but as soon as a valiant scholar produces an index of the whole repertory of names and events (on the lines of Susan Stout's *Index to the Gide–Martin du Gard Correspondence*), the whole exercise will be a delight ...

Further glossing over Gide and music would exceed the already much-abused space. For the same reason, a great many equally intriguing aspects of his tortuous persona – an artist 'divisé contre lui-même' (Mauriac) – had to be discarded. Far from *ADAM* the absurd attempt of solving the, so far, unsolvable Gide puzzle. All that the preceding and following diffuse notes might nevertheless attain – in line with some other contentious issues in the past – is merely to indicate a few points still awaiting expert sifting and coordination.

An absorbing subject is surely the one dealing with *Gide and his women*. Like so many homosexuals in modern literary history, Gide appears to have enjoyed the adulation of the opposite sex, thus justifying Baudelaire's quip, 'L'amour des femmes intelligentes, c'est le plaisir des pédérastes.' Two women in particular, both of unusual intellect, Maria van Rysselberghe and Dorothy Bussy, were fiercely determined to 'own' him, and the many ways in which they tried to outdo each other savour of great fiction. Starting with Dorothy: to George Painter's moving portrayal of the burning *amoureuse* one must add Jean Lambert's masterly introduction to the English edition of the *Selected Letters* (1983). Taking little heed of her husband's belief that here was possibly a high priest 'qui trichait avec le Diable', she fell hopelessly in love with Gide when, aged fifty-three, she first met him in 1918, at the time he had eloped to this country with his eighteen-year-old lover, Marc Allegret. What a scenario! Her thirty years of anguish were truly Racinean in their poignancy.

Of Gide's two competing ladies, Dorothy perhaps had the edge of jealousy. As she never received the faintest response to the declarations of love flowing from her letters, she once exploded, 'Don't you ever give a thought to what love and passion are?'. Gide's priceless comment: 'Elle a peut-être raison! J'aurais cinquante et un ans dans deux jours et je ne me connais pas encore!'

Another outburst in the correspondence occurred when Gide seemed to have disregarded a manuscript she had sent him in December 1933. 'I have written a book,' she confided, *"deadly secret"*. It isn't long and won't take you half an hour to read.' It is doubtful, though, whether he realised the artistic qualities of this little masterpiece: a largely autobiographical novel which came out anonymously, *Olivia* by Olivia (Hogarth Press, London 1949), amid general acclaim. The author's understandable scorn and irony – 'By now, perhaps you will have the glory of having rejected two bestsellers, Proust and yours truly' – must have shaken Gide, for he tried to expiate in his inimitable way. 'J'ai commis parfois de si grossières, de si impardonnables erreurs vis-à-vis de Proust et Dorothy Bussy.'

For years Mme Bussy was dying to embrace him, but each time she came near him, she would freeze before the rigid mask on his face. Towards the end of her life, she finally found the courage to kiss ... the lapel of his overcoat! 'It was a greater pleasure to me, oh much, than kissing your face,' she wrote afterwards; 'and I daresay that in reality that's a symbol of my whole attitude. I like watching your face. I know it so well. I have such a collection of its expressions. There's one missing. I deeply horribly regret it ... – but don't let me become like your Youra!'

Through her exquisite translations of most of his major works, Dorothy Bussy did more than anyone else to consolidate Gide's fame in the Anglo-Saxon world. (Painter dedicated his translation of *Prométhée mal enchaîné*, 1952, to DB, 'incomparable translator, one of the most remarkable women of her generation'.) However, during Gide's visit to Oxford in 1947, to receive his Honoris Causa doctorate, she tried everything to keep him only for herself. In restrained but amusing language, Lambert recalled the ostracism he and his wife Catherine (Gide's daughter) had to endure while awaiting the day of Convocation. Mme Bussy also contrived, but with limited success, to minimise the decisive role played by an impassioned rival, Dr Enid Starkie. A full-blooded *éminence grise* – the *Listener* called her a 'master canvasser' – Enid fought tooth and nail to beat the Establishment and secure Gide's election.

It didn't take Dr. Starkie long to show that she, too, could assert her own proprietory rights. I was to experience this at first hand! Indeed, once the ceremony at the Sheldonian was over, I felt somehow gratified that I had succeeded in persuading an old acquaintance, Norman Miller, staff photographer on the *Oxford Mail*, to swap a local football match for the historical event taking place the same afternoon. As he came out of the Rotunda in his impressive robe, the ecstatic Gide began addressing the Lamberts and the admiring crowd with 'Ça y est' and 'Ça me va', then, self-admiringly, proceeded towards the display of his books at Blackwell's. I joined the procession in Broad Street leading to Somerville, where Gide was staying, hoping for a chance of exchanging a few words with him, when my way was brusquely barred. The Cerberus was none other than the minute but pugnacious Enid. Typically, years later at a commemoration of Emile Verhaeren (the subject of her doctoral thesis), she still relished the recollection of the episode.

• • •

Gide expressed annoyance when he heard that François Mauriac had been honoured, also at the Sheldonian, but five days *before* him! Back in Paris, he told all his friends that few photographs of himself had ever given him as much pleasure as those taken by Miller. Much to my surprise, in a letter dictated to his secretary, Yvonne Davet, he pointed out that the pictures I had sent him only showed his ceremonial robe as far as the knees, and he wondered whether I could send him new ones showing him in full regalia! He was impatient to see them, for, in a subsequent letter dated July 5th, he wrote: 'Je pensais attendre votre venue à Paris pour vous remercier. Mais il n'est pas certain que j'y sois encore. Dans le cas où je ne serais plus à Paris, puis-je vous prier de remettre à Mme Davet les photos promises et très impatiemment attendues, dont je vous remercie d'avance.' He added: 'Mieux vous écrire aussitôt l'intérêt que je prends à votre revue et vous féliciter de l'excellent choix qu'*ADAM* a su, grâce à vous, réunir.'

The new pictures soon became the most widely reproduced portraits of Gide – his own favourites. They brought me, anyway, a renewed invitation for tea at his Paris apartment.

• • •

I have already confessed in another issue (*ADAM*, No. 337, 1970) the unforgivable blunder I had committed by calling at 1 bis rue Vaneau accompanied by a young lady pianist who, like Gide, had studied the rarely-played Dukas *Variations* and who was hoping to exchange a few notes with the Maître. I didn't know at the time how inhibited he felt when playing in front of other people – particularly strangers. Alas, it was not to be. However, if I myself was denied the privilege of hearing him play, I was richly compensated when, a few months ago, I received a revealing letter from the distinguished composer and pianist Maurice O'Hana. Here is an excerpt:

'Il avait un phrasé très bien pensé, et ses tempi dans Chopin éclairaient d'un jour nouveau les œuvres que les "trop habiles virtuoses" défiguraient en les jouant trop vite. Il avait surtout une manière d'aborder les tempi rapides, en hésitant sur les premières notes, puis en arrivant assez vite au tempo, qui a été pour moi une révélation. Sa sonorité était assez belle.' *(See front cover [of this issue].)*

One hopes that Yvonne Davet, the cultured but totally enslaved secretary, will one day receive well-documented treatment when the definitive Gide biography is eventually written. She was smitten with her employer, exhaustingly so. In a letter to Dorothy Bussy (21 December 1943), Gide unburdened himself: ' … Mme YD, jeune et charmante personne du reste, que je suis *forcé* [my italics] de tenir précautionnement à distance, mais pour qui j'ai beaucoup de sympathie et de *pitié*.' Now in her eighties, she is a forgotten *pensionnaire* in an old people's home outside Paris – symbolically called Maison Gallimard. I was hoping that she might reminisce on her years of working for Gide, but she kept repeating in a faint, remote voice, 'Oh Monsieur, ça c'est du passé.'

Gidean scholars will find Professor Charlotte Wardi's book *Le juif dans le roman français* (280 pages, Nizet, 1985) of particular interest. It seems that Gide wouldn't accept gladly the idea that Jews could be considered true Frenchmen. While acknowledging the talent of many of his Jewish contemporaries, he regarded their writings as belonging to a *littérature avilissante*. Remarkably, irritated as he always was by the 'question juive obsédante et angoissante', he couldn't help stressing Léon Blum's generosity: 'Je lui sais gré de ne pas me tenir grief des passages assez durs de mon *Journal* au sujet des Juifs et de lui-même (que du reste je ne puis renier, car je continue de les croire *parfaitement exacts*' [my italics]. Although he stated that 'L'antisémitisme a sa raison d'être', Charlotte Wardi thinks that 'Gide ne fut pas antisémite au sens que nous donnons à ce mot.' She stresses, though, 'le silence angoissant qui pèse dans son *Journal* sur l'immense tragédie juive'. On the other hand, Professor Wardi quotes an intriguing statement Gide made in December 1938: 'Mais du moins puis-je déclarer mon indignation profonde devant un crime collectif qui dépasse en férocité, en perfidie et en lâcheté, ce que l'on pouvait craindre d'un régime d'oppression.' (See Arnold Mandel's article, 'André Gide et le racisme' (*Evidences*, February 1951).

Several other avenues must be left for others to pursue. Suffice it to mention that nothing but Gide and England alone is a subject on which fresh data have emerged in recent years. A last-minute discovery: an English translation of *Corydon* published by GMP (Gay Modern Classics).

At the end of this seemingly endless journey, during which one came across younger writers such as Philippe Sollers describing Gide as 'le plus grand des écrivains sans génie', or Pierre de Boisdeffre deciding in *Métamorphoses de la littérature* that Gide 'n'influence plus, n'agit plus, a cessé d'inquiéter', one feels like Emmanuel Berl when speaking of Proust, that 'Gide est pour nous *un mort obsédant*'. Particularly so since the Supreme Sacred Congregation of the Holy Office has decreed: 'Let his work be condemned in no uncertain terms.'

Assuming finally that one gets a passport *up there*: might one bump into Gide and Duhamel in the Elysium? Passionate amateur musicians both, reconciled at last, trying their hand at some celestial chamber music ...?

CONTRIBUTORS

Patrick POLLARD – *André Gide: A musical chronicle (including Select Bibliography)*
Sixty-Eight Letters (plus Appendix) between GIDE and DEBUSSY, MILHAUD,
    STRAVINSKI, DUKAS, Ida RUBINSTEIN and Florent SCHMITT
Desmond HARMSWORTH – *Egyptian Thebes* [poem]
George D. PAINTER – *Dorothy Bussy and Gide*
Philip OUSTON – *'All discord, harmony not understood'* – *Five in Search of God Himself*
Bernard DUHAMEL – *Une famille de médicins et musiciens*

NOTES

1. In *L'Orchestre de la rue Vauquelin* (*Figaro Littéraire*, April 1966), Henri Jourdan, a former Director of the Institut Français in London, evoked the atmosphere of these gatherings: 'Le petit orchestre qui s'assemblait rue Vauquelin une fois la semaine et dont je fis partie au début des années vingt s'éblouissait littéralement dans la chaleur d'un foyer familier. Le soir où j'arrivai je ne me doutais pas que mon violoncelle allait être la caisse de réso- nance d'une amitié qui durerait près d'un demi-siècle. Il s'en fallait de beaucoup que l'orchestre fût au complet ou tout au moins équilibré. Nous avions la flûte du maître de maison, assis à son bureau, l'oeil et l'oreille aux aguets. L'effort comptait plus que le résul- tat. Et chaque fois, en effet, le miracle se renouvelait: la musique nous parlait à travers des imperfections, car elles étaient nos imperfections. Belle revanche sur la technicité des machines reproductrices des sons, ces faiseuses d'anges parfaits.'
2. Little did I know then that Vaudoyer was the young man Proust had asked on May 24th 1921 to escort him to the Jeu de Paume to have a last look at Vermeer's *View of Delft* – 'the most beautiful painting in the *world*' (Painter, vol. II, p. 320). Like so many other Proustians, he became a Nazi sympathiser, but, much to Duhamel's disgust, this did not prevent the French Academy from receiving him, in 1950, among the immortals. 'Un siège venait d'être déclaré vacant. Les amis de Vaudoyer commençaient à s'agiter. Nous étions en séance quand, soudain, Mauriac demanda la parole. Voilà mon François qui se lève et qui commence à faire, de sa voix déchirée, une petite déclaration surprenante pour expli- quer que l'Académie semblait avoir pris la décision de ne pas nommer des collaborateurs. Cette intervention fut le signal d'une sourde guerre dans laquelle il eut contre lui tous les amis de Vaudoyer, les collaborateurs et les autres. Puis les mois passèrent encore et Octave Aubry étant mort, l'Académie commença de s'occuper de lui trouver un successeur. Rien ne se fait à ciel ouvert dans cette noble maison' (*Le livre de l'amertume*). Vaudoyer was elect- ed, and, following Duhamel's *Diary*, one is bemused to learn that, during a subsequent ses- sion, the same fearless Mauriac sprang a *coup de théâtre*: 'Mauriac s'est levé et lui a fait devant tout le monde des excuses et une affirmation d'amitié, plus forte que les diver- gences d'opinion. Vaudoyer a éclaté en sanglots.'
3. During a heated debate at the first international congress of writers in exile, held in London in 1941 (the first issue of bilingual *ADAM* was launched to coincide with, and in honour of, this impressive gathering), I heard H. G. Wells and Rebecca West describing the irascible, quarrelsome Jules Romains as a 'sad case'. On the other hand, he was generous to *ADAM* by contributing five short essays, one of them entitled 'Le rôle de l'esprit dans les affaires du monde'...

4. D. H. Lawrence, 'rotten and rotting others, incapable of what is ordinarily called thinking' – T. S. Eliot, *After Strange Gods*, 1934.

5. However, the waters of literary generosity 'are sometimes notoriously shark-infested' (Rosemary Friedman).

6. I happened to be in Paris at the time, and Blanche Albane most graciously invited me to attend a tea party on the Sunday following the election. Alas, I couldn't resist the temptation of going to hear Arthur Schnabel, the same afternoon, play Beethoven's *Emperor Concerto*, so I went to Salle Pleyel first. By the time I reached rue de Liège all the guests had already left. Unforgivably, I missed Mauriac and Valéry among others!

7. Barbara Wall, author of a series of evocative Paris sketches, and her late husband, the novelist and critic Bernard Wall, were neighbours of the Duhamels at Naze-Valmondois (Oise). She remembers the country house and its owner at the height of his moral crisis: 'He loved the whole area and referred to it as "notre douce vallée". Duhamel's house was surrounded by herbaceous borders, *très anglais*. It was exciting to go inside the large wooden gates that fronted onto the road totally concealing the riches within from the passersby, as in all French villages. He asked Bernard about the rating of various English writers, and whenever Bernard told him that they were temporarily in eclipse, Duhamel said that as soon as writers died they were put in the *frigidaire* for a time, or when they got old perhaps. This was his constant metaphor, offered with a wry smile. Perhaps he thought *he* was in the frigidaire.'

8. Youra Guller was married to Jacques Schiffrin, a brilliant publisher, who, among other achievements, launched the *Bibliothèque de la Pléïade*, subsequently taken over by Gallimard; 'le seul juif pour qui j'ai eu de l'affection' – Gide to Julien Green, Jan 1951.

INDEX

Abarbanel, Isaak, 103
Abbott à Beckett, Gilbert, 94
Abraham, Gerald, 163
ADAM (Art, Drama, Architecture and
    Music), Anglo-French edition (first,
    1968), 62; and Debussy, 166; and
    Dostoevsky, 162–3; 45th birthday tribute,
    167–9; and Gascoyne, 83; and George
    Enescu Biennial Prize, 154, 163; and
    Gide, 172; and Hobson, 104; jubilee exhi-
    bition (1965), 129; and Mauriac, 98; office
    surroundings, 114; on poetry, 121; prizes,
    57–8; and Proust, 45, 47, 51, 101; and
    Sartre, 86
Adler, Robert, 160
Agnon, S. Y., 40; *Das Krumme wird ja gerade*,
    41
Alain (Emile Auguste Chartier), *En lisant
    Dickens*, 92
Albane, Blanche, 174, 197n6
Aldington, Richard, 119
Alibert, François-Paul, 186
Allegret, Marc, 192
American Bollingean Foundation, 116
Anderson, Margaret, 55
Antoine, André, 12
Arab writing, 110–12
Arnold, Matthew, 4
Astruc, Yvonne, 148
atavism, Jewish, 102
Athaenaeum, the, 12, 30, 161
'atrocity writing', 36
Auden, W. H., 23
Austen, Alfred, 4
Austin, Richard, *End of Summer*, 122
authors *see* dramatists; novelists; poets

Baker, John, *Strange Genius of David Lindsay*,
    89
Balzac, Honoré de, 71, 72, 93; and George
    Moore, 5
Bandy, T. W., 74
Barnard, Jean-Jacques, 11
Barney, Natalie Clifford, 46, 119, 131, 185
Barraud, Henry, 70
Barrault, Jean-Louis, 10, 104
Barrow, Thomas (Charles Dickens' uncle),
    95
Bartok, Béla, 83, 147; *Third Piano Concerto*,
    81
Barzun, Jacques, 68, 69

Bates, Alan (poet), 105
Baudelaire, Charles Pierre, 71, 72, 74; and
    Berlioz, 70; *Fusées*, 141; *Les Fleurs du Mal*,
    71, 75, 77, 143; on *Liaisons Dangereuses*,
    143; *Œuvres Complètes*, 74; *Parfum
    Exotique*, 74–5; *Richard Wagner et
    Tannhäuser*, 70
Baudelaire Symposium, 76
Bayley, Jon, 163n1
Beckett, John, 81
Beckett, May, 81
Beckett, Samuel, 22, 80, 82, 83; *Endgame*, 81;
    Malacoda, 81; *Waiting for Godot*, 81
Beerbohm, Max, 23
Beethoven, Ludwig van, 97; bicentenary of,
    90; *Choral Symphony*, 95; and Dickens, 95;
    Die Geschöpfe des Prometheus, 95–6; *Eroica
    Symphony/Eroica Piano Variations*, 96;
    Ninth Symphony, 80, 95; Rolland on, 173;
    Second Symphony, 174; *Seventh Symphony*,
    81; *Sonata in B/B flat major*, 95
Beilis Murder Trial, 160
Belinski, Vissarion, 156
Bell, Goerge, 32
Berg, Alban, 83
Berlin, Pavel, 158–9
Berlioz Centennial Year, 67, 77
Berlioz, Hector Louis, 70, 71, 75; *Carnaval
    Romain*, 68; *Gluck's Orphée*, 72; *Les Soireés
    de l'Orchestre*, 72; *Mémoires*, 73; *Roi Lear*,
    68
Berlioz letters, 68
Berlioz Society of America, 78n1
Berlioz treasure, and Heinrich Rosenthal
    Antiquariat, 67
Bernac, Pierre, 167
Bernard, Jean-Jacques, 19
Bernard, Tristan, 19
Beyle, Henry, 141
Beyle, Marine Henri (Stendhal), 4
Bibesco, Elisabeth, 118
Bibescu, Marthe, 131
Bible, 64, 165
Bibliothèque de l'Arsenal, 11
Bibliothèque Nationale, 2
Bidou, Henri, 15
Blakiston, Noel, 137
Blémont, Emile, 5
Block, Albert (friend of Proust), 102
Blow, Simon, 126, 137
Boissy, Gabriel, 18

Art, Drama, Architecture and Music
An Anthology of Miron Grindea's ADAM
Editorials, Volume I
Selected and Edited by Rachel Lasserson

- First English Edition
- 'A Symbiosis of English and French Culture'
- Chopin in England
- T. S. Eliot's The Aims of Poetic Drama – 'So *ADAM* is 200 Issues Old!'
- Mostly French – Plus D. H. Lawrence
- Our Dylan Thomas Memorial Number – A Telegram from Edith Sitwell
- Marcel Proust: A World Symposium and Our 25th Year
- The Amazon of Letters (A World Tribute to Natalie Clifford Barney)
- In Memory of Jean Cocteau
- Virginia Woolf – Granite and Rainbow
- Our 400th Issue – A Tribute to the London Library
- Auberjonois – Auden – Schönberg – Stravinsky
- 'Sabra' Writings: Hebrew and Arab
- Frederic Raphael and Others
- A Mozartian Pilgrimage
- Proust Concordance, Part II (Frances Stern) – Richard Berenson, Proust et al.